BUDDHIST TEACHING IN INDIA

Studies in Indian and Tibetan Buddhism

THIS SERIES WAS CONCEIVED to provide a forum for publishing outstanding new contributions to scholarship on Indian and Tibetan Buddhism and also to make accessible seminal research not widely known outside a narrow specialist audience, including translations of appropriate monographs and collections of articles from other languages. The series strives to shed light on the Indic Buddhist traditions by exposing them to historical-critical inquiry, illuminating through contextualization and analysis these traditions' unique heritage and the significance of their contribution to the world's religious and philosophical achievements.

STUDIES IN INDIAN AND TIBETAN BUDDHISM

BUDDHIST TEACHING IN INDIA

Johannes Bronkhorst

WISDOM PUBLICATIONS • BOSTON

Wisdom Publications
199 Elm Street
Somerville MA 02144 USA
www.wisdompubs.org

This book is an English translation of a text that was originally published in German as "Die buddhistische Lehre" in the book *Der Buddhismus I: Der indische Buddhismus und seine Verzweigungen*, volume 24, number 1 of the series *Die Religionen der Menschheit* (Stuttgart–Berlin–Köln: W. Kohlhammer, 2000). This translation has been published with the permission of the German publisher.

Library of Congress Cataloging-in-Publication Data
Bronkhorst, Johannes.
Buddhist teaching in India / by Johannes Bronkhorst.
p. cm.—(Studies in Indian and Tibetan Buddhism)
Translation of: Die buddhistische Lehre, originally published in Der Buddhismus I. Stuttgart : W. Kohlhammer, 2000.
Includes bibliographical references and index.
ISBN 0-86171-566-7 (pbk. : alk. paper)
1. Buddhism—India—Doctrines—History. I. Buddhismus I. English. Selections. II. Title.
BQ336.B76 2009
294.3'420954—dc22
2009010816

13 12 11 10 09
5 4 3 2 1

Cover photo © The Trustees of the British Museum. The Buddha ordains his brother Sundarānanda. Detail from limestone relief, approx. one foot high. Hadda, Gandhara, Afghanistan, second-third century A.D.

Cover and interior design by Gopa&Ted2. Set in Diacritical Garamond Pro, 11.4/14.5.

Wisdom Publications' books are printed on acid-free paper and meet the guidelines for permanence and durability of the Production Guidelines for Book Longevity of the Council on Library Resources.

Printed in the United States of America.

This book was produced with environmental mindfulness. We have elected to print this title on 30% PCW recycled paper. As a result, we have saved the following resources: 10 trees, 3 million BTUs of energy, 950 lbs. of greenhouse gases, 4,578 gallons of water, and 278 lbs. of solid waste. For more information, please visit our website, www.wisdompubs.org. This paper is also FSC certified. For more information, please visit www.fscus.org.

Publisher's Acknowledgment

THE PUBLISHER gratefully acknowledges the generous help of the Hershey Family Foundation in sponsoring the publication of this book.

Contents

Preface

THE AIM OF THIS BOOK is to give an overview of Buddhist teaching in India. There is a basic distinction between Buddhist teaching and Buddhist philosophy. These two are not to be taken as identical, even though they are closely related. *Philosophy* is a Western term[1] that might be applied to some, but by no means all, Buddhist teachings. The Buddha himself was clearly averse to any kind of speculation, and he positively avoided "philosophically" important questions. One might conclude from this that the Buddha, and some later Buddhists as well, did not teach philosophy as such. But teach he did, and therefore there is definitely a Buddhist *teaching*.

This is not to deny that important "philosophical" developments took place in Buddhism.[2] Indeed, it appears that the rise of philosophy in India was largely due to Buddhism, and as we will see below, certain Buddhist teachings were definitely of great philosophical importance. Nonetheless, anyone undertaking a description of *Buddhist philosophy* will primarily be interested in "philosophically interesting" teachings and in this way will apply an outside criterion.

This is further complicated by the fact that from a certain point onward, various Buddhist schools tried to systematize their teachings. For the philosopher a systematized teaching is more interesting than a jumble of non-systematic teachings. The philosophically inclined

1 Halbfass 1981: 296–97; 1988: 263–64.

2 Or should we in this context speak of "theological" developments, as Olivelle (1993: 7n1) suggests with regard to the Brahmanical tradition?

scholar might therefore turn his attention to these Buddhist attempts at systematization and ignore many of the other teachings.

A description of the *teachings* of Buddhism, on the other hand, aims at using inner criteria: a particular teaching is not described because it is of philosophical interest to us or because it is thought out systematically, but because Buddhists themselves considered it important. The importance of a teaching in Buddhism is primarily related to how essential a role it plays in the process of liberation. This book therefore is not an overview of Buddhist philosophy but a presentation of what Buddhists have historically considered to be central to the path.[3]

Insight or wisdom (often called *prajñā*), for instance, is one teaching that has played a central role in Buddhism. The Buddhist gains this wisdom while progressing on the path to liberation, most often at its end. Attainment of this wisdom is crucial for the attainment of liberation. It is hardly surprising that the highest wisdom, the key to the highest goal of the Buddhist religion, is frequently described in the texts. For those Buddhists who believe that the highest insight cannot be expressed in words, this description of the highest wisdom is only approximate and not precise. This does not alter the fact that a part of Buddhist teaching is, or claims to be, a description of the wisdom that leads to the ultimate liberation.

However, that is not all there is to Buddhist teaching. Highest wisdom may produce liberation for those Buddhists who are far advanced on the path, but one first has to know how to get to this advanced stage. Buddhist teaching has much to say about that, too. The ideal behavior of devout Buddhists, primarily monks and nuns, is prescribed in the so-called *Vinaya-piṭaka*. Then there are the concepts and notions of buddhas and bodhisattvas, who personify the ideal and serve as models for devout Buddhists. Buddhist teaching in a narrower sense contains

3 Steinkellner (1978: 122) states: "Simplifying greatly, but in a manner that is yet supported by tradition, one can say that this [immense quantity of dogmatic and practical teachings, an overview of which hardly exists at present] is nothing but the interpretation of the insight acquired by the Buddha and of the road that leads to it."

numerous instructions in spiritual practice. These are mainly found in the discourses (*sūtra*)[4] collected in the *Sūtra-piṭaka*, or "basket of discourses." In other words, Buddhist teaching is not solely concerned with the insight that leads to liberation; there are many additional things one needs to know in order to follow the path to liberation.

Moreover, Buddhist teaching includes those beliefs whose relevance to liberation is not immediately clear. For example, the cosmological ideas of the Indian Buddhists, which found widespread acceptance, do not at first seem to have much to do with liberation and the Buddhist religion in a narrow sense, and indeed, many were not exclusive to Buddhists in India. In this arena, it is not always obvious which ideas are religious and which are not. At first glance, ideas about astronomy, cosmology, geography, and the like can appear to have little if anything to do with religion generally, or with Buddhism in particular. As we will see later, however, certain cosmological concepts are closely related to specific Buddhist meditative states. Consequently they, too, deserve at least some attention in a presentation of Buddhist teaching.

In chapter 1, after a discussion of methodology, this book begins with an attempt to discern the teachings of the historical Buddha by subjecting the earliest texts to critical analysis. It shows how his goal of liberation grew out of the śramana ascetic movements of his day while yet modifying it in some important respects. In chapter 2, we see how developments after the Buddha's death led to greater systematization of his teachings in the catalogs of the various Abhidharma texts and a projection back on to the Buddha's teachings of the so-called *dharma theory* division of reality into atomic units of mind, matter, and time. In chapter 3, we see how the doctrine of emptiness of all dharmas came to be associated with the ethic of the bodhisattva ideal, how seemingly non-empty conceptions of buddha nature emerged simultaneously, and how the introduction of logico-epistemological approaches

4 The suggestion that *sūtra* is a wrong Sanskrit rendering for Middle Indic *sutta*, which should have been rendered as *sūkta* ("well-spoken"), does not convince. Cf. Hinüber 1994c: 132 and note 28.

allowed Buddhists to prove their positions and engage in debate among Buddhist schools and with non-Buddhists. Finally, in chapter 4, we review the hermeneutical landmarks of Buddhism's early development and show how it was not only a product of its environment but helped shaped the other religious cultures of its time and place.

Given the scope of the present book, it would be impossible to exhaustively describe all the Buddhist teachings that ever existed in India. The selection here has been guided by the intention to illuminate the links between certain key teachings, with the aim of helping the reader understand these selected teachings in their historical, cultural, and intellectual context.

Acknowledgments

Several people have collaborated in bringing about this translation of the original German. They are, in alphabetical order, Danielle Feller, Rupert Gethin, Rita Langer, Joy Manné, and the undersigned. Subsequently David Kittelstrom, from Wisdom Publications, suggested numerous improvements. Thanks are due to all. Thanks are also due to the De Boer Foundation at the University of Lausanne, for financial assistance.

Johannes Bronkhorst

1. The Teaching of the Buddha

Preliminary Remarks on Methodology

IN THE CHAPTER on teaching in his groundbreaking 1881 work *Buddha: His Life, His Doctrine, His Order* (published first in German as *Buddha, sein Leben, seine Lehre, seine Gemeinde*), Hermann Oldenberg curiously speaks throughout about "the teachings of Buddhism" rather than "the teaching(s) of the Buddha." Helmuth von Glasenapp later emphasized this detail in his concluding note to the thirteenth edition of this book, which came out in 1959. Glasenapp points out that this choice of phrase reveals Oldenberg's view that we do not know anything for certain about what the Buddha actually taught. Indeed, the material available to us is only sufficient to establish what the earliest community may have understood Buddhist teaching to be.

Glasenapp, while generally agreeing with Oldenberg's view, thinks there is reason to believe that the most important ideas of the tradition can be traced back to the Blessed One himself. Glasenapp finds these ideas expressed in the so-called *dharma theory*, which finds its classic expression many centuries after the Buddha in the *Abhidharmakośa* of Vasubandhu (ca. fifth century CE). The dharma theory, which is taken up in more detail in the next chapter, is the view, presented in many Buddhist texts, that a number of metaphysical features, or dharmas, comprise reality; more recent forms of Buddhism ascribed this theory to the Buddha himself.[5] Previous scholars, in their enthusiasm

5 As we will discuss in more detail in chapter 2, the word *dharma* has several

about the discovery of the dharma theory, had gone so far as to believe that the teachings of the *Abhidharmakośa* corresponded largely, even though not in every detail, to the oldest teaching. Glasenapp names Theodor Stcherbatsky and Otto Rosenberg as holding this view, and he himself had followed in their footsteps in his article "Zur Geschichte der buddhistischen Dharma-Theorie" ("On the History of the Buddhist Dharma Theory") published in 1938. Here Glasenapp had come to the conclusion that the philosophical basis developed in the *Abhidharmakośa* constitutes the basis of the whole of Buddhism:

> However much the Buddhist schools differ from each other in many details, in the general principles of their teaching they all agree with each other. The oldest layer that we can get to of Buddhist tradition already contained the essential ideas that found refined expression in the *Abhidharmakośa*. There is reason to assume that already the teaching of Gotama Buddha corresponded in its essence to that what we find in the great Buddhist philosophers of the classical period, even though the latter have adapted it to the way of thinking of their own time and have further elaborated it and worked it out in detail.

Glasenapp criticizes other scholars for assuming that Buddhism was not grounded in any kind of metaphysical concept. He finds this assumption unlikely in view of the fact that all other religious and philosophical systems in India accept a larger or smaller number of ultimate realities. He argues that if Buddhism wanted to compete with these other systems, it could not restrict itself to being a practical doctrine of liberation only; it, too, had to provide answers to numerous metaphysical questions.

This editorial note by Glasenapp prompted an almost immediate response by the American scholar Franklin Edgerton. In his article,

---

different meanings, and within the Buddhist tradition, that meaning evolved over time. *Dharma* in this case does not refer to the Buddha's doctrine.

published in 1959, the same year as Glasenapp's concluding note, Edgerton points out that the same ancient texts that Glasenapp studied also contain passages stating that the Buddha explicitly refuses to engage in philosophical speculations. Probably the best-known passage of this kind is found in the *Cūḷamāluṅkya Sutta* of the Majjhima Nikāya of the Pāli *Sutta-piṭaka*.[6] Oldenberg paraphrases this passage as follows:

> The venerable Māluṅkyāputta comes to the Master and expresses his astonishment that the Master's discourse leaves a series of the very most important and deepest questions unanswered. Is the world eternal or is it limited by the bounds of time? Is the world infinite or does it have an end? Is the living being identical with the body or different from it? Does the Perfect One (*tathāgata*) live on beyond death? Does the Perfect One not live on beyond death? It pleases me not, says the monk, that all this should remain unanswered, and I do not think it right; therefore I am come to the Master to interrogate him about these doubts. May it please the Buddha to answer them if he can. "When anyone does not understand a thing and does not know it, then a straightforward man says: I do not understand that, I do not know that."
>
> The Buddha answers: "What have I said to thee before now, Māluṅkyāputta? Have I said: Come, Māluṅkyāputta, and be my disciple; I shall teach thee, whether the world is everlasting or not everlasting, whether the world is finite or infinite, whether the vital faculty is identical with the body or separate from it, whether the Perfect One lives on after death or does not live on, or whether the Perfect One lives on and at the same time does not live on after death, or whether he neither lives on nor does not live on?"
>
> "That thou hast not said, sire."
>
> "Or hast thou," the Buddha goes on, "said to me: I shall

6 MN I.426–32; sutta no. 63.

> be thy disciple, declare unto me, whether the world is everlasting or not everlasting, and so on?"
>
> This also Māluṅkyāputta must answer in the negative.
>
> A man, the Buddha proceeds, was struck by a poisoned arrow, and his friends and relatives called in a skillful physician. What if the wounded man said: "I shall not allow my wound to be treated until I know who the man is by whom I have been wounded, whether he is a noble, a brahman, a vaiśya, or a śūdra"; or what if he said: "I shall not allow my wound to be treated until I know what they call the man who has wounded me, and of what family he is, whether he is tall, or small, or of middle stature, and how the weapon with which he struck me was made." What would the end of the case be? The man would die of his wound.
>
> Why has the Buddha not taught his disciples whether the world is finite or infinite, whether the accomplished one lives on beyond death or not? Because the knowledge of these things does not conduce to progress in holiness, because it does not contribute to peace and enlightenment. What contributes to peace and enlightenment the Buddha has taught his own: the truth of suffering, the truth of the origin of suffering, the truth of the cessation of suffering, the truth of the path to the cessation of suffering.
>
> "Therefore, Māluṅkyāputta, whatsoever has not been revealed by me, let that remain unrevealed, and what has been revealed, let it be revealed."[7]

There are other passages that indicate that the Buddha did not answer the questions whether the world is everlasting or not everlasting, whether the world is finite or infinite, whether the living being is identical with the body or separate from it, whether the Perfect One lives on after death or does not live on, or whether the Perfect One lives

7 Oldenberg 1971: 274–75. For the original German, see Oldenberg 1961: 256–57.

on and at the same time does not live on after death, or whether he neither lives on nor does not live on.[8]

What can we conclude from the coexistence of passages in which metaphysical speculations are rejected and passages in which a kind of dharma theory is proclaimed or assumed? In his reply to Edgerton's critique, Glasenapp (1960) points out that the fact that specific questions remained unanswered does not allow the general conclusion that all metaphysical problems were regarded as unsolvable, or that occupying oneself with them was regarded as fruitless. However, in the centuries following the Buddha's demise, the dharma theory gained ever more importance in the eyes of those who were responsible for the collection and preservation of his words. This may suffice to explain its supposed presence in the oldest texts. The existence of passages like the one from the *Cūḷamāluṅkya Sutta*, on the other hand, passages that are *not* in agreement with such later priorities, should for this reason be given greatest importance. Even though we cannot exclude the possibility that the seeds of what later became the dharma theory may have been present in the teaching of the Buddha, we must abandon the idea that these approached anything resembling a full-blown metaphysical framework.[9] Besides, the evidence for the existence of the dharma theory in the ancient sūtras is far less conclusive than Glasenapp assumed.

The controversy between Edgerton and Glasenapp allows us to draw some important methodological conclusions. First, it shows that not every word attributed to the Buddha in the ancient discourses should necessarily be taken as having been pronounced by him. If we want to learn about the teaching of the Buddha, we cannot avoid examining the ancient discourses with a critical eye.

Second, the discussion suggests a possible method by which—in some cases at least—older parts of the teaching can be distinguished from later additions and developments. What is involved is a layering

8 Cf. Oetke 1994: 85–120.

9 Frauwallner (1973a: 369 = 1953: 464) calls this an "untenable anachronism."

of teachings rather than a layering of texts.[10] Two types of passage were mentioned in the controversy between Edgerton and Glasenapp: on the one hand, those in which all metaphysical speculations are rejected, and on the other hand, those in which the dharma theory is expressed or at least assumed. These two types of passages contradict each other, at least according to Edgerton. If he is right, then only one of the positions represented in those passages can be original. The Buddha did not reject metaphysical teachings while at the same time teaching a metaphysical doctrine himself. One has to choose: *either* the Buddha rejected metaphysical teachings *or* he taught a metaphysical doctrine himself. The same choice is required wherever we encounter contradictions in the ancient canon.[11] The choice is relatively easy where one is able to identify the origin of a contradictory teaching in a later development of Buddhism or in non-Buddhist currents of the time. In the case of the dharma theory, for example, the origin is easy to identify: as we will see below, dharmas—here meaning the building blocks of reality—become a major preoccupation of later Buddhism. Nevertheless, it is not possible to reduce this method to a mechanical process. As we have seen above, where Edgerton saw a contradiction, Glasenapp saw none. Besides, even in relatively clear cases, where this method can be employed without problems, one could question the result. Can one

10 Schmithausen (1992: 110–12; 1990: 1–3) discusses three methods of distinguishing between what is earlier and what is later. He mentions "layering of texts" as one of them but not "layering of teachings."

11 This approach is, of course, not the only possible one. Especially in the context of the actual practice one could argue that the Buddha might have accepted a certain practice while at the same time rejecting its excessive exercise. Gombrich (1994: 1080) uses this argument when he seeks to justify certain practices described in the ancient discourses. However, the ancient texts never actually say that only the excessive exercise of a particular practice is rejected, or that it is rejected *only on the grounds of its excessive exercise*. This kind of justification seems therefore unlikely, even though not logically impossible. The same applies to the approach of Vetter (1996: 56), who judges that it is "not impossible" that the Buddha employed certain practices which he had originally classified as useless in a different context. Vetter is more or less forced into this approach by his decision to give much weight to the words ascribed to the Buddha himself, particularly to his so-called first sermon.

really attribute the teaching arrived at in this manner to the historical Buddha? Perhaps the Buddha did not reject *all* metaphysical theories even if he did not teach the dharma theory.

One might criticize Glasenapp and other scholars for projecting later Buddhist teachings onto the historical Buddha. However, they did search for the teaching of the Buddha in the corpus of discourses attributed to him. Other authors try to show that very little of the original teaching of the Buddha has been preserved in the Buddhist canon. They claim that, in order to qualify as remains of what they call "precanonical Buddhism," passages and teachings have to be in contradiction with generally recognized canonical positions.[12]

Some other scholars are of the opinion that the true nature of earliest Buddhism is not found in the ancient discourses at all but only in the inscriptions of Aśoka (third century BCE).[13]

Closely related to this is another opinion that states that it is outright impossible to know anything definite about the teaching content of the discourses before the fourth century CE.[14]

These scholars might be accused of throwing out the baby with the bath water, as they do not even take into consideration passages that are *not* contradicted by other passages. It is indeed in the non-contradicted passages where we should expect to find information about earliest Buddhist teaching.

We, cautiously, opt for the general principle that the teaching that the ancient discourses ascribe to the Buddha can indeed be ascribed

12 This point of view was taken by Stanislaw Schayer in particular. Cf., e.g., Schayer 1935 and 1937; also Regamey 1957 with references to further literature. See also Schneider 1967. Vetter (1996: 50) argues in a similar vein when he claims that the only chance to find a historical line with the help of external criteria are passages that are enclosed in and utilized by differently oriented but relatively old surrounding material; if the way they are utilized in their particular context is unconvincing, then this might be an indication that these passages cannot have been original to that context.

13 For a discussion of these views and further references, see Schmithausen 1992: 130.

14 Cf. for example Schopen 1984: 9–22.

to him.[15] Only where there are reasons to doubt the authenticity of a certain teaching—because it contradicts other canonical statements, for example—should we deviate from this principle.

Following this method to the extent possible, we now turn to the actual teaching of the Buddha. Our point of departure, as indicated, is the assumption that positions that are found in the early discourses and are not contradicted in these texts can be attributed to him. However, in cases where teachings are presented in the form of lists, the possibility of later scholastic influence has to be taken into account, given the later scholastic tendency to present all the teachings it ascribed to the Buddha in lists. Where two or more contradictory opinions are ascribed to the Buddha, we have to examine two possibilities. One is that one of the contradicting opinions is also found in another religious movement current at the time. Another possibility is that one of the contradicting opinions belongs to a later phase in the development of Buddhism.[16] In both cases the opinion in question can be left out of consideration in our attempt to reconstruct the teaching of the Buddha. We have already drawn attention to the weak sides of the method and need not repeat them here.

A danger accompanying the study of early Buddhism is the attempt, frequent in scholarly research, to reduce Buddhist terms to concepts current in the West. The large number of publications dealing with the

15 In this respect one has to agree with Richard Gombrich. Gombrich (1988: 20–21; cf. 1990: 6ff.) is unfortunately of the opinion that the ancient texts must first of all be interpreted according to the tradition (although Gombrich 1992 seems to voice a different opinion). Snellgrove (1987: 31), too, is of the opinion that "[a]ll one can fairly do is to accept the whole tradition as presented in any particular sect of Buddhism at its face value." Fortunately scholarship does have the possibility to penetrate into earlier times, even if with difficulty and not always with completely certain results.

16 It needs to be emphasized that simply finding a position mirrored in another religious movement at the time of the Buddha does not in itself disqualify it from being an authentic teaching of the Buddha, as Gombrich (1994: 1072) seems to think. Such a teaching must also be contradicted in the Buddhist texts themselves.

Buddhist *nirvāṇa* illustrates this.[17] Such studies obscure the fact that much in the ancient canonical texts leaves little to be desired in terms of clarity. We will therefore let the texts speak for themselves wherever possible. Comparative studies of different versions of a passage, often preserved in both Pāli and Chinese, will, where they exist, be mentioned. In cases, however, where the differences between versions are of little or no relevance for our presentation, we will only quote a translation from the Pāli. While relying on existing English translations for many scriptural quotations, these have been modified so as to achieve greater consistency in terminology and style.

Main Teachings

Let us now examine the details of the teaching of the Buddha. The first question to ask is: if the Buddha did not teach a metaphysical system, what then did he teach? The passage from the *Cūḷamāluṅkya Sutta* quoted above gives the following answer. The Buddha preached what is conducive to the holy life and to peace and enlightenment: the truth of suffering, the truth of the origin of suffering, the truth of the cessation of suffering, the truth of the path leading to the cessation of suffering. This is repeated frequently in different ways. Some examples: "Monks, both formerly and now what I teach is suffering and the cessation of suffering."[18] "[...] for it is praise of the Tathāgata [the 'Perfect One'] to say of him: 'When he teaches the Dharma to anyone, it leads him when he practices it to the complete destruction of suffering.'"[19] The teaching of the buddhas, according to other passages, is suffering, its origin, its cessation, and the path leading to cessation.[20]

---

17 Cf. Welbon 1968.

18 MN I.140 (tr. Ñāṇamoli & Bodhi 1995: 234); SN IV.384; see also AN I.176.

19 MN I.69, 72 (tr. Ñāṇamoli & Bodhi 1995: 164); cf. DN II.80, etc.

20 DN I.110, 148, II.41; MN I.380, II.41, 145; AN IV.186, 213; Vin I.16, 18, 19, 181, 225, II.156; Ud 49. It has often been assumed that this fourfold categorization has been adopted from the field of medicine. See for example Frauwallner 1953: 184. However, it has been shown by Wezler (1984: 312–13) that there are no grounds for such an assumption.

The four truths referred to are known as the *four noble truths*. Perhaps their most beautiful exposition is found in the following story of the ancient canon:

> On one occasion the Blessed One was dwelling at Kosambī [Skt. Kauśāmbī] in a *siṃsapā* [Skt. *śiṃśapā*] grove. Then the Blessed One took up a few *siṃsapā* leaves in his hand and addressed the monks thus: "What do you think, monks, which is more numerous: these few leaves that I have taken up in my hand or those in the grove overhead?"
>
> "Venerable sir, the leaves that the Blessed One has taken up in his hand are few, but those in the grove overhead are numerous."
>
> "So, too, monks, the things I have directly known but have not taught you are numerous, while the things I have taught you are few. And why, monks, have I not taught those many things? Because they are without benefit, irrelevant to the fundamentals of the spiritual life, and do not lead to disenchantment, to dispassion, to cessation, to peace, to direct knowledge, to enlightenment, to nibbāna [Skt. *nirvāṇa*]. Therefore I have not taught them.
>
> "And what, monks, have I taught? I have taught: 'This is suffering'; I have taught: 'This is the origin of suffering'; I have taught: 'This is the cessation of suffering'; I have taught: 'This is the way leading to the cessation of suffering.'"[21]

The topic of liberation from suffering is never contradicted in the Buddhist texts.[22] We conclude from this that it constituted a main

21 SN V.437–38 (tr. Bodhi 2005: 360).

22 This fact is sometimes overlooked by scholars. Zafiropulo (1993: 184–85), for example, in the concluding part of his otherwise remarkable book, restricts the goal of the Buddha's teaching to liberation from rebirth. Vetter (1995: 222; 1996: 67) is of the opinion that the four noble truths should be regarded as related to the this-wordly aspect of the "*amata*-experience"; according to him there is only an otherworldly aspect in the four noble truths. However, the this-wordly

theme of the teaching of the Buddha. It is often presented as part of a list, the four noble truths. This may be due to the influence of later scholastics. But this later influence concerned the form, not the content: the Buddha taught a method to put an end to suffering.

The so-called first sermon of the Blessed One contains the following explanation of these four noble truths:

> This, O monks, is the noble truth of *suffering*: birth is suffering, old age is suffering, sickness is suffering, death is suffering, to be united with the unloved is suffering, to be separated from the loved is suffering, not to obtain what one desires is suffering; in short the fivefold clinging (to the earthly) is suffering.
>
> This, O monks, is the noble truth of the *origin of suffering*: it is the thirst (for being), which leads from birth to birth, together with lust and desire, which finds gratification here and there: the thirst for pleasures, the thirst for being, the thirst for nonexistence.
>
> This, O monks, is the noble truth of the *cessation of suffering*: the cessation of this thirst by the complete annihilation of desire, letting it go, expelling it, separating oneself from it, giving it no room.
>
> This, O monks, is the noble truth of the *path that leads to the cessation of suffering*: it is this noble eightfold path, to wit: right views, right resolution, right speech, right action, right living, right exertion, right mindfulness, right concentration.[23]

---

aspect of the liberation from suffering (or from that from which one suffers, as Vetter puts it) seems undeniable. The achievement of *amata*, the "deathless," might relate to a part of the liberation from suffering, perhaps the liberation from the fear of death. The four noble truths could in this way be looked upon as an encompassing framework.

23 This explanation is found in the Vinaya of the Theravādins (Vin I.10), of the Mahīśāsakas (TI 1421, vol. 22, 104b23–104c7), and of the Dharmaguptakas (TI 1428, vol. 22, 788a9–20); these passages have all been translated into French by Bareau (1963: 172–76). The translation from the Pāli presented here has been taken from Oldenberg 1971: 211–12.

This explanation still lacks clarity. The noble eightfold path, in particular, provides no details of the method taught by the Buddha. The canonical texts fortunately contain a more detailed description of the path to liberation, which is repeated at several places:

> Here a Buddha (*tathāgata*) appears in the world, accomplished (*arhat*, Pa. *arahaṃ*), perfectly enlightened (*samyaksaṃbuddha*, Pa. *sammāsaṃbuddha*), perfect in true knowledge and conduct, fortunate (*sugata*), knower of worlds, unsurpassed leader of persons to be tamed, teacher of gods and humans, venerable (*bhagavat*), blessed. Having realized with his own direct knowledge this world with its gods (*sadevaka*), Māra (*samāraka*), and Brahmā (*sabrahmaka*), this population with its ascetics and brahmans, with its gods and humans, he makes it known to others. He preaches the teaching that is good in the beginning, good in the middle, and good in the end, with the right meaning and expression; he reveals a holy life (*brahmacarya*, Pa. *brahmacariya*) that is perfectly complete and purified.
>
> A householder or householder's son or one born in some other clan hears that teaching. On hearing the teaching he acquires faith (*śraddhā*, Pa. *saddhā*) in the Buddha. Possessing that faith, he considers thus: "Household life is crowded and dusty; life gone forth (*pravrajyā*, Pa. *pabbajjā*) is wide open. It is not easy, while living in a home, to lead the holy life utterly perfect and pure as a polished shell. Suppose I shave off my hair and beard, put on the ochre robe, and go forth from the household life into homelessness." On a later occasion, abandoning a small or a large fortune, abandoning a small or a large circle of relatives, he shaves off his hair and beard, puts on the ochre robe, and goes forth from the household life into homelessness.
>
> Having thus gone forth and possessing the monk's training and way of life, abandoning the destruction of life (*prāṇātipāta*, Pa. *pāṇātipāta*), he abstains from the

destruction of life; with rod and weapon laid aside, conscientious, merciful, he dwells compassionate to all living beings. Abandoning the taking of what has not been given (*adattādāna*, Pa. *adinnādāna*), he abstains from taking what has not been given; taking only what has been given, expecting only what has been given, by not stealing he abides in purity. Abandoning sexual relations (*abrahmacarya*, Pa. *abrahmacariya*), he observes celibacy, living apart, abstaining from the coarse practice of sexual intercourse.

Abandoning false speech (*mṛṣāvāda*, Pa. *musāvāda*), he abstains from false speech; he speaks truth, adheres to truth, is trustworthy and reliable, one who is no deceiver of the world. Abandoning malicious speech (*piśunā vāk*, Pa. *pisuṇā vācā*), he abstains from malicious speech; he does not repeat elsewhere what he has heard here in order to divide [those people] from these, nor does he repeat to these people what he has heard elsewhere in order to divide [these people] from those; thus he is one who reunites those who are divided, a promoter of friendships, who enjoys concord, rejoices in concord, delights in concord, a speaker of words that promote concord. Abandoning harsh speech (*paruṣā vāk*, Pa. *pharusā vācā*), he abstains from harsh speech; he speaks such words as are gentle, pleasing to the ear, and loveable, as go to the heart, are courteous, desired by many and agreeable to many. Abandoning idle chatter (*sambhinnapralāpa*, Pa. *samphappalāpa*), he abstains from idle chatter; he speaks at the right time, speaks what is fact, speaks on what is good, speaks on the teaching (*dharma*, Pa. *dhamma*) and the discipline; at the right time he speaks such words as are worth recording, reasonable, moderate, and beneficial.

He abstains from injuring seeds and plants. He eats only one meal a day, abstaining from eating at night and outside the proper time. He abstains from dancing, singing, music, and unsuitable shows. He abstains from wearing garlands, smartening himself with scent, and embellishing himself with unguents. He abstains from high and large couches. He abstains from accepting gold and silver. He abstains from accepting raw grain. He abstains from accepting raw meat. He abstains from accepting women and girls. He abstains from accepting men and women slaves. He abstains from accepting goats and sheep. He abstains from accepting fowl and pigs. He abstains from accepting elephants, cattle, horses, and mares. He abstains from accepting fields and land. He abstains from going on errands and running messages. He abstains from buying and selling. He abstains from false weights, false metals, and false measures. He abstains from cheating, deceiving, defrauding, and trickery. He abstains from wounding, murdering, binding, brigandage, plunder, and violence.

He becomes content with robes to protect his body and with almsfood to maintain his stomach, and wherever he goes, he sets out taking only these with him. Just as a bird, wherever it goes, flies with its wings as its only burden, so too the monk becomes content with robes to protect his body and with almsfood to maintain his stomach, and wherever he goes, he sets out taking only these with him. Possessing this aggregate of noble moral discipline (*śīlaskandha*, Pa. *sīlakkhandha*), he experiences within himself a bliss of blamelessness.

On seeing a form (*rūpa*) with the eye, he does not grasp at its signs and features. Since, if he left the eye faculty unguarded, evil unwholesome states of longing (*abhidhyā*, Pa. *abhijjhā*) and dejection (*daurmanasya*, Pa. *domanassa*) might invade him, he practices the way of its restraint, he guards the eye faculty, he undertakes the restraint of the eye faculty. On hearing a sound (*śabda*) with the ear [...] On smelling an odor (*gandha*) with the nose [...] On tasting a flavor (*rasa*) with the tongue [...] On feeling a tactile object (*spraṣṭavya*) with the body [...] On cognizing a mental property[24] (*dharma*, Pa. *dhamma*) with the mind (*manas*), he does not grasp at its signs and features. Since, if he left the mind faculty unguarded, evil (*pāpaka*) unwholesome (*akuśala*, Pa. *akusala*) states of longing and dejection might invade him, he practices the way of its restraint, he guards the mind faculty, he undertakes the restraint of the mind faculty. Possessing this noble restraint of the faculties, he experiences within himself an unsullied bliss.

He becomes one who acts with clear awareness when going forward and returning; who acts with clear awareness when looking ahead and looking away; who acts with clear awareness when flexing and extending his limbs; who acts with clear awareness when wearing his robes and carrying his outer robe and bowl; who acts with clear awareness when eating, drinking, chewing, and tasting; who acts with clear awareness when defecating and urinating; who acts with clear awareness when walking, standing, sitting, falling asleep, waking up, talking, and keeping silent.

Possessing this aggregate of noble moral discipline, and this noble restraint of the faculties, and possessing this noble mindfulness and clear awareness, he resorts to a secluded resting place: the forest, the root of a tree, a mountain, a ravine, a hillside cave, a charnel ground, a jungle thicket, an open space, a heap of straw. On returning from his almsround, after his meal he sits down, folding his legs crosswise, setting his body erect, and establishing mindfulness (*smṛti*, Pa. *sati*) before him.

Abandoning longing (*abhidhyā*, Pa. *abhijjhā*) for the world, he dwells with a mind (*cetas*) free from longing; he purifies his mind (*citta*) from longing. Abandoning ill will (*vyāpāda*) and hatred (*pradveṣa*, Pa. *padosa*), he dwells with a mind free from ill will, compassionate for the welfare

---

24 On this translation, see Schmithausen 1976: 246n14. See further the discussion in chapter 2.

of all living beings; he purifies his mind from ill will and hatred. Abandoning dullness (*styāna*, Pa. *thīna*) and drowsiness (*middha*), he dwells free from dullness and drowsiness, having clear consciousness (*ālokasaṃjñin*), mindful and clearly comprehending; he purifies his mind from dullness and drowsiness. Abandoning restlessness (*auddhatya*, Pa. *uddhacca*) and remorse (*kaukṛtya*, Pa. *kukkucca*), he dwells free from agitation with a mind inwardly peaceful; he purifies his mind from restlessness and remorse. Abandoning doubt (*vicikitsā*, Pa. *vicikicchā*), he dwells having gone beyond doubt, unperplexed (*akathaṃkathin*) about wholesome mental properties (*kuśala dharma*); he purifies his mind from doubt.

Having thus abandoned these five hindrances (*nīvaraṇa*) and the secondary defilements (*upakleśa*, Pa. *upakkilesa*), secluded from sensual pleasures, secluded from unwholesome mental properties (*akuśala dharma*), he enters and dwells in the first stage of meditation (*dhyāna*, Pa. *jhāna*), which is accompanied by deliberation (*vitarka*) and reflection (*vicāra*), with pleasure (*prīti*) and joy (*sukha*) born of seclusion (*vivekaja*). [...]

Again, with the subsiding of deliberation and reflection, a monk enters and dwells in the second stage of meditation, which has internal quiet (*adhyātmasaṃprasāda*, Pa. *ajjhattaṃ sampasādanaṃ*) and unification of mind (*cetasa ekotībhāvaḥ*, Pa. *cetaso ekodibhāvo*) without deliberation and reflection, with pleasure and joy born of concentration (*samādhija*). [...]

Again, with the fading away as well of pleasure, he dwells equanimous (*upekṣaka*, Pa. *upekkhaka*) and, mindful (*smṛtimat*, Pa. *sata*) and fully aware (*saṃprajānat*, Pa. *sampajāna*), he experiences joy with the body; he enters and dwells in the third stage of meditation, of which the noble ones (*ārya*, Pa. *ariya*) declare: "He is equanimous, mindful, one who dwells joyfully." [...]

> Again, with the abandoning of joy (*sukha*) and suffering (*duḥkha*, Pa. *dukkha*), and with the previous passing away of joy (*saumanasya*, Pa. *somanassa*) and dejection (*daurmanasya*, Pa. *domanassa*), he enters and dwells in the fourth stage of meditation, which is neither suffering nor joyful and includes the purification of mindfulness by equanimity (*upekṣāsmṛtipariśuddhi*, Pa. *upekkhāsatipārisuddhi*).[25]

This part of the description of the path to liberation may coincide, in its contents, with what was taught by the historical Buddha. Its precise *form*, on the other hand, may owe its origin to the influence of later scholasticism, especially there where lists are involved, such as with the five hindrances and the four stages of meditation.[26] The description of the third stage of meditation, moreover, cannot in this form go back to the historical Buddha himself, as it contains the phrase: "on account of which the noble ones declare." The noble ones can only be Buddhists, as there is no evidence that the path of the four stages of meditation existed before the historical Buddha. Since, then, this description quotes earlier Buddhists, we have to assume that it was given its final form by later Buddhists. Contentwise, however, we may look upon it as, by and large, original.

The concluding part of the description, presented below, requires more caution. It describes the insights that are acquired at the moment

---

25 Tr. Bodhi 2005: 246–48. Meisig (1987) has compared the longer versions (Chinese, Sanskrit, Pāli) of this explanation as found in the *Śrāmaṇyaphala Sūtra* and identified a number of later insertions in the different versions. However, his analysis does not affect what is presented here. Manné (1995) interprets this presentation of the path to liberation as a "case history."

26 Zafiropulo (1993: 74ff.) doubts whether the four stages of meditation constitute part of the oldest Buddhist tradition. However, apart from their outer form, the criteria outlined above give us no reason to assume that the four stages of meditation are not authentic. The passages cited by Zafiropulo that do not mention them can be explained by developments that will be discussed below. Other passages speak of *dhyāna* in general without any mention of *four* stages of meditation. These only suggest, if anything, that the grouping into four stages did not exist at the beginning of the tradition; but even this is in no way conclusive.

of liberation. These insights are the most important items of knowledge there are in Buddhism. They were soon regarded as the essence of the Buddhist teaching. Not surprisingly, whatever came to be looked upon at any time as most important in the Buddhist teaching was subsequently claimed to have been discovered by the Buddha at the time of his liberation. We will return to this issue in a following chapter. Here we shall present the concluding part of the above description, leaving out portions that comparison of different versions has identified as later additions:[27]

> When his mind is thus concentrated, purified, bright, unblemished, rid of defilement, malleable, wieldy, steady, and attained to imperturbability, he directs it to knowledge of the destruction of the taints (*āsravakṣayajñāna*, Pa. *āsavakkayañāṇa*). He understands as it really is: "This is suffering. This is the origin of suffering. This is the cessation of suffering. This is the way leading to the cessation of suffering." He understands as it really is: "These are the taints. This is the origin of the taints. This is the cessation of the taints. This is the way leading to the cessation of the taints."
>
> When he knows and sees thus, his mind is liberated from the taint of desire (*kāmāsrava*, Pa. *kāmāsava*), from the taint of existence (*bhavāsrava*, Pa. *bhavāsava*), and from the taint of ignorance (*avidyāsrava*, Pa. *avijjāsava*).[28] When

27 Cf. Bareau 1963: 81–82; Schmithausen 1981: 221–22n75; Vetter 1988: xxiv n. 8; Bronkhorst 1993: 119–21; Zafiropulo 1993: 95–96. The passages left out deal with the knowledge of previous births and knowledge of the death and rebirth of beings. Gombrich (1994: 1085) does not believe these passages to be later additions because, if they were, there would not be "three knowledges" (*tisso vijjā*). He argues that the Buddha needed three knowledges to mock the Brahmans who also have three knowledges, namely the three Vedas. One could turn this argument around and use it to show why the final version of the text had to have three knowledges.

28 Zafiropulo (1993: 101–2) gives reasons to think that the division into three or four types of taints is of a later date; see also below. Zafiropulo further comes up with an original interpretation of the difference between the part concerning the four noble truths and the part concerning the taints (p. 125).

> [the mind] is liberated there comes the knowledge: "I am liberated."[29] He understands: "Birth is destroyed, the spiritual life has been lived, what had to be done has been done, so that I will not again return here."[30]

This passage shows that liberation takes place during the practitioner's lifetime and not at the moment of death. Other passages confirm this. The goal of the religious life is repeatedly described as attainable in this life and even as "not connected with death."[31] However, as we will see later, not all texts agree on this point.[32]

Various features of the ancient texts can be explained by the fact that at the beginning of its development, Buddhism was subject to strong influence from other movements. For instance, the most problematic part of the passage just presented deals with liberating knowledge; it is around this topic in particular that ideas originally alien to Buddhism found their way in. We now turn to this topic.

Self and Liberating Knowledge

The ancient texts tell us that the Buddha went to various teachers before his enlightenment as part of his search for the end of suffering—Ārāḍa Kālāma and Udraka Rāmaputra are mentioned by name. On each occasion he rejected their teachings after examination.[33] After his

---

29 Translation adjusted according to Schmithausen's latest interpretation of the phrase; see Zafiropulo 1993: 152. Cf. also Schmithausen 1981: 219–20n69.

30 Tr. Bodhi 2005: 249. Translation of the last phrase in accordance with Hinüber 1968: 182.

31 Bronkhorst 1993: 96–97; 1984: 187–90.

32 Norman (1994: 212 and 214) claims that nirvāṇa is indeed attained only at the time of death and that a person who has been liberated during his lifetime "has attained *nibbāna* (temporarily) but has relinquished it for as long as his life remains." However, in support of this he adduces mainly philosophical rather than philological arguments.

33 Zafiropulo (1993: 22ff.) is probably right in pointing out that there is no reason to assume that Ārāḍa Kālāma and Udraka Rāmaputra were not historical figures. See also Gombrich 1994: 1074–75.

enlightenment he was—again according to the ancient discourses—frequently involved in discussions with people who held other opinions. This suggests that the Buddha shared certain opinions with other teachers of his time. It is also likely that he proclaimed new teachings that went beyond these shared opinions. We will first delineate the common background and then discuss some important differences that the Buddhist texts themselves emphasize. In the process we will discover that some non-Buddhist teachings exerted an influence on the development of Buddhist teaching.

The belief in rebirth features in the explanation of the four noble truths and in the path to liberation. It cannot be regarded as something new taught by the Buddha because there are good reasons to think that he accepted it as a point of departure for his quest. It is an important presupposition of his teaching. This is not surprising. We know that in India this belief was not restricted to Buddhism. We find it in various non-Buddhist movements such as Jainism and the old Upaniṣads of the Veda. It also seems certain that Jainism existed already before the time of the historical Buddha.[34] He may also have been familiar with the contents of some Upaniṣads or of parts of them.[35] Our method, too, gives us no reason to doubt that the founder of Buddhism held this belief.[36] It follows that the belief in rebirth existed when the Buddha started his career as a teacher. We may assume that for him rebirth was not only a certainty but also an important facet of the problem to which he believed he had found a solution.

The doctrine of rebirth as it is presupposed in the Buddhist texts,

---

34 A predecessor of Mahāvīra by the name of Pārśva (Pāsa) supposedly lived and died 250 years before Mahāvīra, the Jaina teacher who was a contemporary of the Buddha; see Schubring 1935: 24–25. Simson (1991) points out that compared to other religious movements of the time, Buddhism originated relatively late.

35 See below.

36 Hirakawa (1990: 6) does not believe that rebirth constitutes an indispensable part of the Buddha's teaching. For Vetter (1996: 54) it seems likely that the Buddha first realized and taught the deathless (*amṛta*, Pa. *amata*) and only later discovered the doctrine of rebirth—or he was aware of the doctrine but started to engage with it only afterward. See also below.

however, is not identical with what we find, for example, in the Jaina texts. Both religions share the idea that the actions of a person determine how he or she will be reborn, but they differ in the way these actions are understood. In Jainism actions are understood as concrete, or physical; in Buddhism intention (*cetanā*) also plays a role: "Monks, I say that intention is action. It is with a certain intention that one acts, whether with body, speech, or mind."[37] This is understandable. The second noble truth says of thirst, i.e. desire, that it leads from birth to birth. Desire and intention are closely related. Actions, on the other hand, may result from intention—and therefore desire—but they do not have to.

This may explain the apparent difference between the four noble truths and the account quoted above of the path to liberation. In the four noble truths, thirst, i.e. desire, is regarded as the cause of rebirth. According to the path to liberation, however, beings are reborn each in accordance with his or her actions (*karman*). This difference confirms that karma is not conceived of as concrete or physical in these texts, because it is thirst that drives humans to act. Nevertheless, on the basis of these and similar passages some scholars raise the question whether karma played any role at all in the teaching of rebirth in early Buddhism.[38] We will not dwell on this question, however, because our criterion is contradiction between passages, and there is none in this case, so that we have no grounds to exclude the belief in karma.[39]

Another point shared by Buddhism and some of the other teachings of the time is the search for liberation from the cycle of rebirths. Once again it has to be said that in this respect, too, the Buddha's teaching was not original. Nor do the Buddhist texts make any such claim. The

37 AN III.415. See also McDermott 1984: 26ff.; 1980: 165–92. Bareau (1951: Index-Glossaire, p. 31 s.v. *cetanā*) translates the term *cetanā* as "*entendement*." This meaning may be suited to the *Dhammasaṅgaṇi* but not to the passage at hand. Cf. Kapani 1992: I.184n36; Abhidh-k(VP) p. 2n3.

38 See Schmithausen 1986: 205ff.

39 For the same reason we will not discuss the theory that originally karma could only lead to rebirth in a heaven or a hell; cf. Vetter 1988: 77ff. Schmithausen (1992: 137ff.) discusses these theories in the light of Aśoka's inscriptions.

novelty in the teaching of the Buddha is not the search for liberation or the belief in rebirth but rather the specific method taught.

Not all of ancient India's religions were based on the two premises of rebirth and search for liberation. The ancient and traditional religion of the brahmans in particular, the Vedic religion, had very different conceptions and goals. Rebirth and liberation belonged to a different, non-Vedic culture, which has not left us much in terms of scriptures[40] but which exerted much influence at the time. The Upaniṣads, even though they are associated with the Veda, were influenced by these non-Vedic ideas: they contain an amalgam of Vedic thinking combined with the belief in rebirth and the search for liberation.[41] Buddhism clearly belongs to that non-Vedic culture, even though its teachings differ considerably at times from other currents that belong to it.

The fact that Buddhism accepted the teaching of rebirth as a given shows that it did not originate in a historic vacuum. The Buddha shared this belief with his contemporaries; the same is probably true of a number of other beliefs, some of which may remain unidentifiable. In order to understand the ways in which the Buddha's method for achieving liberation differed from what came before, an understanding of certain non-Buddhist teachings and methods is necessary. The same is true when it comes to understanding passages in the Buddhist canon that criticize non-Buddhist methods, sometimes in ways that are not immediately obvious.

To illustrate this, let us turn to a problem that has played a central role both in the later history of Buddhism and in modern scholarship. It concerns the question of a self in ancient Buddhism. Most later Buddhists in India simply denied the existence of a self, a position we will take up later on. Here we have to ask whether the ancient discourses actually deny the existence of a self. Among modern scholars studying

---

40 Mainly it is the canons of the Jainas and Buddhists that remain.

41 Cf. Bronkhorst 1993a. Hinüber (1994: 6–7) speaks of a second, non-Vedic tradition of literature in ancient India whose early history goes back to the time of Vedic literature and which finds expression in the ancient texts of Buddhism and Jainism.

the passages in question, some believe that ancient Buddhism did not deny a self,[42] others believe that it did.[43] Instead of examining the controversy, let us take a look at some of the passages concerned and try to interpret them in the light of what we know of the time of the Buddha. The most important of these passages is supposed to preserve the words that the Buddha addressed to his first five disciples shortly after his enlightenment:

> And the Exalted One spake to the five monks thus:
>
> "Material form (*rūpa*), O monks, is not the self (*anātman*, Pa. *anattā*).[44] If material form were the self, O monks, material form could not be subject to sickness, and a man should be able to say regarding his material form: my body shall be so and so; my body shall not be so and so. But inasmuch, O monks, as material form is not the self, therefore material form is subject to sickness, and a man cannot say as regards his material form: my body shall be so and so; my body shall not be so and so.
>
> "The sensations (*vedanā*), O monks, are not the self [...]"—and then the very same exposition which has been given regarding material form is repeated with regard to the sensations. Then comes the detailed explanation regarding the remaining three aggregates (*skandha*, Pa. *khandha*), [namely] the ideations (*saṃjñā*, Pa. *saññā*), the conditioned factors (*saṃskāra*, Pa. *saṃkhāra*), [and] consciousness (*vijñāna*, Pa. *viññāṇa*). Then the Buddha goes on to say:
>
> "What think ye then, O monks, is material form permanent or impermanent?"

42 E.g., Frauwallner 1973a: 176–77 (1953: 222–23); Schmithausen 1969: 157–70; Bhattacharya 1973; Pérez-Remón 1980; Oetke 1988: 59–242.

43 E.g., Collins 1982: 250–71; 1982a; Gombrich 1988: 21 and 63.

44 Oldenberg translates *anattā* "not the self," Bareau "dépourvu de soi," that is "without self." We will discuss these two possible interpretations below. Here it must suffice to say that the context in this passage supports Oldenberg's interpretation.

"Impermanent, sire."

"But is that which is impermanent, sorrow or joy?"

"Sorrow, sire."

"But if a man duly considers that which is impermanent, full of sorrow, subject to change, can he say: that is mine, that is I, that is myself?"

"Sire, he cannot."

Then follows the same exposition in similar terms regarding sensations, ideations, conditioned factors, and consciousness: after which the discourse proceeds:

"Therefore, O monks, whatever in the way of material form (sensations, ideations, etc.) has ever been, will be, or is, either in us or in the outer world, whether strong or weak, low or high, far or near, it is not the self: this he must in truth perceive, who possesses real knowledge. Whosoever regards things in this light, O monks, being a wise and noble hearer of the word, turns away from material form, turns away from sensation and ideation, from conditioned factors and consciousness. When he turns away from them, he becomes free from desire; by the cessation of desire he obtains deliverance; when [the mind] is liberated there comes the knowledge: 'I am liberated.' He understands: 'Birth is destroyed, the spiritual life has been lived, what had to be done has been done, so that I will not again return here.'"[45]

We cannot tell with certainty, on the basis of this passage, whether the existence of a self is denied or not. It is not explicitly denied; there is no statement to the effect that "the self does not exist." All that is said

45 This passage is found in the Vinaya of the Theravādins (Vin I, pp. 13–14), in the Vinaya of the Mahīśāsakas (TI 1421, vol. 22, 105a15–24), and in the Vinaya of the Dharmaguptakas (TI 1428, vol. 22, 789a12–789b1), and elsewhere, for example SN III.67–68; see also SN III.48–49, etc. (for further references see Oetke 1988: 88–89 and 105; Pérez-Remón 1980: 158ff.). The various Vinaya versions have been translated into French by Bareau (1963: 191–92). We here follow Oldenberg's (1971: 213ff.) paraphrase.

is that the five aggregates that constitute the physical and mental basis of a human being are not the self. However, we can learn something else from this passage. Regardless of its existence or nonexistence, a specific *concept* of the self presents itself: the self that is being talked about is permanent, joyful, and not subject to change. Furthermore, it is clear from this passage that knowledge of the self is not the path to liberation. On the contrary, liberation is achieved by turning away from what might erroneously be regarded as the self.

Among non-Buddhists in ancient India, knowledge of the self was often recognized as the principal means to achieving liberation. In those non-Buddhist circles, this self was described in the same terms we also meet in this Buddhist passage: it is permanent, not subject to change, and often joyful. This cannot be a coincidence. Most of these individuals and currents, like Buddhists, held in common the goal of escape from the cycle of rebirth and the belief that rebirth is determined by actions (*karman*) performed in a previous life. Unlike their Buddhist counterparts, however, they concluded from this that one must either suppress all actions or discover that the core of the human (or even nonhuman) being, its true self, has no part in these actions and is, therefore, permanent and not subject to change.[46]

We will deal later with the adherents of ascetic movements who tried to suppress, fully or in part, their bodily and mental activities. Here we are interested in those currents in which knowledge of the true self was looked upon as the primary condition for liberation, for these will enable us to correctly evaluate the passage from the Buddhist canon quoted above. They find expression, in the early period, primarily in the Upaniṣads and in the great epic, the *Mahābhārata*. It is not impossible, though far from certain, that the Buddha was familiar with the contents of some Upaniṣads or of some of their parts, and perhaps with other Vedic texts.[47] In the *Bṛhadāraṇyaka Upaniṣad* (4.4.20),

46 Bronkhorst 1993: 31–67.

47 See Norman 1981: 19–29; Gombrich 1988: 77; 1990: 14ff. On the familiarity of the Pāli canon with the Veda and Vedic sacrifices, see Falk 1988: 225–54 (with references).

for example, it is said: "The self is unborn, great, and permanent." The *Maitrāyaṇī Upaniṣad* (2.7) and the *Śvetāśvatara Upaniṣad* (1.9) emphasize the inactivity of the self. (We have already indicated that it is likely that the Upaniṣads borrowed these ideas from other, non-Vedic movements.) The joyful nature of the self, too, is mentioned in the old Brahmanical texts. What defines the self is joy and bliss (*ānanda*), we read in the *Taittirīya Upaniṣad* (2.5). The same is said about Brahman in the *Bṛhadāraṇyaka Upaniṣad* (3.9.28), and the identification of Brahman with the self is well attested.

All this shows that the passage quoted above criticizes first and foremost an alternative method of liberation. The fact that in the Buddhist texts this view of the self is sometimes explicitly attributed to others confirms this. We read, for example, of ascetics and brahmans who regard that which is pleasant in the world as permanent, joyful, the self, free of illness, and at ease.[48] These ascetics and brahmans commit a mistake, it is added, because in this way thirst, i.e., desire, becomes stronger. Another passage is worth quoting for its humorous comparison. It is put in the mouth of the Buddha:

> There are some ascetics and brahmans who declare and believe that after death the self is entirely happy and free from disease. I approached them and asked if this was indeed what they declared and believed, and they replied: "Yes." Then I said: "Do you, friends, living in the world, know and see it as an entirely happy place?" and they replied: "No." I said: "Have you ever experienced a single night or day, or half a night or day, that was entirely happy?" and they replied "No." [...] It is just as if a man were to say: "I am going to seek out and love the most beautiful girl in the country." They might say to him: "Well, as to this most beautiful girl in the country, do you know whether she belongs to the khattiya [Skt. *kṣatriya*], the brahman, the merchant, or the artisan class?"

48 SN II.109; cf. MN I.135–36; III.64, etc.; see also Oetke 1988: 157; Norman 1981.

> and he would say: "No." Then they might say: "Well, do you know her name, her clan, whether she is tall or short or of medium height, whether she is dark or light-complexioned or sallow-skinned, or what village or town or city she comes from?" and he would say: "No." And they might say: "Well then, you don't know or see the one you seek for and desire?" and he would say: "No." Does not the talk of that man turn out to be stupid?[49]

The aim of the teaching of the Buddha is evidently not to discover the real self. On the contrary, the preoccupation with the true nature of the self has to be given up. Only then one is ready to follow the path shown by the Buddha.[50] Seen from this practical point of view, the question as to the existence of the self is of minor importance. The main thing is that knowledge of the self plays no useful role on the Buddha's path to liberation. In view of the fact that certain non-Buddhist currents asserted a permanent self not subject to change because only knowledge of such a self could be useful to the attainment of liberation, it is probably justified to assume that the Buddha did not accept the existence of such a self.[51]

Note that the passage quoted above is not only negative. Acquiring the insight that the various components of the person are not the self causes a wise and noble listener to turn away from material form, and so on; as a result he becomes free from desire and attains liberation. In this

---

49 DN I.192–93; tr. Walshe 1995: 166. Cf. also Glasenapp 1983: 65–66.

50 Schmithausen (1973a: 178) was probably right in stating that the Buddha's negative attitude with regard to the self was purely spiritual-practical. Vetter (1991: 187), too, rightly observes that the fact that the existence of the *ātman* is not recognized in the ancient texts is not merely an expression of denial but should be seen as a case of avoidance of the *ātman* in the description of aim and result of the path. However, his reasoning does not convince when he claims that the *ātman* was too much surrounded by myths, which were perceived as inappropriate or even as a hindrance.

51 Nevertheless, Oetke (1988: 153) is no doubt right in thinking that the thesis according to which the Buddha explicitly rejected or denied a self is unfounded.

way the criticism of other, non-Buddhist paths serves a positive purpose. The rejection of the liberating knowledge of others becomes itself a liberating knowledge. This will be discussed in more detail below.

In the passage on not-self above, it is stated that the five aggregates (*skandha*, Pa. *khandha*)—that is material form (*rūpa*), sensations (*vedanā*), ideations (*saṃjñā*, Pa. *saññā*), conditioned factors (*saṃskāra*, Pa. *saṃkhāra*), and consciousness (*vijñāna*, Pa. *viññāṇa*)—are not the self. The aggregates are, in our text, components of the person, which should not be confused with the concept of the self, and it seems natural to assume that the five aggregates are all there is to a person. This, at any rate, is how the later Buddhists understood it. The person (*pudgala*, Pa. *puggala*), seen this way, is a conglomerate of these aggregates.[52]

It is impossible to determine whether the aggregates, and the analysis of the person based on, or inspired by, them, was part of the original teaching of the Buddha. One could conceive of the path to liberation described so far without the assumption of the aggregates, but they are, as far as I am aware, never criticized in the ancient texts.[53] One thing however is certain, namely, that the list of aggregates became extremely important for the later development of the teaching, as will be shown below. The same is true of other lists in the ancient discourses. Take another look at the following passage from the description of the path to liberation quoted above: "On seeing a form with the eye, he does not grasp at its signs and features. [...] On hearing a sound with the ear [...] On smelling an odor with the nose [...] On tasting a flavor with the tongue [...] On feeling a tactile object with the body [...] On cognizing a mental property with the mind, he does not grasp at its signs and features." This passage describes how the monk must behave with regard to the objects of his sense organs. It also contains a list of the sense organs and sense objects. These are the eye (*cakṣus*) and form (*rūpa*), the ear (*śrotra*) and sound (*śabda*), the nose (*ghrāṇa*) and odor (*gandha*), the

52 The distinction between the person and the self is taken up in more detail in chapter 2.

53 Oetke (1988: 121) considers it possible that the relationship between person and *skandha*s was not very clearly defined in earlier times.

tongue (*jihvā*) and flavor (*rasa*), the body (*kāya*) and tactile objects (*spraṣṭavya*), the mind (*manas*) and the mental property (*dharma*). All together these are six pairs, or twelve realms (*āyatana*), which is the designation by which they are known in the Buddhist texts and gain in importance. An extension of this list is the one of eighteen elements (*dhātu*). It contains not only the above six sense organs and six sense objects but also the six corresponding classes of consciousness: eye consciousness (*cakṣurvijñāna*), ear consciousness (*śrotravijñāna*), nose consciousness (*ghrāṇavijñāna*), tongue consciousness (*jihvāvijñāna*), body consciousness (*kāyavijñāna*), and mind consciousness (*manovijñāna*).

We are now ready to deal with the problem of liberating knowledge. We have seen that, during the formation of Buddhism, knowledge of the self constituted a path to liberation that competed with Buddhism. This path to liberation was close to Buddhism in that it, too, had liberation from the cycle of rebirths as its aim. The early Buddhists were familiar with this other path, and they were inevitably confronted with the question as to what constituted the liberating knowledge of the Buddhist path. This question was all the more important because there was one further important religious tradition at the time that, even though it did not accept liberation from rebirth as a goal, nevertheless gave great importance to insight. This was Vedic religion. In Vedic literature, especially in the so-called Brāhmaṇas, mention is often made of the power of knowledge, particularly in the context of the magical identifications common there.[54]

A few examples must suffice to illustrate this. We read, for example, in the *Aitareya Brāhmaṇa* (1.5.1): "The one who desires energy or Brahmanic illustriousness should [...] use the two *gāyatrī* stanzas. The *gāyatrī* is energy and Brahmanic illustriousness. Energetic and illustrious does he become who *knowing thus* uses the two *gāyatrī* stanzas."[55] The *Jaiminīya Brāhmaṇa* (1.122) contains the following passage: "Rūra [...], desiring cattle, performed austerities. He saw this melody (*sāman*). He praised with it. He used this (word) *iḷā* (as finale). *Iḷā* means cat-

54 See Smith 1989.

55 Tr. Gonda 1975: 372; cf. Oldenberg 1919: 5–6.

tle. Then he obtained cattle. Therefore this melody procures cattle. *He who knows this* obtains cattle and becomes rich in cattle. And because Rūra [...] saw it, therefore also it is called Raurava."[56] From the same Brāhmaṇa (JB 1.11) we learn the following: "When now he offers these two morning oblations, [the sun] lifts him up by means of these two. As an elephant rises together with him who is sitting on the elephant seat, so this deity rises together with him who offers *knowing thus*. It makes him go to its own world, of which there is none supreme. Whatever is beyond the sun, that is immortality. That he wins."[57] And again: "*He who knows* the 'divine' chariot comes into possession of a chariot. The 'divine' chariot is sacrifice."[58] In the next example, this one from the *Taittirīya Brāhmaṇa* (3.11.8.7–8), a connection between persons and things is "etymologically" established: "Prajāpati (the creator god) did not know how to give the sacrificial fee (*dakṣiṇā*). He put it in his right hand (*dakṣiṇaḥ*). He took it, speaking the ritual formula (*mantra*): 'For fitness (*dakṣa*) I take you, the sacrificial fee (*dakṣiṇā*).' Therefore he became fit (*adakṣata*). The one who *knowing thus* receives the sacrificial fee (*dakṣiṇā*) becomes fit (*dakṣate*)."[59] There are numerous examples of this kind in Vedic literature. They demonstrate that the Vedic religion also attributed great value to knowledge.

What was the liberating knowledge of the Buddhists? There are indications that the Buddhists themselves were divided over this question. This is already true of the authors of the ancient discourses, which provide different answers. In the description of the path to liberation quoted above, we find the knowledge of the destruction of the taints (*āsrava*); in several versions the knowledge of past lives and the knowledge of the passing away and reappearance of beings are added. In the passage on not-self quoted above, it is rather the knowledge that the five aggregates (*skandha*) are not mine, not I, and not my self that leads to liberation. Elsewhere it is the thought that the five aggregates

56 Tr. Bodewitz 1990: 69.

57 Tr. Bodewitz 1973: 42.

58 JB 1.129; tr. Bodewitz 1990: 73–74. Cf. Gonda 1960: 178.

59 Tr. Witzel 1979: 13. Cf. Gonda 1991: 177.

appear and disappear, or the insight that the aggregates are empty, void, and without substance, that leads to this goal.[60] In some texts, doctrinal points that have meanwhile gained in importance become part of the liberating knowledge. Examples are the doctrines of conditioned origination (*pratītyasamutpāda*) and of the selflessness of the person ([*pudgala-*]*nairātmya*),[61] which are discussed below.

If we examine more closely the knowledge of the destruction of the taints, a number of irregularities become apparent.[62] In the passage quoted above this knowledge was described as follows: "He understands as it really is: 'This is suffering. This is the origin of suffering. This is the cessation of suffering. This is the way leading to the cessation of suffering.' He understands as it really is: 'These are the taints. This is the origin of the taints. This is the cessation of the taints. This is the way leading to the cessation of the taints.' When he knows and sees thus, his mind is liberated from the taint of desire (*kāmāsrava*, Pa. *kāmāsava*), from the taint of existence (*bhavāsrava*, Pa. *bhavāsava*), and from the taint of ignorance (*avidyāsrava*, Pa. *avijjāsava*)." This knowledge includes the four noble truths, which are presented here as the liberating knowledge. But these same four noble truths are also the content of the first sermon delivered by the Buddha after his enlightenment, if we can trust the tradition on this point.[63] This means, no doubt, that it was considered that these truths could motivate a listener to enter the path to liberation. They cannot therefore constitute the liberating knowledge that manifests itself at the end of this path.

There is something else. In several versions of the first sermon the

---

60 Schmithausen 1981: 219–21.

61 Schmithausen 1981: 211–12. Several of these knowledges have in common that one reaches liberation only when one has stopped identifying with the changing components of the person. In this respect these insights are not very different from the cognition of the unchanging nature of the self, criticized by the Buddha.

62 Vetter (1996: 66–67) attempts to prove that the *āsrava*s cannot have been part of what constituted the oldest layer of the canon ("kein Buddhawort"). Schmithausen (1992: 123–24) discusses the multifaceted meaning of the word *āsrava* in Buddhist as well as non-Buddhist literature.

63 Cf. Bareau 1963: 172–73; Féer 1870; Waldschmidt 1951.

Buddha explains to the group of five disciples how, at his enlightenment, he had fully realized the four noble truths which comprise three "turnings" (*parivarta*)—i.e., of the wheel of the doctrine—and twelve aspects (*ākāra*), four for each turning:[64]

The first turning:

1. this is suffering;
2. this is the origin of suffering;
3. this is the cessation of suffering;
4. this is the path leading to the cessation of suffering

The second turning:

5. suffering must be fully known;
6. its origin must be destroyed;
7. its destruction must be accomplished;
8. the path leading to its destruction must be traveled.

The third turning:

9. suffering has been fully known;
10. its origin has been destroyed;
11. its destruction has been accomplished;
12. the path leading to its destruction has been traveled.

These explanations are probably later additions.[65] But it is in this form that the texts portray knowledge of the four noble truths as liberating knowledge, for they continue: "O monks, as soon as the [pure] eye that sees the four noble truths with its three turnings and twelve aspects arose, along with the certainty, the knowledge, and the insight, I was liberated, relieved, released from this world with its gods, its *māra*s, and its *brahmā*s, from its human beings with their ascetics and

64 CPS pp. 146–48. I here follow Lamotte (1977: 289), who also provides references to parallel versions.

65 See Féer 1870: 429–35; Schmithausen 1981: 203. Zafiropulo (1993: 118), while denying the possibility that these explanations themselves, along with the four noble truths, might have constituted the content of liberating knowledge, understands these explanations as a not very successful description of part of the process that leads to liberation.

their brahmans. I established myself firmly in the state of mind that is free from confusions, and from that moment, O monks, I knew that I had attained the highest and perfect enlightenment." These elaborations show that there were Buddhists for whom the unaugmented four noble truths could not be the liberating knowledge. What led the Buddha to his enlightenment was rather the knowledge of the first truth, the destruction (of the content) of the second truth, the realization of the third truth, and the practice of the fourth truth.[66]

It has already been observed that the interest of the early Buddhists in some form of liberating knowledge can easily be explained with reference to the religious milieu of the time. The vacillating attitude of the texts with regard to the exact content of this knowledge gives rise to the suspicion that the early Buddhist tradition had little or nothing to offer in this respect. That would not be surprising. In the above-quoted description of the path to liberation, a number of meditative, one might say mystical, states are depicted that precede the liberating knowledge; this knowledge is therefore attained in such a state. It is however known that mystical states cannot always be accurately described in words. Perhaps the oldest tradition did not talk about a liberating knowledge at all, or if it did, it talked about a knowledge without specifying its content. This latter suspicion is supported by the fact that in some versions of the first sermon—probably the older ones—the four noble truths or other forms of liberating knowledge are not mentioned at all. The Buddha is here portrayed as someone who teaches his disciples in private. Liberating knowledges, or any other knowledges for that matter, are not formulated.[67]

---

66 Rospatt (1996: 84) points out that the certainty of one's liberation from suffering cannot possibly precede the experience of liberation itself.

67 See Bronkhorst 1993: 102–11; Zafiropulo 1993: 161, 183. Zafiropulo (1993: 120) suspects that in the oldest texts it is the term *ājñā/aññā* rather than *prajñā* that points at this ineffable liberating knowledge. Cf. also Vetter 1988: 30. Even if we accept that originally the liberating knowledge was not, or could not be, put in words, we cannot conclude from this that the Buddha did not have a teaching that could be expressed in words, as Gombrich (1994: 1072) believes. Cf. also Zafiropulo 1993: 111–12.

In most versions of the first sermon the listeners are five monks. In the versions belonging to the *Vinaya-piṭaka*, these five monks attain the goal of the teaching, namely, liberation from the taints, during the second sermon of the Buddha.[68] That is to say, like the Buddha, the five monks become arhats. We have already come across this second sermon, which is so important for the five monks. It is the discourse on not-self, whose most important parts have been quoted above. In that connection we have also pointed out that the knowledge of not-self is regarded there as liberating knowledge. Now we see that this liberating knowledge enabled the five monks to become arhats while still listening to the sermon.

It is difficult to conceive of a starker contrast than the one between the path to liberation as discussed above and the process of liberation described here. In the preceding account liberation was attained in solitude, in a mystical state, and presumably without the help of knowledge formulated in words. In the present one it suffices to listen to the liberating knowledge, in the presence of others, in order to immediately become an arhat. This contrast shows that various ideas about the path to liberation found a place side by side in the ancient Buddhist texts.

The same contrast also appears elsewhere in the Buddhist discourses and plays a significant role in the further development of Buddhism. The famous Belgian scholar Louis de la Vallée Poussin emphasized this in 1937 in an important article that draws attention to two monks, Musīla and Nārada.[69] In a sūtra of the Saṃyutta Nikāya / Saṃyuktāgama,[70] first Musīla is questioned about his spiritual state. It becomes clear that he knows through his own knowledge and insight the causal relationships found in the chain of *conditioned origination* (*pratītyasamutpāda*, Pa. *paṭiccasamuppāda*, to be discussed below). He knows from the same

68 Pāli *imasmiñ ca pana veyyākaraṇasmiṃ bhaññamāne* (Vin I.14) indicates simultaneity: "While the teaching was being spoken"; the same goes for the Chinese parallels (TI 1421, vol. 22, 105a24; TI 1428, vol. 22, 789b1; MĀ p. 778c6).

69 La Vallée Poussin 1937b: 189–222. Cf. Gombrich 1996: 96ff.

70 SN II.115–16; SĀ pp. 98c–99a.

source that the cessation of becoming is nirvāṇa. If this is true, the questioner concludes, the venerable Musīla is an arhat, one whose taints are destroyed. Musīla's silence betrays his agreement with this. Next Nārada asks to be questioned in the same way. He answers the same questions in exactly the same words. He rejects, however, the conclusion that he is an arhat, one whose taints are destroyed. He explains this with the help of a simile. Just as when a man who is hot and thirsty finds a well in the wilderness, he sees the well and knows that it contains water, but alas, he cannot reach and touch the water. In the same way he, Nārada, even though he knows that the cessation of becoming is nirvāṇa, is no arhat, and his taints have not been destroyed.

As said before, the contrast between the two processes of liberation is too pronounced to go unnoticed. It makes a great deal of difference whether enlightenment is only to be found in the solitude of the forest, in a mystical state induced by meditation exercises, or alternatively, by means of the attainment of certain knowledges, possibly in the company of other people. It is even more telling that the Buddhists themselves do not know who is an arhat and who is not. In Musīla's case the texts give the impression that he maintains in good faith that he is an arhat. The sūtra does not state that he was wrong. It does, however, state that, under the same circumstances, Nārada did not consider himself to be an arhat.

We have repeatedly pointed out that the presence in the Buddhist texts of a liberating knowledge that can be expressed in words can, without difficulty, be explained by the important role such items of knowledge played in several non-Buddhist religious movements of the time. This is particularly clear in the case of the liberating knowledge of not-self. This knowledge, as we have seen, is expressed in the following words:

> Therefore, O monks, whatever in the way of material form (sensations, ideations, etc., respectively) has ever been, will be, or is, either in us or in the outer world, whether strong or weak, low or high, far or near, it is not the self: this he must in truth perceive, who possesses real knowledge. Whosoever

> regards things in this light, O monks, being a wise and noble hearer of the word, turns away from material form, turns away from sensation and ideation, from conditioned factor and consciousness. When he turns away from them, he becomes free from desire; by the cessation of desire he obtains deliverance; when [the mind] is liberated there comes the knowledge: "I am liberated." He understands: "Birth is destroyed, the spiritual life has been lived, what had to be done has been done, so that I will not again return here."

The non-identity of the person with anything that is involved in actions is here emphasized. This hardly differs from the knowledge of the self of certain non-Buddhists. Their self was that part of the person which does not participate in actions. Seen this way, this liberating knowledge of the Buddhists is hardly more than a mirror image of the liberating knowledge of the self of those non-Buddhists. In this case the Buddhist texts have not just borrowed the concept of a liberating knowledge expressible in words, they have also borrowed its content from their opponents.[71]

It follows that the discrepancy mentioned above, which was noticed by the Buddhists themselves, need not be ascribed to the teaching of the historical Buddha. It is far more likely that, contrary to what happened later, no explicitly formulated liberating knowledge was part of the original teaching. This does not exclude that some kind of liberating knowledge may have played a role in Buddhism from the beginning. The texts frequently speak about *prajñā* (Pa. *paññā*), which may be translated as "wisdom." It is, for example, described as follows:

71 See Bronkhorst 1995. I do not subscribe to the point of view of Schneider (1967: 253–54; 1980: 69–70), who in some publications ascribes to the Buddha the teaching that one has to abstain from accumulating karma in order to avoid rebirth. Schneider quotes in this context also the first sermon of the Buddha. This teaching is precisely *not* part of original Buddhism.

> Right view (*samyagdṛṣṭi*, Pa. *sammādiṭṭhi*), I say, is twofold: there is right view that is affected by taints, partaking of merit, ripening on the side of attachment; and there is right view that is noble, taintless, supramundane, a factor of the path. [...] And what, monks, is the right view that is noble, taintless, supramundane, a factor of the path? The wisdom (*prajñā*, Pa. *paññā*), the faculty of wisdom (*prajñendriya*, Pa. *paññindriya*), the power of wisdom (*prajñābala*, Pa. *paññābala*), the enlightenment factor of understanding the doctrine (*dharmavicayasaṃbodhyaṅga*, Pa. *dhammavicayasambojjhaṅga*).[72]

It is not hard to imagine that the occurrence of this term in the oldest stratum of the tradition prompted attempts to define the precise content of this "wisdom."[73]

For the modern scholar it is possible, as we have just demonstrated, to explain discrepancies in the canonical texts with the help of the assumption that non-Buddhist movements exercised an influence on Buddhist teaching. For a Buddhist, who takes the texts as the word of the Buddha, the situation is different. Discrepancies like the ones mentioned above require an explanation in his case too, but this explanation should not simply be a historical one. Only a systematic solution might be regarded as satisfactory by the tradition. It would have to show how the contradictory teachings are parts of a wider, more encompassing vision, in which they no longer contradict, but rather support and strengthen each other. It looks as if the doctrine of conditioned origination had a role to play here.

Let us examine the situation in more detail. If one believes that there is an item of knowledge that liberates human beings from the cycle of rebirths, or even from suffering itself, then clearly, the absence of this knowledge must be the reason why humanity finds itself in its sorry state. To phrase it differently: the absence of

72 MN III.72; tr. Ñāṇamoli & Bodhi 1995: 934–35. Cf. also Lamotte 1977: 293.

73 Bronkhorst 1993: 107–8.

knowledge—ignorance—is the original cause of rebirth and suffering. This is of course different from what we encountered in the four noble truths. There it was thirst that was the root of all suffering and that had to be destroyed. How do thirst and ignorance relate to each other? The answer is found in the doctrine of conditioned origination, which is expounded and explained in discourses such as the following one:

> The Blessed One said this: "And what, monks, is conditioned origination? With (1) ignorance as condition, (2) conditioned factors [come to be]; with conditioned factors as condition, (3) consciousness;[74] with consciousness as condition, (4) name-and-form; with name-and-form as condition, (5) the six realms of the senses; with the six realms of the senses as condition, (6) contact; with contact as condition, (7) sensation; with sensation as condition, (8) thirst, i.e. craving; with thirst as condition, (9) clinging; with clinging as condition, (10) existence; with existence as condition, (11) birth; with birth as condition, (12) aging-and-death, sorrow, lamentation, suffering, dejection, and despair come to be. Such is the origin of this whole mass of suffering. [...]
>
> And what, monks, is aging-and-death (*jarāmaraṇa*)? The aging of the various beings in the various orders of beings, their growing old, brokenness of teeth, greyness of hair, wrinkling of skin, decline of vitality, degeneration of the faculties: this is called aging. The passing away of the various beings from the various orders of beings, their perishing, breakup, disappearance, mortality, death, completion of time, the breakup of the aggregates, the laying down

74 Already in the ancient Buddhist texts *vijñāna* has two meanings: "cognition" and "consciousness." The choice of how to translate the term may sometimes be somewhat arbitrary, because the texts themselves do not always make a clear distinction between the two meanings. The ambiguity of the term led in later times to developments that will be discussed below. Cf. Waldron 1994.

of the carcass: this is called death. Thus this aging and this death are together called aging-and-death.

And what, monks, is birth (*jāti*)? The birth of the various beings into the various orders of beings, their being born, descent [into the womb], production, the manifestation of the aggregates, the obtaining of the realms of the senses. This is called birth.

And what, monks, is existence (*bhava*)? There are these three kinds of existence: existence in the sphere of desire (*kāma*), existence in the sphere of form (*rūpa*), existence in the sphere of non-form (*arūpa*). This is called existence.

And what, monks, is clinging (*upādāna*)? There are these four kinds of clinging: clinging to sensual pleasures, clinging to views, clinging to rules and vows, clinging to a doctrine of self. This is called clinging.

And what, monks, is thirst (*tṛṣṇā*, Pa. *taṇhā*)? There are these six classes of thirst: thirst for forms, thirst for sounds, thirst for odors, thirst for flavors, thirst for tangibles, thirst for mental properties. This is called thirst.

And what, monks, is sensation (*vedanā*)? There are six classes of sensation: sensation born of eye-contact, sensation born of ear-contact, sensation born of nose-contact, sensation born of tongue-contact, sensation born of body-contact, sensation born of mind-contact. This is called sensation.

And what, monks, is contact (*sparśa*, Pa. *phassa*)? There are six classes of contact: eye-contact, ear-contact, nose-contact, tongue-contact, body-contact, mind-contact. This is called contact.

And what, monks, are the six realms of the senses (*ṣaḍāyatana*, Pa. *saḷāyatana*)? The eye realm, ear realm, nose realm, tongue realm, body realm, mind realm. These are called the six realms of the senses.

And what, monks, is name-and-form (*nāmarūpa*)? Sensation, ideation, volition, contact, attention: this is called name. The four great elements and the form derived from the four great elements: this is called form. Thus this name and this form are together called name-and-form.

And what, monks, is consciousness (*vijñāna*, Pa. *viññāṇa*)? There are six classes of consciousness: eye consciousness, ear consciousness, nose consciousness, tongue consciousness, body consciousness, mind consciousness. This is called consciousness.

And what, monks, are the conditioned factors (*saṃskāra*, Pa. *saṅkhāra*)? There are these three kinds of conditioned factors: the bodily conditioned factor, the verbal conditioned factor, the mental conditioned factor. These are called the conditioned factors.

And what, monks, is ignorance (*avidyā*, Pa. *avijjā*)? Not knowing suffering, not knowing the origin of suffering, not knowing the cessation of suffering, not knowing the path leading to the cessation of suffering. This is called ignorance.

Thus, monks, with ignorance as condition, conditioned factors [come to be]; with conditioned factors as condition, consciousness [...] Such is the origin of this whole mass of suffering. But with the remainderless fading away and cessation of ignorance comes cessation of conditioned factors; with the cessation of conditioned factors comes cessation of consciousness; with the cessation of consciousness comes cessation of name-and-form; with the cessation of name-and-form comes cessation of the six realms of the senses; with the cessation of the six realms of the senses comes cessation of contact; with the cessation of contact comes the cessation of sensation; with the cessation of sensation comes the cessation of thirst; with the cessation of thirst, comes the cessation of clinging; with the cessation of clinging comes the cessation of existence; with the cessation of existence come the cessation of birth; with the cessation of birth comes the cessation

> of aging-and-death, sorrow, lamentation, suffering, dejection, and despair. Such is the cessation of this whole mass of suffering.[75]

In this enumeration ignorance occurs at the beginning, thirst in the eighth position. This means that ignorance is a condition for all of the other elements in the enumeration, including thirst. And the destruction of thirst is only possible if ignorance is destroyed first. Therefore only subordinate importance can be assigned to the destruction of thirst, and the original path to liberation now becomes a relatively unimportant part of the new method, whose most important part is the liberating insight.[76]

Despite its usefulness for the coherence of the teaching, this enumeration of the causal links of conditioned origination (*pratītyasamutpāda*, Pa. *paṭiccasamuppāda*) poses great challenges to the understanding. Already in the ancient discourses it is described as very profound and difficult to comprehend.[77] And when the disciple Ānanda believes that he has grasped the causal sequence, the Buddha is reported to say to him:

> Do not say that, Ānanda, do not say that! This conditioned origination is profound and appears profound. It is through not understanding, not penetrating this doctrine that this generation has become like a tangled ball of string, covered as with a blight, tangled like coarse grass, unable to pass

75 SN II.2–4; tr. Bodhi, 2000: 534–36. Cf. Mylius 1985: 201–2. The doctrine of conditioned origination has many forms, especially in the Saṃyutta Nikāya; cf. Zafiropulo 1993: 104ff.; Mori 1991: (742)–(733) (= 39–48). Zafiropulo (1993: 108) points out that ignorance is often missing in the different versions and concludes that ignorance was not from the beginning regarded as the main cause of all suffering.

76 It is of course tempting to suspect that the distinction between the taint of desire (*kāmāsrava*, Pa. *kāmāsava*) and the taint of ignorance (*avidyāsrava*, Pa. *avijjāsava*), which we encountered in the description of the event of liberation, cited earlier, is not original either.

77 CPS § 8.2, p. 440; cf. Bernhard 1968: 53.

> beyond states of woe, the ill destiny, ruin, and the round of birth-and-death.[78]

Probably the best modern attempt at explaining the chain of conditions is found in Erich Frauwallner's *History of Indian Philosophy*. After a detailed analysis of the different elements of the chain, Frauwallner sums up his explanation in the following manner:

> The ultimate cause of entanglement in the cycle of existence is ignorance (*avidyā* [1]), i.e. the lack of acquaintance with the releasing knowledge, namely, the four noble truths. For in the person who does not possess this knowledge, conditioned factors (*saṃskāra* [2])[79] originate that are directed at the sense-objects and the earthly personality. Driven by these conditioned factors, consciousness (*vijñāna* [3]), which is, like a fine body, the carrier of rebirth, enters after death into a new womb. Connected with this consciousness, the body and the psychical factors (name-and-form, *nāmarūpa* [4]) develop, and finally also the six realms of the senses (*ṣaḍāyatana* [5]) of the new being, which in this way comes into existence. When this new being is born, the fateful contact (*sparśa* [6]) of the sense organs with their objects ensues. Sensations (*vedanā* [7]) of different kinds arise and awaken the passions, above all thirst (*tṛṣṇā* [8]), which clings (*upādāna* [9]) to the sense-pleasures and the supposed "I" and leads, therethrough, to new bondage and a new existence (*bhava* [10]). Once again this leads to rebirth (*jāti* [11]) and entanglement in the sorrow of existence (*jarāmaraṇa,* etc. [12]), and this goes on in an endless chain, as long as the releasing knowledge and the destruction of thirst do not put an end to the cycle.[80]

78 DN II.55; tr. Walshe 1995: 223. Cf. also Bernhard 1968: 54; La Vallée Poussin 1913: vi.

79 For a detailed analysis of this term in Buddhism, see Kapani 1992: 169ff.

80 Frauwallner 1973a: 165 (1953: 208–9). Cf. also Glasenapp 1938: 63–64. For an overview of the various attempts at explanation, see La Vallée Poussin 1913: 34ff.

In this explanation—as in most others—the links of the chain are distributed over three lives. Two rebirths are depicted, but in very different ways. This somewhat strange state of affairs is best explained with the help of Frauwallner's assumption that the chain with twelve links is the result of a fusion of two different chains.[81] The second part, from thirst to old age, dying, and so on (8–12), is content-wise merely an elaboration of the basic idea of the first two noble truths: old age, dying, and so on (12)—i.e., suffering—are conditioned by birth (11) and new existence (10) and have as their cause thirst (8) on account of clinging (9).[82]

The first part of the chain, from ignorance to sensation (1–7), describes how a new being is born. In this process consciousness (*vijñāna*) is the carrier that after death enters the next incarnation in the cycle of rebirths.[83] One can indeed imagine that consciousness, driven by conditioned factors (*saṃskāra*), enters into a new womb. Following this, a new body with mental factors (name-and-form, *nāmarūpa*) and realms of the senses (*ṣaḍāyatana*) develops, which, through contact (*sparśa*) with outer objects, has sensations (*vedanā*). The main problem with regard to understanding this first part is to explain the relationship between ignorance (*avidyā*) and the conditioned factors (*saṃskāra*). It is not at all obvious that conditioned factors are conditioned by ignorance, or that the knowledge of the four noble truths leads to the destruction of the conditioned factors. Indeed, in a passage from the Majjhima Nikāya, taints are put in the place of ignorance.[84] Without ignorance the two parts of the causal chain conflict less with each other and describe more or less the same thing, though in different terms. The conditioned factors (or perhaps the taints) are now the

81 Frauwallner 1973a: 166–67 (1953: 210–11); Bernhard 1968. In Frauwallner's opinion it was the Buddha himself who reshaped his teachings in order to take into account the importance of liberating insight in other religious movements.

82 See Bernhard 1968: 56. Zafiropulo (1993: 110–11) quotes some passages which do indeed contain the chain beginning with "thirst" and ending in "old age, dying, etc.," without the preceding links.

83 Frauwallner 1973a: 162 (1953: 204–5).

84 MN I.54; cf. Bernhard 1968: 56.

original cause for rebirth in the first part, in the same way as thirst is in the second part.

These thoughts on the original form and meaning of the causal chain are necessarily speculative. The main conclusion to be drawn is that we are not likely to learn much about the teaching of the Buddha from the doctrine of conditioned origination. In its classical form it is not part of the original teaching of the Buddha. Although we cannot exclude the possibility that one, perhaps even both, of its parts do not contradict the original teaching of the Buddha, the chain as a whole belongs to a time when attempts were made to reconcile new ideas about liberating knowledge with the old teaching.[85]

In spite of this, the doctrine of conditioned origination became ever more important. The ancient discourses already contain the following statement: "One who sees conditioned origination, sees the teaching; one who sees the teaching, sees conditioned origination."[86] We have also seen that some texts present conditioned origination as the content of liberating knowledge. We will come across this doctrine again while dealing with further developments of the teaching.

Asceticism and Meditation

The first sermon describes the Buddha's path to liberation as the Middle Path:

> O monks, one who has gone forth from worldly life should not indulge in these two extremes. What are the two? There is indulgence in desirable sense objects, which is low, vulgar, worldly, ignoble, unworthy, and unprofitable, and there is devotion to self-mortification, which is painful, unworthy, and unprofitable. O monks, avoiding both these extremes, the Buddha (*tathāgata*) has realized the Middle Path. It

85 The doctrine of conditioned origination in its classical form may well be inseparable from the dharma theory, as Hirakawa (1990: 54) observed.

86 MN I.191; tr. Ñāṇamoli & Bodhi 1995: 284.

> produces vision, it produces knowledge, it leads to calm, to higher knowledge, to enlightenment, to nirvāṇa. And what is that Middle Path, O monks, that the Buddha has realized? It is the noble eightfold path, namely: right views, right resolution, right speech, right action, right living, right exertion, right mindfulness, right concentration.[87]

It is reasonable to suppose that the expression "indulgence in desirable sense objects" does not characterize a specific religious movement that existed during the Buddha's lifetime, but rather the common man, who does not "indulge in desirable sense objects" in order to reach a religious goal. However, the opposite extreme no doubt presupposes ascetics who used "devotion to self-mortification" as a method to reach a religious goal. It has been suggested that the doctrine of the Middle Path might reflect the legend of the life of the Buddha before his enlightenment: wasn't he born a prince, who lived for a long time a life of pleasure before dedicating himself to asceticism, without getting anything useful out of either?[88] Since this book deals with the teachings of Buddhism, not the life of its founder, there is no need to go into the question whether this legend is as old as the doctrine of the Middle Path.

The Buddhist discourses contain many passages that show that the Buddha regularly came in contact with ascetics who dedicated themselves to self-mortification. In such passages, these ascetics are often Jainas—described in the sources as *nirgrantha* (Pa. *nigaṇṭha*) "free from all ties or hindrances"[89]—who followed the instructions of the teacher Jñātṛputra (*Pa.* Nāt(h)aputta). These passages, along with what we know from the old texts of the Jainas and from other sources, convey a clear image of these ascetics' motivations and practices. The main aim pursued by them was release from the cycle of rebirths. Since they held that rebirth is determined by the actions carried out in a previous life,

87 Vin I.10; tr. Rewata Dhamma 1997: 17. Cf. Mimaki & May 1979: 456ff.

88 Mimaki & May 1979: 457.

89 MW p. 541 s.v. *nirgrantha*.

they believed that liberation could be reached by suppressing all activities. The following passage describes the Buddha's meeting with such ascetics:

> Now, Mahānāma, on one occasion I was living at Rājagaha (Skt. Rājagṛha) on the mountain Vulture Peak. On that occasion a number of Nigaṇṭhas living on the Black Rock on the slopes of Isigili were practicing continuous standing, rejecting seats, and were experiencing painful, racking, piercing sensations due to exertion.
>
> Then, when it was evening, I rose from meditation and went to the Nigaṇṭhas there. I asked them: "Friends, why do you practice continuous standing, rejecting seats, and experience painful, racking, piercing sensations due to exertion?"
>
> When this was said, they replied: "Friend, the Nigaṇṭha Nātaputta is omniscient and all-seeing and claims to have complete knowledge and vision thus: 'Whether I am walking or standing or asleep or awake, knowledge and vision are continuously and uninterruptedly present to me.' He says thus: 'Nigaṇṭhas, you have done evil actions in the past; exhaust them with the performance of piercing austerities. And when you are here and now restrained in body, speech, and mind, that is doing no evil actions for the future. So by annihilating with asceticism past actions and by doing no fresh actions, there will be no consequence in the future. With no consequence in the future, there is the destruction of action. With the destruction of action, there is the destruction of suffering. With the destruction of suffering, there is the destruction of sensation. With the destruction of sensation, all suffering will be exhausted.' This is [the doctrine] we approve of and accept, and we are satisfied with it. [...]
>
> "Friend Gotama, pleasure is not to be gained through pleasure; pleasure is to be gained through pain. For were pleasure to be gained through pleasure, then King Seniya

> Bimbisāra of Magadha would gain pleasure, since he abides in greater pleasure than the venerable Gotama."[90]

During another meeting with Jainas, the Buddha expresses himself in the following ironic way: "If the pleasure and pain that beings feel are caused by what was done in the past, then the Nigaṇṭhas surely must have done bad actions in the past, since they now feel such painful, racking, piercing sensations."[91]

In these passages, the Jainas' practices are explicitly criticized. Elsewhere, in a passage that presumably describes the Buddha's efforts before his enlightenment, when he was still a bodhisattva, they are criticized implicitly.[92] We are told that the bodhisattva, since his discipleship with two teachers had proved to be in vain, decided to practice asceticism alone. He found an appropriate place and started to practice the "meditation without breathing" (Pa. *appānaka jhāna*; Skt. *aprāṇaka dhyāna*). This meditation is described in all its horrifying particulars, and it leads to a situation where some gods believe that the bodhisattva is dead. After this meditation without breathing, the bodhisattva decides to fast, and in fasting, too, he goes to extremes. (Characteristically, the bodhisattva does not die of starvation, as some Jainas did, because the gods prevent this.) After all these trials, he reaches the following conclusion:

> Whatever recluses and brahmans in the past have experienced painful, racking, piercing sensations due to exertion, this is the utmost, there is none beyond this. And whatever recluses and brahmans in the future will experience painful, racking, piercing sensations due to exertion, this is the

---

90 MN I.92–93; tr. Ñāṇamoli & Bodhi 1995: 187–88; cf. Bronkhorst 1993: 26–27, with references to Chinese parallels.

91 MN II.222; tr. Ñāṇamoli & Bodhi 1995: 832.

92 MN I.242–46; II.93; 212 (in the last two passages the whole text is not repeated in the edition of the Pali Text Society; but it is repeated in the Nālandā Edition, NDPS II, pp. 326–31 and 490–94). This passage and its Chinese parallel (EĀ S. 670c18–671b4) are translated and discussed in Bronkhorst 1993: 1ff.

> utmost, there is none beyond this. And whatever recluses and brahmans at present experience painful, racking, piercing sensations due to exertion, this is the utmost, there is none beyond this. But by this racking practice of austerities I have not attained any superhuman states, any distinction in knowledge and vision worthy of the noble ones. Could there be another path to enlightenment?[93]

The aim of this supposedly autobiographical description is clear: it shows that the Buddha knows from his own experience the ascetic path presumably leading to liberation, and that he has followed this path as far as, or even further than, the rival ascetics themselves. He therefore also knows from personal experience that this path is of no use and does not lead to the desired goal. It is of particular interest to note that this path, which was purportedly tried by the Buddha, is in all details identical to that of the Jainas. This is further emphasized by the fact that this autobiographical episode is once narrated during a conversation with a Jaina. This conclusion is furthermore justified by its contents, for it is the Jainas who sought liberation by means of fasting and suppressing breath. There are other details that support this position as well.[94]

It is clear from what precedes that the Buddha made a distinction between his teaching and the ascetic mode of life primarily followed by the Jainas. Surprisingly, elsewhere in the discourses the Buddha himself propounds this rejected mode of life, sometimes in exactly the same words.[95] In a passage from the Aṅguttara Nikāya, for example, the Bud-

---

93 MN I.246; tr. Ñāṇamoli & Bodhi 1995: 340.

94 For references to the old Jaina texts and a more detailed discussion, see Bronkhorst 1993: 31ff. One cannot rule out, as Gombrich (1994: 1073–74) remarks, that this autobiographical representation really originated with the historical Buddha himself; but this is neither certain, nor even likely.

95 It is not only in the discourses that this mode of life is shown in a positive light. Gombrich (1994: 1078–79) shows how Jaina influence is noticeable in many verses of the Buddhist canon. We should not forget that many of these verses originally came from collections belonging to groups of wandering ascetics, some of whom were non-Buddhists, as de Jong (1991: 7) astutely observes.

dha instructs the Jaina Vappa as follows: "As these taints come about as a result of bodily activities [...], as a result of activities of speech [...], as a result of activities of mind, in the case of one who abstains from bodily activities [...], from activities of speech and mind that cause vexation and distress, it follows that those taints causing pain do not exist in him. He carries out no fresh action; as to his former action, he wears it out by constant contact with it."[96] From this we must conclude that such ascetic practices, although criticized by the Buddha, were nevertheless adopted by certain Buddhists.[97]

The aim of the ascetic practices described above was to subdue one's actions, words, and thoughts. The efforts to suppress the sense organs are related to these. These practices, too, are mentioned in the Buddhist discourses, once again critically. Thus we hear about a teacher who taught a practice of cultivation of the sense organs that brought a result where the practitioner would neither see forms with the eye nor hear sounds with the ear. When the Buddha was informed about this, he commented that if this were cultivating the sense organs, then the blind and the deaf were cultivating their sense organs.[98] We have already noticed the same kind of irony in the story of the standing Jainas. It is therefore all the more remarkable to observe that the Buddha himself is supposed to have undertaken such practices. The *Mahāparinirvāṇa Sūtra*, which describes the end of the Buddha's life,[99] relates the following discussion between the Buddha and a certain Putkasa (Pa. Pukkusa). The latter is a disciple of the teacher Ārāḍa Kālāma (Pa. Āḷāra Kālāma), and the sūtra tells the following story about him:[100]

96 AN II.197; tr. Woodward 1973: 208–9. Cf. AN I.221; MĀ p. 434b23–24.

97 The same opinion is voiced by Ruegg 1989: 142–43.

98 MN III.298–99; cf. SĀ p. 78a22–23.

99 The terms *nirvāṇa* and *parinirvāṇa* initially meant the same thing. Only later the term *parinirvāṇa* came to designate the Buddha's death. Cf. Bronkhorst 1993: 97–98, with references to further literature; Kubo 1992: 3.

100 DN II.130–32; tr. Walshe 1995: 258–59; Bareau 1970: 282ff.; Waldschmidt 1950–51: 270ff.

> Once, Lord, Āḷāra Kālāma was going along the main road and, turning aside, he went and sat down under a nearby tree [...]. And five hundred carts went rumbling by very close to him. A man who was walking along behind them came to Āḷāra Kālāma and said: "Lord, did you not see five hundred carts go by?" "No, friend, I did not." "But didn't you hear them, Lord?" "No, friend, I did not." "Well, were you asleep, Lord?" "No, friend, I was not asleep." "Then, Lord, were you conscious?" "Yes, friend." "So, Lord, being conscious and awake you neither saw nor heard five hundred carts passing close by you, even though your outer robe was bespattered with dust?" "That is so, friend."
>
> And that man thought: "It is wonderful, it is marvelous! These wanderers are so calm that though conscious and awake, a man neither saw nor heard five hundred carts passing close by him!" And he went away praising Āḷāra Kālāma's lofty powers.

We easily recognize here the "cultivation of the sense organs bringing it about that one can neither see forms with the eye nor hear sounds with the ear," and we would expect the Buddha to reject it here too. But this does not happen, for he answers:

> "Well, Pukkusa, what do you think? What do you consider is more difficult to do or attain to—while conscious and awake not to see or hear five hundred carts passing nearby or, while conscious and awake, not to see or hear anything when the rain god streams and splashes, when lightning flashes and thunder crashes?"
>
> "Lord, how can one compare not seeing or hearing five hundred carts with that—or even six, seven, eight, nine, or ten hundred, or hundreds of thousands of carts to that? To see or hear nothing when such a storm rages is more difficult...."
>
> "Once, Pukkusa, when I was staying at Ātuma, at the

> threshing floor, the rain god streamed and splashed, lightning flashed, and thunder crashed, and two farmers, brothers, and four oxen were killed. And a lot of people went out of Ātuma to where the two brothers and the four oxen were killed.
>
> "And, Pukkusa, I had at that time gone out of the door of the threshing floor and was walking up and down outside. And a man from the crowd came to me, saluted me, and stood to one side. And I said to him: 'Friend, why are all these people gathered here?' 'Lord, there has been a great storm and two farmers, brothers, and four oxen have been killed. But you, Lord, where have you been?' 'I have been right here, friend.' 'But what did you see, Lord?' 'I saw nothing, friend.' 'Or what did you hear, Lord?' 'I heard nothing, friend.' 'Then, Lord, were you conscious?' 'Yes, friend.' 'So, Lord, being conscious and awake you neither saw nor heard the great rainfall and floods and the thunder and lightning?' 'That is so, friend.'
>
> "And, Pukkusa, that man thought: 'It is wonderful, it is marvelous! These wanderers are so calm that they neither see nor hear when the rain god streams and splashes, lightning flashes, and thunder crashes!' Proclaiming my lofty powers, he saluted me, passed by to the right, and departed."

Again we notice that practices that were explicitly rejected by the Buddha nevertheless found a way into Buddhism.[101] In this last case, it is also clear that rivalry between religious groups played a role, as it was obviously impossible for the Buddhists to admit that non-Buddhist teachers had skills the Buddha did not possess.

This last passage mentions the teacher Ārāḍa Kālāma, whose name is also known from another part of the Buddha legend. For Ārāḍa

---

101 Gombrich (1994: 1077) thinks that the Buddha, who was weakened by illness and about to die, may here exceptionally have boasted about practices he otherwise did not agree with.

Kālāma was one of his two teachers at the time when he was still a bodhisattva and had not yet reached enlightenment. We have seen how a so-called autobiographical episode of the Buddha was used to prove the uselessness of the Jainas' self-torturing practices. We are therefore entitled to suppose that the description of the Buddha's study under Ārāḍa Kālāma and Udraka, the son of Rāma, may likewise contain elements of propaganda. And this is indeed the case. What the bodhisattva learns from Ārāḍa Kālāma and subsequently from Udraka, the son of Rāma, is the following: from Ārāḍa Kālāma he learns the *realm of nothingness* (*ākiñcanyāyatana*), and from Udraka, the son of Rāma, he learns the *realm of neither ideation nor non-ideation* (*naivasaṃjñānāsaṃjñāyatana*). His studies are so successful that Ārāḍa Kālāma suggests that they should, both of them, instruct his students together; Udraka, the son of Rāma, even offers him the sole leadership of his school. But in both cases the bodhisattva refuses, and he justifies this with the remark that these doctrines do not lead to renunciation, to lack of passion, to cessation, to peace, to knowledge, to enlightenment, and to nirvāṇa, but only to the realm of nothingness, or, respectively, to the realm of neither ideation nor non-ideation.[102]

On the basis of the mere names of these realms, it is impossible to get an exact idea of their particular nature and of the differences between them. But the names suggest that they are states in which thoughts and other mental activities are suppressed. This is confirmed by the circumstance that the same name Ārāḍa Kālāma is also mentioned in connection with the suppression of the sense organs described above. Furthermore, it is important to note that the same autobiographical passages that describe how the bodhisattva rejects the realm of nothingness and the realm of neither ideation nor non-ideation continue to narrate how he (re)discovers the first stage of meditation and immediately understands that this is the path to enlightenment. These two realms are thus contrasted with the stages of meditation; only the latter lead to nirvāṇa.

In spite of this, the realms taught by Ārāḍa Kālāma and by Udraka,

---

102 Klimkeit 1990: 81.

the son of Rāma, managed to find a way into the Buddhist tradition. Consider the account of the Buddha's death:

> These were the Buddha's last words.
>
> Then the Lord entered the first stage of meditation (*dhyāna*, Pa. *jhāna*). And leaving that he entered the second, the third, the fourth stage of meditation. Then leaving the fourth stage of meditation, he entered the realm of infinity of space (*ākāśānantyāyatana*), then the realm of infinity of consciousness (*vijñānānantyāyatana*), then the realm of nothingness (*ākiñcanyāyatana*), then the realm of neither ideation nor non-ideation (*naivasaṃjñānāsaṃjñāyatana*), and leaving that he attained the cessation of ideation and feeling (*saṃjñāvedayitanirodha*).
>
> Then the venerable Ānanda said to the venerable Anuruddha: "Venerable Anuruddha, the Lord has passed away." "No, friend Ānanda, the Lord has not passed away, he has attained the cessation of ideation and feeling."
>
> Then the Lord, leaving the attainment of the cessation of ideation and feeling, entered the realm of neither ideation nor non-ideation, from that he entered the realm of nothingness, the realm of infinity of consciousness, the realm of infinity of space. From the realm of infinity of space he entered the fourth stage of meditation, from there the third, the second, and the first stage of meditation. Leaving the first stage of meditation, he entered the second, the third, the fourth stage of meditation. And, leaving the fourth stage of meditation, the Lord finally passed away.[103]

---

103 DN II. 156; tr. Walshe 1995: 270–71; Bareau 1971: 150–56; cf. Waldschmidt 1950–51: 394–97. Zafiropulo (1993: 68–67) cites reasons that go against the supposition that there was already an organic relationship between the non-authentic realms before they were taken over by Buddhism. Gombrich (1994: 1077) concludes, on the basis of this death scene, that the sojourn in what we call the "non-authentic" realms was the least disagreeable way to bear physical pain; he does not believe that these realms were non-authentic, i.e., that they were not

These same mental states are also mentioned once (and once only) in connection with the Buddha's enlightenment. According to a passage from the Aṅguttara Nikāya, the bodhisattva gradually entered into the nine stages mentioned above, up to the highest of them, namely, the cessation of ideation and feeling. Here his taints were destroyed, having been seen with wisdom. The Buddha concludes this autobiographical passage with the words:[104]

> And so long, Ānanda, as I attained not to, emerged not from these nine attainments of gradual abidings (*samāpatti*), both forward and backward, I realized not completely, as one wholly awakened, the full perfect awakening, unsurpassed in the world with its gods, Māra, and Brahmā, on earth with its ascetics, brahmans, gods, and men; but when I attained to and emerged from these abidings suchwise, then, wholly awakened, I realized completely the full perfect awakening unsurpassed. [...] Then knowledge and vision rose up within me: Mind's release for me is unshakable, this birth is final, there is now no becoming again.

Since no mental processes take place in the cessation of ideation and feeling, the highest enlightenment cannot take place in that realm. The Buddha only realized that he had gained enlightenment after he emerged again from these realms. It is apparently also impossible to pass from the cessation of ideation and feeling into the nirvāṇa that takes place at death. These considerations support the claim, made above, that the aim of these realms—from the realm of infinity of space up to the cessation of ideation and feeling—was to suppress thoughts and other mental activities. Such realms, or the efforts made to reach

---

taught by the historical Buddha, but admits that they may not have led to the goal directly.

104 AN IV.448; tr. Hare 1935: 295; cf. La Vallée Poussin 1937b: 219–20. Zafiropulo (1993: 32–33, 66–67n30) stresses the exceptional nature of this passage; there are, on the other hand, innumerable passages in which the four stages of meditation (*dhyāna*) are connected with the Buddha's enlightenment.

them, correspond quite accurately to the general idea of liberation of the Jainas and other ascetics pursuing similar goals: for them, the main means to reach liberation is to put an end to all activities, even mental ones. Such realms of consciousness (if we may call them that) were rejected by the Buddha, but nevertheless soon found a place among the states Buddhists sought to attain in their mental practice.

In the above passages the cessation of ideation and feeling is the highest stage. Sometimes only the four stages that precede it are mentioned together, namely, from the realm of infinity of space to the realm of neither ideation nor non-ideation. These are the *four formless states* (*ārūpya*, Pa. *arūpa*), among which the realm of neither ideation nor non-ideation is the highest. The realm of nothingness is the highest stage in the so-called seven *stations of consciousness* (*vijñānasthiti*, Pa. *viññāṇaṭṭhiti*). None of these series can be taken to be authentic.[105]

What distinguishes the four original stages of meditation from the non-authentic realms? If the suppression of all mental activities characterizes the latter, we must assume that the same does not hold—or at least not to the same extent—for the former. In any case this kind of suppression should not be the main goal of the four stages of meditation. Their goal lies in another dimension, which we may call "the mystical dimension" for want of a better term. From this point of view, the four stages of meditation seek to attain an ever-deeper "mystical" state, whereas the four realms of attainment only aim at suppressing mental activities.

It is of course not ruled out that normal mental activities may become weaker in the deeper "mystical" states. This is indeed what the description of the four stages of meditation suggests. Thought and reflection disappear in the second stage of meditation; satisfaction disappears in the third; well-being, unease, pleasure, and displeasure disappear in the fourth. Equanimity and mindfulness, on the contrary—and apparently consciousness too—remain until the fourth stage. Conversely, there is no reason to suppose that the non-authentic realms of attainment have anything to do with the "mystical" dimension. This is not only

105 Cf. Bronkhorst 1993: xiii, 83; 1985: 308.

suggested by the circumstance that concomitant phenomena, which appear in the stages of meditation under the names of "satisfaction," "well-being," and so on, are not mentioned here. It is more important that the "mystical" dimension has no role to play in practices whose main goal is to put an end to all mental and physical activities.[106]

A few things remain to be said about the non-authentic realms of attainment. We have seen that these originally belong to a set of ideas and practices in which the suppression of all activities is thought to bring about liberation in two different, mutually supporting ways: "by annihilating with asceticism past actions and by doing no new actions," as the Jainas explained to the Buddha. Here liberation presupposes that all previous actions are destroyed and that no new actions take place; this happens only at death. It is therefore easy to understand that in the Buddhist texts, too, these realms of attainment were often associated with the idea of liberation at the time of death. Cessation of ideation and feeling (*saṃjñāvedayitanirodha*), also called *attainment of cessation* (*nirodhasamāpatti*), is therefore sometimes described as similar to nirvāṇa or as touching it.[107]

Recapitulation

The method explained at the beginning of this chapter has allowed us to distinguish between doctrines we can confidently ascribe to the historical Buddha and others that we have good reasons to suppose were not part of his original teaching. It leads to the remarkable conclusion that a sizable part of what came to be ascribed to the Buddha had not been taught by the founder himself. It is worthwhile to recapitulate briefly the teachings in the ancient canon that, by applying this method, turn out to *not* derive from the Buddha.

These teachings are of two kinds. Some deal with the theme of

106 The absence of sensual experiences and mental representations is not here considered to be the main characteristic of mysticism, as is argued, for instance, by Forman (1990: 7). Vetter (1994: 182–83) bases his work on a definition of mysticism that includes in a quasi-automatic way the meditation on the *infinity* of earth and so on. Cf. also Vetter 1984.

107 La Vallée Poussin 1937b: 213–14; Schmithausen 1981: 241, 219n67.

liberating knowledge. There are several of these, because there was no consensus in the Buddhist tradition as to the exact content of liberating knowledge. We have seen that the idea of an explicitly formulated liberating knowledge cannot be considered as original to Buddhism; it rather came about under the influence of non-Buddhist currents. Conversely, the contents of the liberating knowledge were not borrowed from non-Buddhist currents. We have no reason to doubt that the historical Buddha taught the four noble truths, for example. The same holds for the doctrine that there is no self in the five aggregates (*skandha*), although in this case, as we have seen, the assignment of this doctrine to the role of liberating knowledge appears to be indebted to non-Buddhist ideas.

There are many reasons to suppose that the doctrine of conditioned origination (*pratītyasamutpāda*) was not taught by the Buddha in the form in which it is preserved in the canon. This does not alter the fact that this formulation is entirely Buddhist because, as far as we can tell, it has not been borrowed from other sources. The fact that this formulation—like the four noble truths and the doctrine of not-self—could become the content of the liberating knowledge, however, can be explained by the fact that the early Buddhists were looking for a content of their liberating knowledge, being influenced in this respect by certain non-Buddhist religious currents of their time. Furthermore, the doctrine of not-self could easily be reinterpreted so as to become similar to the non-Buddhist doctrines of the self, as we have seen.

Beside the teachings about liberating knowledge, others reveal a close relationship with the ascetic movements of those days. The main theme of these movements was to suppress all bodily and mental processes and bring them to a standstill. In the Buddhist texts, these ideas find expression in certain mental exercises that aim at suppressing mental activities and emotional states. They also find expression in forms of physical asceticism that found a place in the Buddhist tradition.

Louis de La Vallée Poussin pointed out as long ago as in 1937 that these two currents within the Buddhist texts—he calls them opposite theories—are the same as those respectively called Sāṃkhya and Yoga in the *Bhagavadgītā*: in the first, liberation is entirely or primarily obtained by means of knowledge, i.e., intellectual effort; in the second, this goal is reached by means of ascetic practice.[108] This parallelism is not coincidental. As we have seen, the two currents within Buddhism developed under the influence of two currents that existed outside it. This does not mean that there is no difference between Buddhism and the other religious movements that existed at that time. On the contrary, Buddhism succeeded in integrating these outside influences in such a manner that its own specificity was not at risk. This does not alter the fact that the Buddhism that we know from the old texts already contains many elements that do not come from its founder.

The two currents discussed above, the intellectual and the ascetic, were not taught by the Buddha. This does not signify that the Buddha's message is no longer available in the ancient texts and that this precanonical doctrine can only be uncovered by means of deductions and speculative theories. As we have tried to show, the Buddha's original teaching has been transmitted by the Buddhist texts just as efficiently as the non-original material. It included criticism of other intellectual and ascetic movements that existed at its time, elements of which nevertheless managed to find their way into the Buddhist tradition.

It is not easy to get a clear picture of the Buddha's original teaching. Certainly, its aim was to stop suffering and rebirth. To achieve this, the Buddha taught a path in which consciousness played a major role. This is clear from the awareness practices and from the four stages of meditation. In the highest stage of meditation, it is somehow possible, with the help of wisdom (*prajñā*), to bring about a decisive transformation. Once this happens, the goal is attained.

The most astonishing thing about the teaching of the Buddha is that it is in some respects radically different from other teachings that were current in its time and region. The Buddhist texts themselves insist that the Buddha had discovered something new, and that he therefore taught something new. Scholars have often claimed that Buddhism is a special type of Yoga, assuming that a form of Yoga similar to Buddhism existed already at the time of the Buddha. This is incor-

108 La Vallée Poussin 1937b: 189–90, with references to Edgerton 1924: 27.

rect.[109] It is true that classical Yoga has several points in common with Buddhism, but this is due to the influence of Buddhism on Yoga, as we shall see below. There are no indications that classical Yoga, or something like it, existed at the time of the Buddha. The aim of pre-classical Yoga, like that of the practice of the Jainas, was to suppress bodily and mental activities;[110] it has little in common with the practice taught by the Buddha, and it appears that the Buddha regularly tried to make this clear—to no avail.

The Buddha preached a quite new method, whose aim was to put an end to suffering and rebirth. This new method had to find its place alongside the established methods, of which there were several. Among them we can distinguish two in particular. Both share one common premise, namely, that rebirth is caused and conditioned by actions, and that as a result one must somehow get rid of one's actions. This happens either by suppressing all mental and bodily activities—this is the first method—or by realizing that the true self does not participate in any activities—this is the second method. These two methods each propose a solution that fits the problem in an obvious manner. In contrast, it was not at all obvious how and why the method taught by the Buddha could put an end to rebirth. In comparison with its two rivals, the Buddhist method seemed ill suited to the task.

This circumstance is responsible for the fact that, from the start, Buddhist tradition incorporated, in adjusted form, practices and ideas that belonged to the other two methods. The same circumstance also explains why the Buddhist textual corpus contains, side by side, a variety of different methods. The Buddhists had a problem, and this is the way they tried to solve it.

These attempts to solve the problem were only half-hearted, and they could not be otherwise. For the Buddhist tradition also preserved clear statements of the Buddha that rejected the alternative methods.

---

109 This opinion is first found in Senart 1900; then in Beck 1916: 136–37; and in Frauwallner 1953: 173; further references in de Jong 1976: 34; finally King 1992; *contra* Kloppenborg 1990.

110 Cf. Bronkhorst 1993: 45ff.

Buddhism was therefore faced with a problem it could not solve. The doctrine of not-self, in particular, which was too solidly grounded in the tradition to be simply pushed aside, remained a major challenge. The inescapable conflict that resulted lent an internal dynamic to the further development of Buddhism—a topic we examine more closely below.

2. Arranging the Doctrine

The Origin of the Dharma Theory

SHORTLY BEFORE HIS DEATH the Buddha is recorded to have taught his disciple Ānanda in the following manner:[111] "It may come to pass, Ānanda, that you will think: 'The doctrine is deprived of its teacher, we no longer have a master.' You should not think thus, Ānanda. The doctrine (*dharma*) and the discipline (*vinaya*) that I taught you, they shall be your teachers after my demise." The Buddha's disciples knew how to value these words. We owe it to their efforts that the collections of discourses and disciplinary rules ascribed to him were preserved. However, they were not content with merely memorizing these discourses and rules (which were not consigned to writing until several centuries after his death).[112] They also studied the

111 MPS 41a; tr. according to Dutoit 1906: 302; as cited in Klimkeit 1990: 147.

112 The Theravāda canon was probably consigned to writing in the first century BCE in Ceylon; see Falk 1993: 284–85. Norman (1993: 280) is of the opinion that Hīnayāna texts were probably written down already in the second century BCE, either in northern India or in Ceylon; see also Norman 1989: 36 ("There is growing evidence that at a date much earlier than has hitherto been believed there was an increasing use of writing in the Theravādin tradition"); Brough 1962: 218. However, Vetter (1994a) shows that certain Pāli texts were perhaps enlarged upon as late as the first centuries of the Common Era. Meisig (1992: 214–15n1) seems to hold that at least the Dīrghāgama of the Dharmaguptakas was not written down before its Chinese translation in 412–13 CE. A similar remark can be made with regard to the Chinese translations of the Vinaya texts; see Hu-von Hinüber 1994: 96–97.

contents of the Master's teaching, arranging its main points into lists of concepts. Thus we have the four noble truths, the four stages of meditation (*dhyāna*), the five aggregates (*skandha*), the twelve realms of the senses (*āyatana*), the eighteen elements (*dhātu*), and so forth.

The search for such lists of concepts began early. A discourse relates the following in this regard: When the Buddha was still alive, Vardhamāna, the founder of Jainism, died. Soon quarrels arose among Vardhamāna's disciples as to the correct interpretation of his teaching. In order to prevent similar happenings in the Buddhist community, Śāriputra, a senior disciple, composed a long list of all of the Buddha's important doctrines and explained them to the other disciples.[113]

It is not surprising that the search for lists of concepts should already appear in the oldest Buddhist texts. For example, an important work belonging to the *Sūtra-piṭaka* is called Aṅguttara Nikāya in Pāli and Ekottarāgama in Sanskrit. Following Winternitz, these two terms are probably best translated as "the collection of discourses classified in increasing numerical order."[114] In the Pāli version, the discourses—numbering at least 2308—are arranged in eleven chapters (*nipāta*) in such a way that the first chapter deals with things that are unique, the second with things of which there are two, the third with things of which there are three, and so on up to the eleventh chapter, which deals with things of which there are eleven. For instance, in the chapter on twofold things, we find discourses on the two things that one must avoid, on the two dark and two light things, on the two reasons for living in the forest, on the two kinds of buddhas, and so forth; in the part dealing with threefold things, we find discourses on the triad of actions, words, and thoughts; on the three kinds of monks; and so

113 Frauwallner 1995: 121 (= 1971a: 116 [4]). This story is found at the beginning of the *Saṅgīti Sūtra* (Saṅg pt. 1, pp. 44–45); cf. Waldschmidt 1955: 298–318. The death of the founder of Jainism also plays a role in other sūtras; cf. Gethin 1992: 232–33.

114 For the significance of the term *Aṅguttara*, see Hinüber 1996: 39 § 76. It is doubtful whether the extant division of the canon is the oldest, for there are traces of an older division. See Hinüber 1994c.

forth.[115] The Chinese version of the Ekottarāgama is classified according to the same general principles but differs so drastically from the Pāli version in details that we are forced to conclude that the two collections were produced independently of each other.[116]

The same need to preserve the Buddha's teaching and to fit it as neatly as possible in lists of concepts is shown in two sūtras belonging to the "Collection of Long Discourses" (Dīrghāgama, Pa. Dīgha Nikāya), the *Saṅgīti Sūtra* and the *Daśottara Sūtra*.[117] These two sūtras likewise present doctrinal concepts arranged in numerical sequence.

Lists of concepts are also the basis for the texts found in the *Abhidharma-piṭaka*, the "basket of scholasticism."[118] Only the *Abhidharma-piṭaka* of the Theravādins and the *Abhidharma-piṭaka* of the Sarvāstivādins have been fully preserved. They are highly dissimilar.[119] Nevertheless, it is important to note that both piṭakas contain texts that have a close connection with the old discourses. This is true of the *Saṅgītiparyāya*, a commentary in the Sarvāstivāda *Abhidharma-piṭaka* on the above-mentioned *Saṅgīti Sūtra*, and even more true of the *Dharmaskandha* of the Sarvāstivādins and the *Vibhaṅga* of the Theravādins, which are very closely connected and are probably both derived from the same original text, now lost.[120] Both texts have in common that they first introduce a short sūtra text, and then this text and the doctrines it contains are subsequently explained in detail. This shows how the authors of these treatises proceeded. The words of the

115 See Winternitz 1913: 45.

116 Bronkhorst 1985: 312–15; Anesaki 1908: 83–84.

117 Daśo with DaśoE(Trip), Saṅg with SaṅgE; Pauly 1957: 281–92; Pauly 1959: 248–49; de Jong 1966. De Jong draws our attention to the fact that the *Daśottara Sūtra* must have been one of the best-loved Buddhist sūtras. Gombrich (1990: 6) finds it meaningful that the beginning of the *Saṅgīti Sūtra* should narrate how the disciples of the Jina Nigaṇṭha Nātaputta already disagreed on the tenor of his words at the time of his death.

118 Concerning the original and the later significance of the word Abhidharma, see Cox 1995: 3–4; Hinüber 1994a.

119 For a description and analysis, see Frauwallner 1995: chaps. II and III (= 1964 and 1971–72).

120 Frauwallner 1995: 20 (= 1964: 78–79); 39–40, 43–44 (= 1971: 103–4, 107–8)

Buddha transmitted by tradition provided their basis. Nothing new was added except that the doctrines were arranged into lists. The Buddhists of that period were concerned not to add anything new to the teachings of the Buddha. It is therefore all the more surprising to see how these activities were responsible for the arising of fundamentally different teachings in the course of time. As far as we can tell, this happened independently of anyone's conscious will. In the following pages we shall concentrate on the factors that brought about these changes, leaving everything else aside.

The attempts to arrange the Buddha's teaching and to consign its main points to lists have parallels in the Indian context. The canonical texts of Jainism in particular show the same tendency. In the third main section (*aṃga*) of the Jaina canon, the *Ṭhāṇaṃga*, various topics are treated in numerical sequence, from one to ten, as in the Buddhist Aṅguttara Nikāya. The fourth aṅga, the *Samavāyaṃga*, continues in the same way: the contents of the first two thirds of this work are also arranged in categories, like the *Ṭhāṇaṃga*, but here the numbers go beyond ten; they even go beyond a hundred, reaching immense heights.[121]

What makes the Buddhist lists of concepts important for the development of the doctrine, however, is the circumstance that this tendency to enumerate itself gave rise to a new doctrine, the so-called *dharma theory*. This happened at the end of a development we will trace below. To illustrate the new mode of thought, let us first examine a presentation of the path leading to liberation that is repeatedly found in the old discourses, as well as in more recent Buddhist texts. This presentation is composed of seven building blocks. Each of them is an independent list of concepts, and all of these lists of concepts also occur independently in the texts. The new presentation of the path to liberation is in this way a collection of previously existing elements. Together, they contain what was seen by the Buddhists of those days as the essence of the Buddha's teaching.

The lists of concepts collected in this way are:

121 Winternitz 1913: 300; Schubring 1935: 62; Hinüber 1996: 40 § 78.

1. the four applications of mindfulness (*smṛtyupasthāna*, Pa. *satipaṭṭhāna*)
2. the four right exertions (*samyakpradhāna/-prahāṇa*, Pa. *sammappadhāna*)[122]
3. the four constituent parts of supernatural power (*ṛddhipāda*, Pa. *iddhipāda*)
4. the five faculties (*indriya*)
5. the five strengths (*bala*)
6. the seven helpful means to enlightenment (*bodhyaṅga*, Pa. *bojjhaṅga*)
7. the noble eightfold path (*ārya aṣṭāṅga mārga*, Pa. *ariya aṭṭhaṅgika magga*).

These four enumerations contain a total of thirty-seven concepts, which later became known under the common designation of *dharmas helpful to enlightenment* (*bodhipakṣya/bodhipākṣika dharma*, Pa. *bodhipakkhiyā dhammā*).[123] A closer examination of these lists shows that their collection did not produce an organic whole. They can be described as follows:[124]

The *four applications of mindfulness* are: (1) The application of mindfulness to the body, (2) the application of mindfulness to the sensations (*vedanā*), (3) the application of mindfulness to the mind (*citta*), and (4) the application of mindfulness to the dharmas. A comparison of the various versions of the canonical texts reveals that the "dharmas" meant under point 4 were perhaps initially only the seven helpful means to enlightenment (*bodhyaṅga*), to be mentioned below.[125] But

122 For an explanation of the Sanskrit variant *samyakprahāṇa*, which approximately means "right abandonment," see Gethin 1992: 69–70.

123 Most of the old collections of sūtras mention the dharmas helpful to enlightenment without indicating the number thirty-seven. (Exceptions are almost only found in the Ekottarāgama; see Cox 1992: 94–95n34). This is confirmed by a discussion in the *Mahāvibhāṣā*, which tries to explain it; see Cox 1992a: 166.

124 Gethin 1992: part 1; Lamotte 1944–80: III: 1119–20; Cox 1992: 94–95n34.

125 Bronkhorst 1985: 312. Gombrich (1996: 35–36) believes that the dharmas were originally the teachings of the Buddha used in meditation.

perhaps also the five hindrances (*nīvaraṇa*) were included—i.e., the desire for pleasures of the senses, malice, sloth, irritation, and doubt—and the six fetters (*saṃyojana*), which arise from the internal and external realms of perception—i.e., the organs of the senses and the objects of the senses—or from their contact.[126]

The *four right exertions* are the exertions to preserve oneself from bad, unwholesome dharmas that are yet to arise; to abandon bad, unwholesome dharmas that have already arisen; to bring forth wholesome dharmas that are yet to arise; and to protect wholesome dharmas that have already arisen.

The *four constituent parts of supernatural power* are accompanied (1) by concentration originating from *desire* and conditioned factors originating from exertion, (2) by concentration originating from *energy* and conditioned factors originating from exertion, (3) by concentration originating from *mind* and conditioned factors originating from exertion, (4) by concentration originating from *examination* and conditioned factors originating from exertion.

The *five faculties* are faith (*śraddhā*), energy (*vīrya*), mindfulness (*smṛti*), concentration (*samādhi*), and wisdom (*prajñā*).

The *five strengths* are faith (*śraddhā*), energy (*vīrya*), mindfulness (*smṛti*), concentration (*samādhi*), and wisdom (*prajñā*).

The *seven helpful means to enlightenment* (*bodhyaṅga*) are mindfulness (*smṛti*), understanding the doctrine (*dharmapravicaya*), energy (*vīrya*), pleasure (*prīti*), calm (*praśrabdhi*), concentration (*samādhi*), and equanimity (*upekṣā*).

We have already discussed the noble eightfold path: right views, right resolution, right speech, right action, right living, right exertion, right mindfulness (*smṛti*), right concentration (*samādhi*).

These lists of concepts overlap repeatedly. The list of strengths, for instance, is not different from the list of faculties. The difference between these two was obviously not clear to the oldest Buddhist tradition either, and attempts were made to solve the problem.[127] There are

126 See Schmithausen 1976: 247–48.

127 Gethin 1992: 141–42.

other overlaps: concentration (*samādhi*), for instance, is mentioned in four places, mindfulness (*smṛti*) appears in four lists besides the one dedicated to it, and so on. All this is best explained by the assumption that the dharmas helpful to enlightenment were not conceived of together; rather, they were assembled more or less haphazardly by joining preexisting lists. This composite list demonstrates how important it was for the Buddhists in those days to arrange the essential parts of the Buddhist doctrine in lists.

In spite of its obvious weaknesses, this list of thirty-seven dharmas helpful to enlightenment became very important. They are stated to be wholesome (*kuśala*, Pa. *kusala*). They must be cultivated in order to be freed of taints (*āsrava*, Pa. *āsava*). They are said to constitute the "cultivation of the road." They are the jewels of the doctrine.[128] For the Buddhists of those days, taken together they represented the essence of Buddhist doctrine and practice.[129] We shall return later to their role in subsequent developments.

This list was also important for the arrangement of the doctrine. It became the basis for additions and extraneous enlargements. We find it in a more or less enlarged form in the so-called Mātṛkās of the Abhidharma texts of various Buddhist schools. It has also partly determined the internal arrangement of the Saṃyutta Nikāya/Saṃyuktāgama.[130]

Let us now examine the important word *dharma* (Pa. *dhamma*) and its meanings. We have already met this word several times, in very different senses. First of all, *dharma* means "doctrine." The Buddha told his disciples that the doctrine (*dharma*) and the discipline (*vinaya*) would be their teachers after his demise. The word *dharma* is however also used in another sense, which is not easy to define, because the word taken in this second sense underwent a semantic change in the course of time.

We can start with the observation that in many passages (perhaps the oldest) the word *dharma* means something akin to "mental

128 Bronkhorst 1985: 305 with references; Gethin 1992: 229n2.

129 Gethin 1992: 232; Warder 1980: 81–82 and 1983: 16.

130 Bronkhorst 1985.

property, characteristic of the mind." Consider how the word is used in the long depiction of the path leading to liberation, discussed in the "Main Teachings" section above. Two extracts should be considered:

> On seeing a form with the eye, he does not grasp at its signs and features. Since, if he left the eye faculty unguarded, evil unwholesome states of longing and dejection might invade him, he practices the way of its restraint, he guards the eye faculty, he undertakes the restraint of the eye faculty. On hearing a sound with the ear [...] On smelling an odor with the nose [...] On tasting a flavor with the tongue [...] On feeling a tangible with the body [...] On cognizing a *mental property* (*dharma*) with the mind, he does not grasp at its signs and features. Since, if he left the mind faculty unguarded, evil unwholesome states of longing and dejection might invade him, he practices the way of its restraint, he guards the mind faculty, he undertakes the restraint of the mind faculty. Possessing this noble restraint of the faculties, he experiences within himself an unsullied bliss.

Furthermore:

> Abandoning longing for the world, he dwells with a mind free from longing; he purifies his mind from longing. Abandoning ill will and hatred, he dwells with a mind free from ill will, compassionate for the welfare of all living beings; he purifies his mind from ill will and hatred. Abandoning dullness and drowsiness, he dwells free from dullness and drowsiness, having clear consciousness, mindful and clearly comprehending; he purifies his mind from dullness and drowsiness. Abandoning restlessness and remorse, he dwells free from agitation with a mind inwardly peaceful; he purifies his mind from restlessness and remorse. Abandoning doubt, he dwells having gone beyond doubt, unperplexed

> about wholesome *mental properties* (*dharma*); he purifies his mind from doubt.
>
> Having thus abandoned these five hindrances and the secondary defilements, secluded from sensual pleasures, secluded from unwholesome *mental properties* (*dharma*), he enters upon and dwells in the first stage of meditation, which is accompanied by deliberation and reflection, with pleasure and joy born of seclusion.

Clearly, the translation "mental property," in the sense of "characteristic of the mind," is appropriate here for *dharma*.

The dharmas are also mentioned in connection with the applications of mindfulness (*smṛtyupasthāna*), of which the fourth is the "application of mindfulness to the dharmas." These dharmas were perhaps initially only the seven helpful means to enlightenment (*bodhyaṅga*): mindfulness, understanding the doctrine, energy, pleasure, calm, concentration, and equanimity. Probably the five hindrances (*nīvaraṇa*)—i.e., desire for pleasure of the senses, malice, sloth, irritation, and doubt—and the six fetters (*saṃyojana*) were also included. Again, the translation "mental property" fits.

The dharmas are again mentioned in the description of the four right exertions (*samyakpradhāna*/*-prahāṇa*). These are the exertions to preserve oneself from bad, unwholesome dharmas which are yet to arise; to abandon bad, unwholesome dharmas that have already arisen; to bring forth wholesome dharmas that are yet to arise; and to protect wholesome dharmas that have already arisen.

It is clear that in all these passages the term *dharma* applies to properties of the mind. The dharmas are the objects of the mind (*manas*), just as form is the object of the eye or sound the object of the ear. These dharmas can be wholesome or unwholesome. A few unwholesome dharmas are mentioned by name: desire, displeasure, perhaps also malice, anger, rigidity, sloth, irritation, regret, and doubt.

The semantic development of this term can be understood as follows. We have seen that the early Buddhists took pains to arrange the elements of the doctrine. This was by producing numerical sequences and lists. Besides, some principles of classification had already begun to be used in the old texts. These are the five aggregates (*skandha*), the twelve realms of the senses (*āyatana*), and the eighteen elements (*dhātu*). These principles, however, do not merely arrange properties of mind. Indeed, in the case of the five aggregates, the first aggregate—that of form (*rūpa*)—contains the physical, i.e., non-mental, aspects of the personality. The case is even more extreme for the realms of the senses. The realms of the senses are the sense organs and their objects. Ten out of the twelve realms of the senses have little to do with the mind and are not properties of mind. A similar observation can be made for the elements, which partly overlap with the realms of the senses. It is extremely unlikely that the aggregates, the realms of the senses, and the elements were originally meant as classifications of the dharmas. They nevertheless came to be seen as such. In the old discourses, the word *dharma* is very seldom used in connection with these classifications. And the few passages in the Pāli *Sutta-piṭaka* that use the term *dharma* in connection with the five aggregates are found almost without exception in the Saṃyutta Nikāya, whose arrangement, as we have seen, was determined by Abhidharma-like lists of concepts and which is, therefore, relatively close to later developments.[131] The collections of dharmas produced in this way had in the end not all that much to do with properties of mind. But the name *dharma* was kept.

One further development came to play a significant role in the subsequent interpretations of the dharma theory. It concerns the concept of the person and the interpretation of passages about not-self. We have already seen that the various components of the person—especially the five aggregates—are not the self. A few frequently repeated passages in the Pāli canon also claim that all the dharmas are not the self (*sabbe dhammā anattā*).[132] This was increasingly interpreted in the

131 SN III.39, 159, 191. Glasenapp (1938: 52) also mentions in this connection MN I.435–36: *so yad eva tattha hoti rūpagataṃ vedanāgataṃ saññāgataṃ saṅkhāragataṃ viññāṇagataṃ te dhamme aniccato [...] samanupassati*, but this sentence is lacking in the Chinese parallel (TI 26, vol. 1, 779c–780a). Schayer (1935: 126–27) has already pointed out the non-identity of *rūpa* and *dharma* but attributed that difference to "pre-canonical" Buddhism.

132 DN I.185, II.64, MN I.228, 136, etc.

sense that the parts constituting a person do not together form a new entity, which would be the person. The person therefore does not exist; only its component parts exist. Instead of a self (*ātman*, Pa. *atta(n)*), the texts now also speak of a person (*pudgala*, Pa. *puggala*).[133] This person is represented as a composite entity, which, for that very reason, does not exist. The negation of the person thus becomes an ontological position: if one could enumerate all that exists, one would not find any persons in that list, because they do not really exist. We should note that the person, whose existence is here denied, is no longer the self as it is represented in certain Upaniṣads and elsewhere outside Buddhism. We are dealing with a completely different concept of the self or person—namely, a self that is a collection of dharmas and that does not exist *because* it is a collection.[134]

This way of thinking has consequences. We have seen how the enlarged meaning of the word *dharma* led to the position that the dharmas were no longer only properties of mind: they now also included things that were not found in the human mind. From this one had to conclude that not only the human mind, but absolutely everything that exists in the world is composed of dharmas. Now, if the person is characterized as not really existing because it is a collection of dharmas, then the same also holds for all other collections of dharmas, i.e., for practically everything that exists, with the exception of the dharmas themselves.[135] This means that all the objects that we know from everyday life do not really exist. Drawing attention to this became one of the favorite themes of Buddhist texts, as we will show with a few examples.

Already in a canonical sūtra a nun called Vajirā declares that a living being (*sattva*) is only a collection of conditioned factors (*saṃskāra*); the living being itself is not found. Just as the word "chariot" is used when the parts of the chariot are united, in the same way the expression

---

133 Cf. Walleser 1925: 79; *contra* Oetke 1988: 80–81.

134 Cf. Kajiyama 1977.

135 This was probably expressed later by means of the pseudo-etymological explanation that the dharmas carry their own characteristics (*svalakṣaṇadhāraṇa*); see Hirakawa 1993. Cf. also Warder 1971.

"living being" is used when all the aggregates (*skandha*) are present.[136] The same comparison, and a reference to the nun Vajirā's words, is found in the Pāli version of the "Questions of Milinda" (*Milindapañha*), which may date back to the second century BCE.[137] This text describes a conversation between the monk Nāgasena and King Menander (Milinda), which starts as follows:

> Then King Milinda approached the venerable Nāgasena; having approached, he exchanged greetings with the venerable Nāgasena; and, having exchanged greetings of friendliness and courtesy, he sat down at a respectful distance. And the venerable Nāgasena greeted him in return so that he gladdened the heart of King Milinda. Then King Milinda spoke thus to the venerable Nāgasena: "How is the revered one known? What is your name, revered sir?"
>
> "Sire, I am known as Nāgasena; brethren in the faith address me, sire, as Nāgasena: But though (my) parents gave (me) the name of Nāgasena or Sūrasena or Vīrasena or Sīhasena, yet it is but a denotation, appellation, designation, a current usage, for Nāgasena is only a name since no person is got at here."
>
> Then King Milinda spoke thus: "Good sirs, let the five hundred Bactrian Greeks and the eighty thousand monks hear me: This Nāgasena speaks thus: 'Since no person is got at here.' Now, is it suitable to approve of that?"
>
> And King Milinda spoke thus to the venerable Nāgasena: "If, revered Nāgasena, the person is not got at, who then is it that gives you the requisites of robe material, almsfood, lodgings, and medicines for the sick, who is it that makes use

136 SN I.135. In the Saṃyuktāgama (TI 99, vol. 2, 327b) the same comparison is made by the nun Śīlā; see Bareau 1962: 114–15. Oetke (1988: 129) rightly underscores the fact that this passage from the *Vajirā Sutta* seems to be practically the only text in the *Sutta-piṭaka* criticizing in a clear and unmistakable way the common conception of living beings.

137 According to de Jong (1996: 383) this date is too early, but he proposes no other.

of them; who is [it] that guards moral habit, practices (mental) development, realizes the ways, the fruits, nirvāṇa; who is it that kills a living thing, takes what has not been given, goes wrongly amid the sense pleasures, speaks lies, drinks liquor; and who commits the fivefold karma (the fruit of which comes with) no delay? Therefore there is not skill, there is not lack of skill, there is not one that carries out or makes another carry out actions that are skilled or unskilled, there is no fruit or ripening of actions well or ill done. If, revered Nāgasena, someone killed you, there would be no murder. Also, revered Nāgasena, you have no teacher, no preceptor, no ordination. If you say: 'Fellow Brahma-farers address me, sire, as Nāgasena,' what here is Nāgasena? Is it, revered sir, that the hairs of the head are Nāgasena?"

"O no, sire."

"That the hairs of the body are Nāgasena?"

"O no, sire."

"That the nails...the teeth, the skin, the flesh, the sinews, the bones, the marrow, the kidneys, the heart, the liver, the membranes, the spleen, the lungs, the intestines, the mesentery, the stomach, the excrement, the bile, the phlegm, the pus, the blood, the sweat, the fat, the tears, the serum, the saliva, the mucus, the synovic fluid, the urine, or the brain in the head are (any of them) Nāgasena?"

"O no, sire."

"Is Nāgasena material shape, revered sir?"

"O no, sire."

"Is Nāgasena sensation...ideation...the conditioned factors? Is Nāgasena consciousness?"

"O no, sire."

"But then, revered sir, is Nāgasena material shape and feeling and ideation and conditioned factors and consciousness?"

"O no, sire."

"But then, revered sir, is there Nāgasena apart from

material shape, sensation, ideation, the conditioned factors, and consciousness?"

"O no, sire."

"Though I, revered sir, am asking you repeatedly, I do not see this Nāgasena. Nāgasena is only a sound, revered sir. For who here is Nāgasena? You, revered sir, are speaking an untruth, a lying word. There is no Nāgasena."

Then the venerable Nāgasena spoke thus to King Milinda: "You, sire, are a noble delicately nurtured, exceedingly delicately nurtured. If you, sire, go on foot at noontime on the scorching ground and hot sand, trampling on sharp grit and pebbles and sand, your feet hurt you, your body wearies, your thought is impaired, and tactile consciousness arises accompanied by anguish. Now, did you come on foot or in a conveyance?"

"I, revered sir, did not come on foot; I came in a chariot."

"If you, sire, came by chariot, show me the chariot. Is the pole the chariot, sire?"

"O no, revered sir."

"Is the axle the chariot?"

"O no, revered sir."

"Are the wheels the chariot?"

"O no, revered sir."

"Is the body of the chariot the chariot... is the flagstaff of the chariot the chariot... is the yoke the chariot... are the reins the chariot... is the goad the chariot?"

"O no, revered sir."

"But then, sire, is the chariot the pole, the axle, the wheels, the body of the chariot, the flagstaff of the chariot, the yoke, the reins, the goad?"

"O no, revered sir."

"But then, sire, is there a chariot apart from the pole, the axle, the wheels, the body of the chariot, the flagstaff of the chariot, the yoke, the reins, the goad?"

"O no, revered sir."

"Though I, sire, am asking you repeatedly, I do not see the chariot. Chariot is only a sound, sire. For what here is the chariot? You, sire, are speaking an untruth, a lying word. There is no chariot. You, sire, are the chief king in the whole of India. Of whom are you afraid that you speak a lie? Let the five hundred worthy Bactrian Greeks and the eighty thousand monks listen to me: This King Milinda speaks thus: 'I have come by chariot.' But on being told: 'If you, sire, have come by chariot, show me the chariot,' he does not produce the chariot. Is it suitable to approve of that?"

When this had been said, the five hundred Bactrian Greeks, applauding the venerable Nāgasena, spoke thus to King Milinda: "Now do you, sire, speak if you can."

Then King Milinda spoke thus to the venerable Nāgasena: "I, revered Nāgasena, am not telling a lie, for it is because of the pole, because of the axle, the wheels, the body of a chariot, the flagstaff of a chariot, the yoke, the reins, and because of the goad that 'chariot' exists as a denotation, appellation, designation, as a current usage, as a name."

"It is well; you, sire, understand a chariot. Even so it is for me, sire, because of the hair of the head and because of the hair of the body... and because of the brain in the head and because of material shape and sensation and ideation and the conditioned factors and consciousness that 'Nāgasena' exists as a denotation, appellation, designation, as a current usage, merely as a name. But according to the highest meaning the person is not got at here. This, sire, was spoken by the nun Vajirā face to face with the Lord:

"Just as when the parts are rightly set
The word 'chariot' is spoken,
So when there are the aggregates
It is the convention to say 'being.'"

> "It is wonderful, revered Nāgasena, it is marvelous, revered Nāgasena. The explanations of the questions that were asked are very brilliant. If the Buddha were still here he would applaud. It is good, it is good, Nāgasena. The explanations of the questions that were asked are brilliant."[138]

Other early texts emphasize the non-existence of the self and of composite objects in general. According to the *Śāriputrābhidharma*, the self (*pudgala/ātman*) is only a name; the parts composing a person are not the self, and there is no self over and above these component parts. Here the self is likened to a hut. "Hut" is but an empty word; its component parts are not a hut, and a hut over and above them does not exist.[139] The *Mahāvibhāṣā*—a text whose importance can be deduced from the fact that the Sarvāstivādins in Kashmir also came to be known as Vaibhāṣikas, "Adepts of the *Vibhāṣā*"—distinguishes between "empirical existence" and "existence through harmonious union." The *pudgala* belongs to the latter category, whereas pot, cloth, chariot, army, forest, and hut illustrate "empirical existence." But only the dharmas have real existence.[140] The *Visuddhimagga*, a text belonging to the Theravāda tradition composed in Sri Lanka in the fifth century CE,[141] compares the terms "living being" (*satta*) and "person" (*puggala*) with expressions such as "chariot," "house," "fist," "sounds," "army," "town," and "tree" and characterizes them as merely conventional designations.[142]

This development turned out to be of the greatest importance for

---

138 Mil 25–26; tr. Horner 1969: 34–38. The Chinese version is found in TI 1670, vol. 32, 696a5–6; 706a9–10; tr. Demiéville 1924: 97–98. Oetke (1988: 185–86) has shown "that no passage of the Chinese version...expresses or alludes to a thesis which would be tantamount to the one which holds that a *pudgala* does not exist."

139 TI 1548, vol. 28, 626c8–9.

140 TI 1545, vol. 27, 42a29–b4. Altogether five categories of existence are distinguished, not all of which are significant in this context. Nakamura (1980: 123–24) mentions this fivefold distinction, but without indicating his sources. Cf. also La Vallée Poussin 1937: 22 (*Mahāvibhāṣā*), 28–29 (Saṃghabhadra).

141 Mori 1984: 7–8, 486–88.

142 Vism(W) XVIII.28; cf. Oetke 1988: 184–85.

the interpretation of the dharma theory. We saw that the dharmas had come to be considered as the component parts of the human person and of all other objects found in the world. This new development implied that only component parts really exist. Composite entities, whether they be persons or some other objects, do not really exist. Henceforth the list of dharmas is not only a list of all the building blocks of the world as it is known to us but also a list of everything that exists. The dharmas therefore became *elements of existence*, and from then on Buddhist doctrine included an exhaustive ontology, a complete enumeration of all that exists.

From the point of view of the Abhidharma Buddhists then, only the dharmas really exist. The other objects that we know from everyday life do not really exist. This forces us to ask the question why and how we can all be misled into believing that they do exist. All human beings are convinced, for instance, that they live in a house, that they ride in a chariot, that they drink water from a pot. If all these objects do not really exist, where does this conviction spring from? The answer is very important for the subsequent history of thought in India, and it has had a lasting influence on ontological thought among Buddhists and non-Buddhists alike. The answer emphasizes the role of language in the construction of the world as we know it. As Nāgasena told King Menander, "chariot" is only a denotation—an appellation, a designation, a current usage, a name—that is used when the requisite components are united, and the same holds for a person. The expression often used in this connection is *prajñapti*, "designation." From this point of view, the objects of the phenomenal world are "mere designation" (*prajñaptimātra*).

The world as conceived of in Abhidharma Buddhism now looks like this. Dharmas make up all that there is. Only dharmas, these building blocks of the world, really exist. Everything else—and this is especially true of collections of dharmas such as persons and macroscopic objects—does not really exist. The reason why all people accept the existence of non-real objects, such as chariots and pots, lies in language. In the end, such objects are mere words. In this regard, the texts often speak of "what exists in a limited sense" (*saṃvṛtisat*) and "what exists in the highest sense" (*paramārthasat*), or of "truth in a limited sense" (*saṃvṛtisatya*) and "truth in the highest sense" (*paramārthasatya*).[143] With respect to these truths, the *Mahāvibhāṣā* of the Sarvāstivādins remarks that in reality there is only one truth, namely the highest. If one nevertheless distinguishes two truths, this is due to one's point of view, not to the thing itself.[144]

The person is thus represented as a collection of dharmas. And we have seen that most Buddhists concluded from this that the person does not exist, because collections do not exist. They believed that in doing so they were doing justice to the words of the Buddha that declare that all dharmas are not the self. This interpretation played a central role in the development of the doctrine according to which no composite entities really exist.

There was, however, a movement in Buddhist thought that was not satisfied with the rejection of the person. It came to be known as Pudgalavāda, and its proponents as Pudgalavādins, "adepts of the doctrine according to which there is a person." We know but little about the origin and subsequent history of this movement. Their literature is almost entirely lost, and we are in part obliged to refer to the critical remarks of their opponents to learn the details of their doctrine. The Pudgalavādins are mentioned in the canonical *Vijñānakāya* of the Sarvāstivādins and may belong to the oldest Buddhist schools.[145] They were still in existence many centuries later: the Chinese pilgrim Xuanzang reports in the first half of the seventh century that among all the Buddhist schools in India, the Pudgalavādins had the greatest number of followers.[146]

We do not have enough information to present the ideas of this school in a complete manner.[147] Nevertheless we see that one theme

---

143 La Vallée Poussin 1937a, with references to Pāli literature and to the literature of the Sarvāstivādins; cf. also Willemen 1975: 85. See further Streng 1971; Freeman 1991.

144 La Vallée Poussin 1937a: 166.

145 La Vallée Poussin 1925: 358–59; Bareau 1955: 114; Cousins 1991: 54–55.

146 Bareau 1955: 121.

147 Thich Thien Chau 1977; also Cousins 1994; Thich Thien Chau 1984; 1987; Bareau 1955: 114–15; Bronkhorst 1992: 70–71. Vetter (1982) claims that

recurs regularly. Our sources claim that the person is neither identical with the aggregates (*skandha*) nor different from them. It is neither inside nor outside the aggregates. Sometimes it is also described as identical with as well as different from the aggregates, the elements (*dhātu*), and the realms of the senses (*āyatana*). These descriptions show that, here too, the person was thought of as a collection of dharmas. The followers of this school, however, were not ready to conclude from this that the person was nonexistent. Numerous canonical citations were used to show that the Buddha himself had often spoken of persons, which therefore had to exist.

The Pudgalavādins were not satisfied with only canonical citations. The descriptions of the person cited above, in particular the first one, made it possible to present the belief in a person as a middle position between two extremes. The **Tridharmakaśāstra* of this school declares: "If the person (*sattva/pudgala*) is different from the dharmas, it is eternal; if it is identical to them, it is non-eternal. These two mistakes should not be made."[148] Here "non-eternal" should probably be taken in the sense of "momentary" (see below). Eternal and momentary are the two extremes. Since the person is neither different from the dharmas nor identical with them, these two extremes can be avoided.

Another text of the school, the **Sāṃmitīyanikāyaśāstra*, adds: "If the person were identical with the aggregates, it would disappear or appear when the aggregates disappear or appear."[149] This confirms the hypothesis formulated above, namely, that in this context non-eternal means "momentary." Since the aggregates are momentary, the person would be so likewise if it were identical with them. But in reality, the person does not disappear when the aggregates disappear, and this is what allows the person to play a role in connection with rebirth

Nāgārjuna attacks the Pudgalavādins in his *Mūlamadhyamakakārikā*. This is, however, unlikely. As we will see, Nāgārjuna attacks the phenomenal world, which is unreal for him, as for most Buddhists. But the phenomenal world of all Buddhists contains an (equally unreal) person, conceived of as a collection of dharmas.

148 TI 1506, vol. 25, 19c3–5.

149 TI 1649, vol. 32, 456b10–11.

and liberation. These are indeed two important functions that the Pudgalavādins attribute to the person: for them rebirth and liberation do not imply a radical break, as they do for most other Buddhists.

We shall below see how the Sarvāstivādins—and most other Buddhists with them—divided everything that exists into two kinds of dharmas, namely the conditioned (*saṃskṛta*) and the unconditioned (*asaṃskṛta*) ones. The conditioned dharmas are momentary, the unconditioned ones eternal. We know that the person is situated between these two extremes. One might think that the person, if it really exists, must be a dharma, like everything else that exists. But then, does the person belong to the conditioned or to the unconditioned dharmas? The masters of the Pudgalavāda school dealt with this question. They decided that the person has its own special category.

In the context of Indian Buddhism, the Pudgalavāda can probably be understood as an attempt to avoid a complete rupture with everyday reality. Indeed, it is the person who makes mistakes, whose activity calls for retribution, and who ultimately keeps the wheel of rebirth revolving. The teaching of the Buddha itself is useless without a person—or so the Pudgalavādins believed. But in spite of the efforts of this school, mainstream Buddhism continued to develop in the direction described above: it accepted the unreal nature of the person and extended that unreal nature to the entire phenomenal world. Subsequent developments, which we will examine in connection with the Mahāyāna, further deepen the gulf between the phenomenal world and reality.

This tendency to look for the highest truth outside the phenomenal world, or even to deny its existence altogether, was peculiar to Buddhism and had no parallels in Brahmanism or Jainism in those days. It can best be explained by the fact that Buddhist liberation demanded a supreme insight but that the contents of that insight had not been fixed clearly by the tradition. In a certain sense, the Buddhists of those days were on the lookout for an insight, and therefore also for a reality hidden behind the phenomenal world. The fact that the Pudgalavāda school still had so many followers in the seventh century proves that the most striking development of Indian Buddhism, which led it ever further away from the phenomenal world, did not find universal approval.

Before turning to the systematization of the dharma theory in Sarvāstivāda, let us briefly note that spiritual practice and cosmology were already interconnected in the old discourses and, under their influence, in later Buddhism as well.[150] Buddhist cosmology cannot be described in detail here. This cosmology, although important in itself, does not constitute Buddhist teaching in the narrow sense of the term, nor is it closely connected with it. An exception is the three planes of existence (*dhātu*), also called worlds (*avacara*, *loka*) or realms of existence (*bhava*)—the plane of desire (*kāmadhātu*), the plane of form (*rūpadhātu*), and the plane of the formless (*ārūpyadhātu*). The plane of the formless is related to the four formless spiritual states (*ārūpya*), and the plane of form to the four stages of meditation (*dhyāna*, Pa. *jhāna*). Nevertheless, these three planes of existence are spatially arranged one above the other. The plane of the formless is situated above the others, and within it, the realm of neither ideation nor non-ideation (*naivasaṃjñānāsaṃjñāyatana*) occupies the highest place.[151] The relation between the various spiritual states and the corresponding world-regions is conceptualized in such a manner that the meditator accesses a region by means of the relevant practice. This way of homologizing "internal" states and "external" situations has parallels in other religions.[152] But it is different from the more rational tendencies characteristic of most later developments of Buddhist thought in India. The belief that states of meditation teach us something about the constitution of the world, however, also occurs later on.

Systematizing the Dharma Theory

The dharma theory outlined above was merely a beginning that could be further refined and systematized. We possess accurate information on

---

150 See, e.g., Glasenapp in Oldenberg 1961: 436–37; W. Kirfel 1920: 207; McGovern 1923: 60–61; Kloetzli 1983, esp. 29–30; Takasaki 1987: 133–34.

151 This is not the only position presented in the literature; see Abhidh-k-bh(P) p. 113.25, Abhidh-k(VP) vol. 2, p. 10.

152 See, e.g., the chapter "Chamanisme et cosmologie" in Eliade 1951: 235–36.

how that happened in the so-called Sarvāstivāda school of Buddhism. This was not the only school that developed in the first centuries of the Buddhist religion; the names of several other schools have come down to us, and we shall briefly examine various points of doctrine of some of them. But first we must recall that only two of these schools have preserved a complete *Abhidharma-piṭaka* ("basket of scholasticism"): the Theravādins (Skt. Sthaviravādins) and the Sarvāstivādins. Of these two, the latter is by far the more important for the subsequent development of Buddhism in India. The Sarvāstivāda school is also the one that went furthest in systematizing the dharma theory. It did so in its canonical *Abhidharma-piṭaka*[153] and in various noncanonical works. Fortunately, several of these noncanonical texts have been preserved in Chinese translations.

We shall first examine the doctrine of momentariness. This doctrine is not the sole preserve of the Sarvāstivādins: it was soon taken over by other Buddhist schools. But in Sarvāstivāda it gave rise to some noteworthy developments.

As the dharma theory developed, the following question became unavoidable: how long do individual dharmas exist, or in other words, how long does it take before a dharma, after coming into existence, disappears again? The Buddhist thinkers sought an answer to this question in the transmitted words of the Buddha, and hit upon the theme of impermanence. Several textual passages deal with it. We have already come across it in the discourse that the Buddha is believed to have preached to his first disciples shortly after his enlightenment. There the Buddha said: "What do you believe, O disciples, is the physical body eternal or not eternal?" "Not eternal, Lord." "And that which is not eternal, is it suffering or bliss?" "Suffering, Lord." The same words are then repeated in connection with the four other aggregates (*skandha*). This passage shows that the old teaching of impermanence was closely related to suffering. It occurs frequently in the canon, and very often, as here, in relation to the aggregates and also to dharmas in general. Another passage, for instance, specifies: "All conditioned factors are

153 On these texts, cf. Cox 1995: 31–32.

impermanent, characterized by production and disappearance. After being produced, they disappear."[154] We have already seen that the conditioned factors (*saṃskāra*), like the aggregates (*skandha*) themselves, had come to be looked upon as dharmas.

Certain Buddhists interpreted this to mean that the dharmas are momentary: they last only a single moment.[155] This new doctrine was not immediately adopted by all Buddhists. It is not found in the *Sutta-piṭaka* of the Theravādins.[156] It first appears in that school in the works of Buddhaghosa (fifth century).[157] Certain Sarvāstivāda texts—e.g., the *Saṃyuktābhidharmahṛdaya* and the *Mahāvibhāṣā*—concede that the Buddha did not speak of moments.[158] Other schools believed that certain dharmas, though non-eternal, were not momentary.[159]

The doctrine of momentariness is of course highly compatible with the dharma theory. The latter denies the existence of composite objects: only their ultimate component parts, the dharmas, really exist. The doctrine of momentariness adds that temporally composite objects do not exist either: from a temporal point of view also only the ultimate component parts, i.e., the momentary dharmas, exist.

We will see that the doctrine of momentariness gave rise to many theoretical discussions, first in the school of the Sarvāstivādins, later in other schools as well.[160] The doctrine of momentariness, although

---

154 SN I.200, etc.; cf. Mimaki 1976: 1 and 209; Silburn 1955: 177–78.

155 See La Vallée Poussin 1934; Rospatt 1995. Schmithausen (1973a: 178–79) holds the view that this doctrine may have been inspired by a certain spiritual practice, perhaps the applications of mindfulness (*smṛtyupasthāna*); Rospatt (1995: 217) rather believes that it is mainly based upon the analysis of change.

156 Glasenapp 1938: 51n9; Kalupahana 1975: 82–83; Rospatt 1995: 16–17.

157 Kalupahana 1975: 148; 1974: 186; 1992: 206–16; Rospatt 1995: 32–33.

158 Dessein 1999: I.140; II.130n588.

159 La Vallée Poussin 1937: 136–37.

160 Rospatt (1995: 15–16) rightly points out that the doctrine of momentariness is explicitly attested at a relatively late date. We assume nevertheless that this doctrine is as old as the Pañcavastuka (see below) and that it finds expression in the characteristics of the conditioned (*saṃskṛtalakṣaṇa*). This is a hypothesis, but it allows for a coherent interpretation of this development; see Bronkhorst 1995a. This hypothesis is furthermore strengthened by the circumstance that already the old *Sūyagaḍa* of the Jainas (1.1.1.17) describes the five Buddhist

not attested in the old discourses, became an inseparable part of the dharma theory, and one that was accepted by most Indian Buddhists. The fact that several schools made an exception for a number of so-called unconditioned (*asaṃskṛta*) dharmas, which are not momentary but eternal, is of minor importance in this context.

Let us now examine the systematization of the dharmas that has been known as Pañcavastuka since Frauwallner gave it that name.[161] It is a new arrangement of the dharmas in five categories. We know that earlier attempts had been made to give each dharma its place in schemes taken from the old discourses. These were the five aggregates, followed by the twelve realms of the senses and the eighteen elements (*dhātu*). However, many dharmas did not fit—or fitted only with the greatest difficulty—into these traditional categories. The Pañcavastuka broke with this tradition and proposed five new categories. We find this new classification in a text of the same name (*Pañcavastuka*), which was preserved as part of the canonical *Prakaraṇapāda* and also independently. We also find it in the older *Dharmaskandha* of the Sarvāstivāda *Abhidharma-piṭaka*.[162] All the later Sarvāstivāda texts know this systematization, even if it occupies a secondary place in them, alongside the division into five aggregates.

The Pañcavastuka, then, is a division of the dharmas into five objects (*vastu*) or categories (*dharma*): (1) form (*rūpa*), (2) mind (*citta*), (3) mental (dharmas) (*caitta/caitasika*), (4) conditioned factors separated from the mind (*cittaviprayukta saṃskāra*), and (5) unconditioned (dharmas) (*asaṃskṛta*). The dharmas numbered from (1) to (4) are conditioned (*saṃskṛta*), those in (5) are unconditioned.

---

aggregates (*skandha*) as *khaṇa-joi* = *kṣaṇayogin*, "which are only linked together for a moment"; see Bollée 1977: 72–73.

161 Frauwallner 1995, chap. VI (= 1963).

162 Imanishi 1969: 13–15; cf., e.g., Dhsk pp. 26.27–27.11. The canonical *Prakaraṇapāda* is found in TI 1541 and TI 1542 (vol. 26). The independent *Pañcavastuka* is found in TI 1556 and TI 1557 (vol. 28). Sanskrit fragments are found in Imanishi 1969. It is likely that the *Pañcavastuka* was first called *Pañcadharmaka* (Imanishi 1969: 12).

As compared to the older classification in five aggregates—called Pañcaskandhaka by Frauwallner—the Pañcavastuka represented clear progress, because it could subsume and classify all the dharmas. Nevertheless, it was not a radical break from the five aggregates, for the aggregates have their place in the new Pañcavastuka, as follows. The first category of the Pañcavastuka, form (*rūpa*), corresponds to the first aggregate, which is likewise called *rūpa*. Sensation (*vedanā*) and ideation (*saṃjñā*) lose their status as separate categories and belong now to the mental dharmas (*caitasika dharma*), the third category of the Pañcavastuka. The fifth aggregate, consciousness (*vijñāna*) is now subsumed under mind (*citta*), the second category of the Pañcavastuka. The aggregate of conditioned factors (*saṃskāra*) belongs primarily to the third category of mental dharmas. But its name also lives on in the fourth category, that of the conditioned factors separated from the mind (*cittaviprayukta saṃskāra*). Indeed, these conditioned factors separated from the mind are already in the old *Dharmaskandha* described as belonging to the aggregate of conditioned factors.[163] But now certain dharmas that only with difficulty found a place in the old system of five aggregates are included in this category.[164] The same applies to the contents of the fifth category, the unconditioned (*asaṃskṛta*) dharmas.

The creation of this new classification was a turning point in the development of Buddhist thinking. It testifies to the readiness to go beyond tradition and to reflect independently on Buddhist teaching. Wherever the traditional teaching showed weaknesses or deficiencies, there was a willingness to change it. This new way of dealing with the teaching is illustrated by certain dharmas that figure in the Pañcavastuka. These dharmas were meant to solve certain difficulties that arose while systematizing the doctrine. Let us look at some of them.

The first category of the Pañcavastuka is material form (*rūpa*). The dharmas in this category are described as follows:

163 Dessein 1999: II:91–92n18.
164 Cf. Abhidh-k-bh(Hi) I, p. XV; also Kapani 1992: 265–66.

> What is material form? The four great elements and [matter] dependent on the four great elements.
>
> What are the four great elements? The element earth, the element water, the element fire, and the element wind.
>
> What is dependent material form? The eye organ, the ear organ, the nose organ, the tongue organ, the body organ, form, sound, odor, flavor, a part of that which can be touched, and [the material form of] non-information (*avijñapti*).[165]

Most of these dharmas are already known to us. Ten out of the twelve realms of the senses (*āyatana*) find a place here, namely the five organs, each with its object. Only the mind (*manas*) and its object, the mental property (*dharma*), are not mentioned. This is understandable, for these two do not belong to the category "material form." Furthermore, the four great elements are present: earth, water, fire, and wind. Their presence in the category "material form" is likewise not surprising. The only element missing is space (*ākāśa*), but this is readily explained by the fact that space was considered an unconditioned and therefore eternal element. The Pañcavastuka keeps it in the fifth category, that of the unconditioned dharmas.

The last dharma listed here is completely different from the other ones: it is the peculiarly named dharma of non-information (*avijñapti*). The function of this dharma can only be understood in the light of the special interpretation of the doctrine of karma in Buddhism. As we have seen, for the Buddhists karma is not only an action but also an intention. An intention can cause a visible, but also an invisible action. In this connection, the *Abhidharmakośabhāṣya* speaks of a person who causes others to act without acting himself. In that person arises "non-information," which forthwith distinguishes him objectively and morally from another person who has not provoked such an action.[166] Henceforth, this "non-

165 Translated according to Imanishi 1969: 6–7.

166 Lamotte 1936: 156–57, 162–63; Abhidh-k(VP) fascicle 3, p. 3n2; Amṛtar(B) p. 30–31; Abhidh-k-bh(Hi) I, pp. XXXV–XXXVI; Sanderson 1994: 38–39.

information" sticks to him and accompanies him until the time when his action will come to fruition.

Other dharmas whose presence points to a further systematization of the dharma theory are found in the fourth category of the Pañcavastuka, that of the conditioned factors separated from the mind (*cittaviprayukta saṃskāra*).[167] This category is the most important innovation of the Pañcavastuka and was created with the aim of classifying those dharmas that could not easily find a place in the old Pañcaskandhaka.[168]

We have spoken above of the momentariness of the dharmas, citing in that connection the old canonical phrase: "All the conditioned factors are impermanent, characterized by production and disappearance. After being produced, they disappear." In Pāli, "characterized by production and disappearance" is *uppādavayadhammino*. This expression contains the word dharma (Pa. *dhamma*) and could also be translated "[all conditioned factors] have production and disappearance as dharmas." It is unlikely that such a meaning was intended in the old days; *dharma* has several meanings, among them, characteristic or quality. Nevertheless, at the time when the dharma theory was fully developed, expressions such as this one could easily give the impression that all the dharmas were accompanied by two more dharmas, namely the dharmas "production" and "disappearance."

It looks as if this statement of the old canon, and other similar ones, was indeed interpreted in this fashion.[169] We find among the conditioned factors separated from the mind (*cittaviprayukta saṃskāra*) the following four dharmas: birth (*jāti*), old age (*jarā*), existence (*sthiti*), and impermanence (*anityatā*). There was no consensus as to the exact number of these so-called "characteristics of the conditioned" (*saṃskṛtalakṣaṇa*): four or three.[170] However that may be, these are the dharmas responsi-

167 Imanishi 1969: 8. The same already happens in the *Dharmaskandha*; see Imanishi 1969: 15–16. A similar list is found in Ghoṣaka's *Amṛtarasa* and elsewhere; see Jaini 1959: 536–37.

168 The list of the conditioned factors separated from the mind is not always the same; see Cox 1995: 70–71.

169 Cf. also Glasenapp 1938: 58–59 for further textual references.

170 See Amṛtar(B) p. 43–44; Cox 1995: 146–47; Bronkhorst 1987: 67–68. The

ble for the production of other dharmas, for their momentary existence, and for their subsequent disappearance. The existence of these dharmas shows that the early Sarvāstivādins were preoccupied with the doctrine of momentariness. The example also shows to what extent Buddhist mentality had changed in the interim. The concepts of birth, old age, and impermanence were used in the old teaching to emphasize the suffering that is inherent in human existence. The same concepts are used here, but their association with suffering has completely disappeared. For our dogmatists, birth, old age, and impermanence are dharmas, that is to say, entities accepted in their ontology that, like other dharmas, exist only for a moment and fulfill a certain function. We will see below that the aridity of this systematization provoked a reaction in other Buddhists. This aridity, however, was not solely a loss. Indeed, the case can be made that this very aridity with regard to feelings accompanied the birth of rational thinking in India. We will return to this later.

It is clear that a radical attempt was made to develop an ontology that, although peculiar, does not contradict the world as we experience it. The issue was to determine what things really exist. Really existing things are necessarily dharmas. The complete list of dharmas should be able to explain our everyday "reality"—which as such does not really exist. We know that dharmas have a beginning, a duration, and an end. The question presents itself whether that beginning really exists or not. If the answer is yes, then that beginning can only be a dharma. If the answer is no, then the dharmas are without beginning and therefore not momentary. This kind of argumentation is rigorously followed with respect to many questions. We find the first manifestations of this way of proceeding in the Pañcavastuka. It is further refined in the later history of the school.

This subsequent refinement is illustrated by the discussion to which

---

canonical founding text of this doctrine, the *Trilakṣaṇa Sūtra*, mentions only three of these characteristics; see Rospatt 1995: 23 (with note 31), 40–41. The *Mahābhārata* knows of four characteristics: birth, growth, decay, and death of the manifested (*vyakta*) (Mhbh 12.228.29–30), and it seems justified to suspect Buddhist influence in this case.

the above-mentioned dharmas gave rise. The question is: If all dharmas possess birth, old age, existence, and impermanence, how about the dharmas birth, old age, existence, and impermanence themselves? These dharmas, too, originate, exist, and disappear, and they, too, should therefore be accompanied by these same dharmas. The later Sarvāstivādins agree with this, and some of them speak about the dharmas "birth of birth" (*jātijāti*), "existence of existence" (*sthitisthiti*), and so on. These new dharmas, however, are not themselves accompanied by further dharmas of birth, old age, existence, and impermanence. This is not necessary, because the first birth also provokes the birth of birth, just as the birth of birth provokes the first birth. The same is true of the remaining dharmas of this kind.[171]

Let us now turn to some other conditioned factors separated from the mind, namely to the word body (*nāmakāya*), the sentence body (*padakāya*), and the sound body (*vyañjanakāya*).[172] The exact explanation of these expressions varies to some extent in the different texts that have come down to us.[173] But all agree that these are linguistic entities. The *word body*, for instance, is the word seen as a unity, and it is not difficult to see what role such a word body could play in the Buddhist worldview. For this worldview has no temporally extended objects, and therefore no place for words and similar linguistic entities. This was apparently a problem for the early Sarvāstivādins. Perhaps it was difficult to believe that there are no words at all, and therefore no words of the Buddha either. Later discussions among Buddhists show that this is indeed a possible explanation.[174] But perhaps they were also thinking

171 Cf. Abhidh-hṛ(A) 2.10, p. 68; Willemen 1975: 19–20. The *Abhidharmahṛdaya* and the *Amṛtarasa* do not use the expressions *jātijāti*, etc.; see Amṛtar(B) p. 44n57.

172 The sound body (*vyañjanakāya*) is lacking in the incomplete manuscript of the *Pañcavastuka* edited by Imanishi (1969: 8) but figures in all the parallel texts. The oldest Chinese translation of this work likewise contains only two, instead of three terms, whose identification is furthermore not unproblematic; see Bronkhorst 1987: 62–63.

173 Bronkhorst 1987: 60–61, with exact textual references; cf. also Jaini 1959a: 97; Amṛtar(B) pp. 61–62.

174 Jaini 1959a: 96.

of the unreal nature of the everyday world, which, as we have seen, is caused by words: a chariot is in reality not observed, it is only a denotation, an appellation, a designation, a current usage, a name, as Nāgasena states in the *Milindapañha*. But if the unreal objects of the everyday world are caused by words, then these words at least should really exist. Unfortunately, the old texts do not reveal to us why the Sarvāstivādins held on to the existence of words and other component parts of language.[175] What we can be certain about is that they were trying to solve the problem of the nonexistence of these language-entities by introducing the above-mentioned linguistic dharmas.

The momentariness of the dharmas also gave rise to the following problem. How can one claim that the innumerable dharmas that constantly appear and disappear have anything in common with each other? How can one grasp exhaustively this unending mass of dharmas with the limited number of names contained in the Abhidharma of the Sarvāstivādins?[176] The answer lies in the dharma named *community-of-being* (*nikāyasabhāga*, also *sabhāgatā*), which also belongs to the conditioned factors separated from the mind. This community-of-being allows us to recognize an aggregate (*skandha*), for example, as such and to name it. It also allows us to recognize and name the various types of beings.[177] Again the need to posit a new dharma to overcome an explanatory gap leads to the expansion of the list of existing things.

The *Pañcavastuka* also mentions under the same fourth category the dharma *obtaining* (*prāpti*). This is the last dharma we shall examine

175 Jaini (1959a: 97–98), with reference to the relevant discussion in the *Abhidharmakośa* of Vasubandhu (Abhidh-k-bh(P) p. 80.24–25), evokes the possibility that physical sounds operate on the *nāman*, while the *nāman* manifests the meaning. However, this role in transmitting meaning is probably a later development; it also appears in non-Buddhist philosophy of language; see Bronkhorst 1998.

176 In later systematizations their number is seventy-five; cf. Abhidh-k-bh(Hi) I p. XII.

177 Abhidh-k-bh(P) p. 67.13–14 along with Abhidh-k-bh(D) p. 230. La Vallée Poussin's translation (Abhidh-k(VP) I.196), according to which there can be a community-of-being only for the dharmas belonging to living beings, is not corroborated by the Sanskrit text. Some texts however only speak about community-of-being in relation to living beings; cf. Abhidh-avat(V) pp. 63–64.

in this section. Its presence shows once again how the Sarvāstivādins attempted to make the world intelligible. A detailed description of this dharma is found, as so often, in the relatively late *Abhidharmakośabhāṣya* of Vasubandhu.[178] According to this text, the existence of the obtaining dharma is proved by the fact that an old discourse claims that by the obtaining of the ten dharmas of an arhat, the accomplished one becomes one who has abandoned the five limbs (*aṅga*).[179] To understand this proof, it is not important to know what the ten dharmas belonging to an arhat or what the five limbs are,[180] only that this passage mentions "obtaining." From this, it was concluded that something like "obtaining" actually exists, and that it is therefore a dharma.

In the context of the Sarvāstivādins' worldview, the use of this dharma is as follows: As we have seen, there are no persons according to the Abhidharma masters. The person is nothing but a collection, a sequence (*saṃtāna/saṃtati*) of dharmas (and therefore does not really exist). Nevertheless, it is indisputable that different persons do not share the same dharmas: different sequences of dharmas make up different persons. It is also clear that the actions of a person have their effects within the sequence that makes up that same person. In other words, dharmas belong to specific persons. What is responsible for their attribution to one person rather than to another? How is the "unity," that is to say, the "belonging together" of a sequence, guaranteed? This is achieved by the dharma obtaining.[181]

This example shows once again how the negation of the person determined to a considerable extent the development of Buddhist

---

178 Abhidh-k-bh(P) p. 62.15–16; Abhidh-k(VP) I.179–80. The definitions in early Abhidharma works are discussed in Cox 1995: 80–81.

179 For the origin of this citation, see Abhidh-k-bh(Pā) p. 33 Nb. [69]. The citation reads *pratilambha* instead of *prāpti*, which once again shows that the old dogmatists were little concerned with the exact denomination of the dharmas; cf. Cox 1995: 79–80. For another citation that supposedly proves the existence of obtaining, see Jaini 1959b: 245.

180 On this, see Abhidh-k(VP) I.181n2.

181 Cf. Mitchell 1974: 195; Cox 1995: 85–86; Jaini 1959b: 238; Buswell & Jaini 1996: 116. See also Waldron 1994: 214–15.

thought. It did so positively—we already know that the dharma theory, for instance, owes its existence to that doctrine. It also gave rise to problems, which the Buddhists sought to solve in various ways that we will examine further below. In this case, it suffices to note that, to a certain extent, the dharma obtaining (*prāpti*) plays the role that would otherwise devolve upon the person—grouping together the dharmas that belong to one person and distinguishing them from other persons.[182]

The dharma obtaining was also used for another purpose, at least in the later texts of the school. Wholesome (*kuśala*) and unwholesome (*akuśala*) dharmas, as well as morally neutral (*avyākṛta*) ones—i.e., mind (*citta*) along with the mental (*caitta*/*caitasika*) dharmas—alternate in a person's stream of thought. Does this mean that wholesome moments of thought can call forth unwholesome ones? Naturally, this cannot be the case. The school does not concede either that wholesome and unwholesome moments of thought can simultaneously appear in one and the same person. How then is the alternation of morally different moments of thought to be explained? Here obtaining plays a useful role. For when a wholesome moment of thought appears, it is accompanied by its "obtaining." Now, when the wholesome moment of thought becomes part of the past but remains in existence as a past dharma,[183] its obtaining causes a series of wholesome obtainings. Subsequently, when an unwholesome moment of thought becomes present, then even though the previous wholesome moment of thought has become past, its obtaining is present and coexists in the same person alongside the unwholesome moment of thought. Owing to this wholesome obtaining, "its" past (but nevertheless existing) wholesome moment of thought can produce a new wholesome moment of thought.[184]

The dharmas discussed so far make clear with how much rigor the early Sarvāstivādins tried to develop and to systematize the dharma theory. These efforts continued over many centuries, so that later texts such

182 See Conze 1962: 141.

183 We discuss the existence of past and future below.

184 Cox 1995: 92–93.

as Vasubandhu's famous *Abhidharmakośabhāṣya*, which may belong to the early fifth century,[185] present a more refined system than the earlier texts. However, the examples discussed above belong to the earlier time. The Pañcavastuka is already present in a few canonical texts of the Sarvāstivāda, and all the dharmas that we have discussed have a place in it. Furthermore, the linguistic dharmas appear to have exerted an influence on the Brahmanical grammarian Patañjali, who lived in the second century BCE.[186] This supports a conclusion that the detailed rationalization of the dharma theory began no later than the second century BCE.

We turn to the unconditioned (*asaṃskṛta*) dharmas. The Sarvāstivādins recognized three of them, namely *space* (*ākāśa*), *cessation not a result of knowledge* (*apratisaṃkhyānirodha*), and *cessation through knowledge* (*pratisaṃkhyānirodha*). We have already observed that unconditioned dharmas are eternal. The Sarvāstivādins looked upon space as a dharma and therefore as something existing. The following can be said about the two cessations (*nirodha*). It may happen that certain dharmas are not produced in the continuum that constitutes a personality because their causes are not present. Liberating knowledge has a similar effect: ignorance and other vices no longer occur in the personality stream; in the end the stream is completely interrupted. In both cases, the Sarvāstivādins explain this by accepting that there are two dharmas: *cessation not a result of knowledge* and *cessation through knowledge*. These prevent the appearance of those other dharmas through being connected with the personality stream.[187]

The doctrine of momentariness gave rise to other questions than those that the Pañcavastuka tried to solve. For instance, if the world is nothing but a succession of distinct momentary dharmas, how can one

---

185 Schmithausen (1992a: 392–97) defends the view that the *Laṅkāvatāra Sūtra*, which was translated into Chinese in 443, cites one of Vasubandhu's late works (the *Triṃśikā*); in the same volume, Lindtner (1992) argues for the opposite view.

186 Bronkhorst 1987: 56–57; 1998a; 1994. See also in chapter 4 below.

187 Frauwallner 1956a: 118; cf. La Vallée Poussin 1930.

explain the undeniable regularity of the world? The traditional answer to this question is the twelvefold causal series of conditioned origination (*pratītyasamutpāda*), which we met above while discussing the old teaching:

> With (1) ignorance as condition, (2) conditioned factors [come to be]; with conditioned factors as condition, (3) consciousness; with consciousness as condition, (4) name-and-form; with name-and-form as condition, (5) the six realms of the senses; with the six realms of the senses as condition, (6) contact; with contact as condition, (7) sensation; with sensation as condition, (8) thirst; with thirst as condition, (9) clinging; with clinging as condition, (10) existence; with existence as condition, (11) birth; with birth as condition, (12) aging-and-death, sorrow, lamentation, suffering, dejection, and despair come to be.

We saw as well that this causal series was interpreted in such a way that its twelve elements were distributed over three births.[188]

The Abhidharma masters attempted to refine the understanding of this causal series. In doing so, they became convinced that each of its twelve elements was a state (*daśā* or *avasthā*) of the five aggregates (*skandha*).[189] The five aggregates are the dharmas that constitute the personality, and the series of conditioned origination must thereby describe the causality operating among these dharmas. Elsewhere it is said that all the conditioned dharmas are conditioned origination, in the sense that they produce all the dharmas that are produced dependently.[190] The *Abhidharmakośabhāṣya* explains that the conditioned dharmas *can* be conditioned origination, in other words that the expression *con-*

188 For interpretations of the causal series, see La Vallée Poussin 1913: 34–45; further Kritzer 1992.

189 Kritzer 1993: 28–29.

190 Abhidh-k-bh(P) p. 133.15, with reference to the *Prakaraṇa* 6.9 (= Prak(Im) 24); further p. 136.9–10.

ditioned origination can refer to the dharmas, because the activity (origination) and the agent (that which originates) are not different from each other.[191] This is true in the dharma theory, for this theory does not number activity among its dharmas: only the bearers of the activity of origination, i.e., the dharmas, really exist. The *Abhidharmakośabhāṣya* further explains that the other (i.e., the older) interpretation of the law of conditioned origination was only propounded in order to put an end to people's confusion over past, present, and future. In reality, the only valid interpretation is the one that is adapted to the dharma theory.[192]

It is true that this new interpretation gives the dharmas their due. Nevertheless it remains unsatisfactory. It does not explain exactly how the dharmas succeed one another at each moment. For this reason, attempts were made early to develop an independent doctrine of causality.[193] Thus the canonical *Vijñānakāya* distinguishes four kinds of conditions (*pratyaya*): the producing condition (*hetu-pratyaya*), the support (*ārambaṇa-* or *ālambana-pratyaya*) or object of knowledge, the immediately contiguous condition (*samanantara-pratyaya*), and the determining condition (*adhipati-pratyaya*).[194] The later but likewise canonical *Jñānaprasthāna* introduces a subdivision into six causes, namely, the causal reason (*kāraṇahetu*), the concomitant cause (*sahabhūhetu*), the common cause (*sabhāgahetu*), the cooperative cause (*saṃprayukta(ka)hetu*), the all-pervading cause (*sarvatragahetu*), and the reason for ripening (*vipākahetu*).[195]

This new doctrine of causality is quite different from the old causal series of conditioned origination and represents a new and independent development.[196] How can we reconcile the old series with the new ideas? In this connection it is interesting to mention the views of Saṃghabhadra. Saṃghabhadra was one of the younger contemporaries

191 Abhidh-k-bh(P) p. 138.15–16; Abhidh-k(VP) II.79.

192 Cf. Abhidh-k(VP) II.67.

193 Lamotte 1944–80: V.2163–64.

194 Frauwallner 1995: 28–29 (= 1964: 88–89); La Vallée Poussin 1913: 52–53.

195 La Vallée Poussin 1913: 54–54; Buswell & Jaini 1996: 110. Tanaka 1985 deals exhaustively with the concomitant condition.

196 A satisfactory interpretation of this theory of causality is still a desideratum.

of Vasubandhu, the author of the *Abhidharmakośabhāṣya*. Both authors probably lived in the fifth century of our era. Saṃghabhadra's *Nyāyānusāra* contains certain ideas about causality that Frauwallner describes as follows:[197]

> According to Saṃghabhadra, causal activity can occur in two ways among the conditioned dharmas (*saṃskṛtadharma*): as cause (*hetu*) and as condition (*pratyaya*). A cause brings about the arising of an effect, while conditions contribute to the process. This is valid for internal as well as external causal processes. The difference between cause and condition is explained by means of the following example: the cause brings about, the conditions furthers, like the mother who bears the child and the foster-mother who brings it up. The condition fosters what the cause has brought forth, the conditions further its development.

In external causal processes, the seed is the cause for the arising of the sprout. Earth contributes as a condition. With the arising of the human embryo, similarly, the first stage of development, the *kalala*, is the cause for the arising of the second, the *arbuda*. Consciousness (*vijñāna*), which according to the law of conditioned origination brings about rebirth, contributes as a condition in the process. Although the *arbuda* does not arise independently of consciousness, it does not arise from consciousness as cause, because they each belong to different causal chains. However, neither can it be said that consciousness does not act as a condition at the arising of the *arbuda*, because its presence and non-presence are based on the former's presence and non-presence.

The last example shows how two elements of the old causal chain—consciousness (*vijñāna*) and name-and-form (*nāmarūpa*)—are related to each other. Consciousness produces name-and-form but as a condition (*pratyaya*), not as a cause (*hetu*). In this way the new doctrine of causality is used to explain the old law of causality.

---

197 Frauwallner 1995: 199–200 (= 1973: 112–13).

The doctrine of momentariness was, in Sarvāstivāda, only part of a more comprehensive understanding of the problem of time. For the doctrine of momentariness only concerns the present. What about the past and the future? Do they exist as well, or does only the present really exist? At an early date, the Sarvāstivāda school had reached the conclusion that all three—past, present, and future—really exist. Its very name expresses this: *sarvāsti* is composed of *sarva* "everything" und *asti* "exists," because the adepts of the school held the view that everything, whether in the past, the present, or the future, exists.[198]

A canonical text, the *Vijñānakāya*, already cites various similar arguments in favor of this school doctrine.[199] They are all based upon the conviction that two moments of mind or consciousness (*citta*, *vijñāna*) cannot occur simultaneously in a single person. The text does not say why this should be so, but this conviction is always presented as the unshakable starting point of the discussion.[200] It is not difficult to understand that some noteworthy conclusions could be drawn from this. Consider the case where a person contemplates his or her desire (*lobha*). Desire and contemplation are two different mental states, which cannot therefore occur simultaneously. This means that if the contemplation takes place in the present, the perceived desire cannot belong to the present; it can only belong to the past or to the future. But the Buddha has declared that desire exists. For desire to exist and to be contemplated, past and future must also exist.

Further arguments are added by later texts.[201] One of these arguments pertains to the consequence that actions would have no effects,

198 Cf., e.g., *Abhidharmakośa* 5.25 (= Abhidh-k-bh(P) p. 296.3–4). It is not at all certain that this school, which was initially a "Vinaya school" (see below), bore this name from the beginning; see Bechert 1985: 44.

199 La Vallée Poussin 1925: 346–58. For later times, see Cox 1988: 44–45.

200 Most of the other schools of the Hīnayāna, with the possible exception of the Mahāsāṃghikas, came to adopt the same position; La Vallée Poussin 1928: 184n2, 186, 411n1; Schmithausen 1967: 113n19; 1987: 45, 46 (part I) and 316n302, 317n314 (part II); Cox 1992: 82–83 with 104n85.

201 See La Vallée Poussin 1937: passim; 1928: I: 187; Schmithausen 1987: I: 4, with II: 248nn25–28.

which contradicts fundamental Buddhist doctrine. The existence of the past also explains how a person, after sojourning for some time in the state of cessation (*nirodha*), in which there is no consciousness, can again become conscious. The problem is that there is in such a case no continuity of mental dharmas, so that the dharmas which appear at the moment of regaining consciousness do not have any directly preceding mental dharmas that could cause them. The existence of the past, and therefore of past mental dharmas, explains their effectiveness over a time gap.

The position according to which past and future exist was debated repeatedly in subsequent developments of the school. The topic is indeed a recurrent one in its most important texts.[202] The question that attracted most attention was: what exactly distinguishes a present dharma from the same dharma while in the past or future? The dharmas were thought to travel through the three times (*adhvan*): from the future they travel into the present, and from the present into the past. The question how to explain this received various answers. The opinions of four teachers—Dharmatrāta, Ghoṣaka,[203] Vasumitra, and Buddhadeva—are regularly cited. Dharmatrāta held that dharmas in the various time zones are distinguished by their state (*bhāva*). For Ghoṣaka the characteristics (*lakṣaṇa*) are responsible: a past dharma is linked with the characteristic of the past, without being devoid of links with the characteristics of the future and present, and analogous conditions hold for present and future dharmas. According to Vasumitra, the three types of dharmas are differentiated by their position (*avasthā*), like calculation sticks (*vartikā*), which, depending on their position, have the value of one, one hundred, or one thousand.[204] According to Buddhadeva, finally, the various dharmas are differentiated by their relation to earlier and later dharmas, just as one and the same woman

---

202 See Frauwallner 1995: chap. VIII (= 1973); La Vallée Poussin 1937.

203 This Ghoṣaka is different from the author of the *Amṛtarasa;* see Amṛtar(B) pp. 12ff.; Dessein 1999: I: lxix ff.

204 This example points to the existence of a decimal place-value system; cf. Bronkhorst 1994a.

can be a mother and a daughter, depending on the relationship one has in mind.[205]

This idea of dharmas traveling through time zones was subsequently abandoned, probably because it presupposes the existence of time. The Sarvāstivādins did not recognize time as something that exists. In their attempt at avoiding the difficulty, they accepted the following solution. Future, present, and past dharmas are differentiated by their efficiency (*kāritra*). If this efficiency has not been activated yet, then the dharmas are future. If it is active, then they are present. And if it has passed, then they are past. The time zones do not really exist; they are really nothing but the dharmas existing in the past, the present, and the future.

The theory of efficiency as a decisive element in the temporal position of the dharmas was over time elaborated and refined by the Sarvāstivādins.[206] It is important to remember that for these thinkers, the existence of past and future dharmas is as real as that of present ones. In other words, a dharma's own-nature (*svabhāva*) is eternal, even though its present manifestation is only momentary.[207]

These developments of the dharma theory are all linked with the doctrine of momentariness and its conception of time in terms of atomic units. Time in this view is a never-ending series of moments that cannot be further subdivided. As we have seen, such a conception aligns well with the dharma theory, which denies the existence of composite entities.

The denial of composite entities led to an atomic conception of not only time but also material form. For each composite entity has parts that are, as a rule, also composite and that therefore do not really exist. This might be used as an argument to prove that the division of matter can continue endlessly without ever producing anything that really exists, and that therefore nothing really exists in the material world. This argument was indeed used in certain later developments of Buddhism,

---

205 Williams (1977) has tried to determine more precisely Buddhadeva's position; Oetke (1995) contradicts him.

206 Frauwallner 1995: 193ff. (= 1973: 106ff.)

207 La Vallée Poussin 1937: 131–32.

but the Sarvāstivādins were not attracted by it. They were not seeking to prove the unreality of the material world. On the contrary, the dharma theory claims to describe the reality behind the unreal everyday objects. The Sarvāstivādins were therefore forced to admit that the subdivision of matter must stop at some point. It stops at the smallest component parts of matter, atoms. The Sarvāstivādins did not concede any spatial extension to their atoms.[208]

There can be no doubt that the atomic representation of matter became part of the worldview of the Sarvāstivādins at an early date. One cannot imagine that these Buddhists would investigate in detail the consequences of the doctrine of momentariness without bothering about the atomic structure of matter. The latter is, after all, a direct consequence of their doctrine of the nonexistence of composite objects. Nevertheless, it appears that atoms are not mentioned in their canonical texts. This can probably be explained by the circumstance that material atoms are not new dharmas and do not provide reasons for postulating new dharmas, as happened in the case of the doctrine of momentariness. The canonical texts primarily concentrate on listing and discussing dharmas; atoms do not contribute anything new to this: like everything else, atoms are composed of dharmas.

Atoms are mentioned in Dharmaśreṣṭhin's *Abhidharmahṛdaya*, which belongs to the early centuries of the Common Era and is probably the oldest noncanonical Sarvāstivāda text that has come down to us.[209] This text explains the relationship between atoms (*paramāṇu*) and dharmas, in the following manner.[210] A distinction is drawn between three types of atoms: first the atoms belonging to the four sense faculties (*indriya*), namely sight, hearing, smell, and taste; second the atoms found in the sense organ that is the body; and third all remaining

208 La Vallée Poussin 1937: 18.

209 Dessein (1999: I: xxxi ff.) has shown that of the two names attributed to this author, Dharmaśrī and Dharmaśreṣṭhin, the latter is to be preferred. He also prefers the title *Abhidharmahṛdaya* instead of *Abhidharmasāra* for his main work (pp. xx–xxi). On the dating of this text, see Dessein 1996; Willemen 1996: 451.

210 TI 1550, vol. 28, 811b4–12; cf. Willemen 1975: 18–19; Abhidh-hṛ(A) pp. 66–67.

atoms. The atoms of the four senses are composed of ten dharmas each. The atoms of the eye, for instance, contains earth (*pṛthivī*), water (*ap*), fire (*tejas*), wind (*vāyu*), form (*rūpa*), odor (*gandha*), flavor (*rasa*), the tangible (*spraṣṭavya*), the sense faculty of the eye (*cakṣurindriya*), and the sense faculty of the body (*kāyendriya*); something similar holds for the remaining senses, i.e., hearing, smell, and taste. The atoms of the body sense organ contain nine dharmas—those given in the example of the eye but without the sense faculty of the eye (*cakṣurindriya*). The remaining atoms, which are not senses, contain eight dharmas each, namely those listed above but without the last two. The text adds that all this is valid for the plane of desire (*kāmadhātu*). On the plane of form (*rūpadhātu*), since it contains neither odor nor flavor, each atom has two fewer dharmas. The Sarvāstivādins, moreover, do not concede any spatial extension to their atoms.[211]

Strictly speaking, atoms cannot be the ultimate components of matter for they are composite themselves. The really ultimate components are the dharmas. This is indeed what we should expect in the light of the dharma theory. There is, however, a problem: the atoms that are not senses all have the same composition. In spite of this, they sometimes behave as earth, sometimes as water, as fire, or as wind. In other words, some of these atoms are hard (*kaṭhina*), others are liquid (*drava*), hot (*uṣṇa*), or mobile (*samudīraṇa*). The *Abhidharmakośabhāṣya* explains this as follows. The dharmas of earth, water, fire, and wind—which are each contained in the atoms—can predominate more or less strongly (*paṭu*). The property that predominates most strongly is the one perceived.[212]

In this conceptualization of matter, it is hard to maintain that there is a difference between substances and properties. If we consider the atom as a substance, we must admit that this substance is nothing but a collection of momentary dharmas. We might feel tempted to call some of these dharmas—such as form and so on—*properties*, and call others—such as earth—*substances*. But this differentiation makes no sense.

211 La Vallée Poussin 1937: 18.

212 Abhidh-k-bh(P) p. 53.9–11, under *Abhidharmakośa* 2.22; cf. Abhidh-k(VP) I.145–46.

Both kinds of dharmas are momentary, and one dharma is not the property of another. We have also seen that the dharmas earth, water, fire, and wind manifest themselves as the properties hardness, fluidity, heat, and movement. The Buddhists themselves were aware of the absence of differentiation. The *Abhidharmakośabhāṣya* deals with the question as follows:[213]

> [Opponent:] Atoms are substances (*dravya*), which are different from the properties form and so on. Therefore, they do not necessarily have to vanish at the same time. [Answer:] The essential difference of these two need in no way be considered as proved. For if we examine them, there is no special earth and so on apart from form and so on. Therefore they are not fundamentally different.

Sarvāstivāda, then, developed an atomistic worldview in which the difference between substances and properties was lost. On the level of dharmas, onc might say that their system knew only properties and no substances. But on the level of atoms (which are substances), substances were seen as nothing but collections of properties.

We have already noted that the Sarvāstivāda doctrine of atoms must be as old as, or perhaps even older than, their doctrine of momentariness. This conclusion is reached not on the basis of textual evidence but on the internal logic of its development. Such conclusions are dangerous and should be drawn with utmost care. However, we have also seen why the doctrine of atoms could not possibly appear in the canonical scholastic texts even if it already existed. Once Buddhist thinkers began moving down the road of the dharma theory, the postulation of atoms, even more than the doctrine of momentariness, was inevitable.

Why, given the Buddha's negative attitude toward metaphysical thought, did the Buddhists of that time rush into the elaboration of an

213 Abhidh-k-bh(P) p. 190.3–5; translated according to Frauwallner 1956a: 101 (with modifications).

ontology? Had the later Buddhists suddenly got rid of this aversion, so as to dedicate themselves wholeheartedly to philosophical questions?

The situation is not quite so simple. The first concern of the Abhidharma specialists was to preserve the Buddha's message and to interpret it correctly. The idea that the Buddha had taught the dharmas had already become widely accepted. Thus we read in the *Mahāvibhāṣā*: "Pārśva says: the Buddha knows the nature and function of all the dharmas."[214] And already a sūtra passage declares that the Buddha teaches all the dharmas without exception. What this passage exactly means by "all the dharmas" is subsequently explained as the dharmas helpful to enlightenment (*bodhipākṣika dharma*).[215] The statement that one cannot put an end to suffering without knowledge of all the dharmas was likewise attributed to the Buddha: "I declare that one cannot put an end to suffering as long as there remains even a single dharma that is not known and rightly understood."[216] By understanding the dharmas, one can practice the four noble truths, understand conditioned origination, know the vices and isolate them, engender their destruction, and thus reach nirvāṇa.[217] This is why the Buddhists were so concerned with identifying and describing all the dharmas. The philosophical development was somehow a byproduct. One could almost say that it happened without conscious intention. We will examine the ways this developed in more detail below. Here it is important to stress that the old canonical Abhidharma texts are not philosophical works.[218] The philosophical dimension remained in the background for a long time and made its appearance only gradually.

When it did appear, it became necessary to deal with the question

214 TI 1545, vol. 27, 247c19–20, 27–28; cf. Dessein 1999: II: 230n414 and n417.

215 Bronkhorst 1985: 305 esp. note 6.

216 Abhidh-k-bh(P) p. 10.25–26 (under *Abhidharmakośa* 1.14); Abhidh-k(VP) I.29. The source of the citation is SĀ, TI 99, vol. 2, 55b7–8, 23–24 (Abhidh-k-bh(Pā) p. 22).

217 Cf. Cox 1992a: 158, with reference to the **Āryavasumitrabodhisattvasaṅgīti-śāstra*. See also Cox 1995: 4–5.

218 The absence of philosophical thought in many of them has been emphasized by researchers. Cf. Frauwallner 1995: 3, 8–11 (= 1964: 59, 65–69).

how exactly liberation is obtained. And inevitably, the Buddhists sought for an answer that would be satisfying in terms of the dharma theory.

Dharmaśreṣṭhin was perhaps the first to attempt to answer this question in detail.[219] His main problem was an old one, and one that we have encountered repeatedly. It is the question of how knowledge can lead to liberation. This problem had been the constant companion of Buddhism from its inception, and had only gained in importance when attempts were made to determine the exact content of this knowledge. We have seen, for instance, how the rejection of the knowledge of a self as a means to liberation was modified in such a way that knowledge of not-self itself became a liberating knowledge. This relation of such knowledge to the problem of rebirth was obvious: it implied non-identification with those parts of the person that perform actions and thereby propel rebirth. We also saw that ignorance—incorrect knowledge—is the primary cause of rebirth in the doctrine of conditioned origination. If ignorance is the primary cause of rebirth, then clearly only correct knowledge can put an end to it.

Dharmaśreṣṭhin follows a path that resembles the doctrine of conditioned origination, in the sense that he too believes that the main problem can be located, at least to a certain extent, in the presence of false views (*dṛṣṭi*). He distinguishes five of these. They are the belief in the existence of the personality (*satkāyadṛṣṭi*), the belief attached to extremes (*antagrāhadṛṣṭi*), the wrong view alone (*mithyādṛṣṭi*), the clinging to false views (*dṛṣṭiparāmarśa*), and the clinging to ceremonial practices (*śīlavrataparāmarśa*). These five views belong to a list of ten attachments (*anuśaya*), which contains five additional elements, namely passion (*rāga*), doubt (*vicikitsā*), disgust (*pratigha*), pride (*māna*), and delusion (*moha*). This list of ten attachments is probably a new creation, but it uses elements taken from the old discourses

219 See Frauwallner 1995: chap. VII (= 1971); Cox 1992b; cf. Willemen 1975: 48–49; Abhidh-hṛ(A) pp. 96–97; Dessein 1999: I: 239ff.; Schmithausen 1978: 104–5. The older works of Abhidharma do not contain a consistent description of the path to liberation; Cox 1992b: 74–75.

and rearranges them. These attachments are of two kinds: one can get rid of six of them—the five views and doubt—by means of discernment (*darśana*) and of the remaining four by practice and contemplation (*bhāvanā*). The objects of this discernment and contemplation are the four noble truths. Liberation occurs when all ten attachments are eliminated.

In their urge to systematize, the Buddhist dogmatists, and Dharmaśreṣṭhin in particular, found it hard to speak of the destruction of the ten attachments by means of the knowledge and contemplation of the four noble truths without indicating which truth was connected with the elimination of which attachment. It was assumed that a knowledge eliminates those attachments which have the same object as that knowledge. In this fashion, the attachments that are eliminated through insight fall into four groups corresponding to the four noble truths. They are eliminated by insight into suffering, the origin of suffering, the end of suffering, or the path leading to the end of suffering. Since most attachments can be directed at multiple objects, and taking into account the three spheres into which the Buddhists divide the world, the attachments were finally enumerated in ninety-eight varieties.

The insight into the four noble truths was likewise subdivided into a succession of moments. For each truth, four "paths" were distinguished, each occupying a single moment. The entire liberating process of knowledge, the vision of the truth (*dharmābhisamaya*), covers in this way sixteen moments of knowledge. Contemplation (*bhāvanā*) is practiced before as well as after the liberating knowledge, but it only takes effect through that knowledge. In this way the decisive significance of the path of discernment (*darśanamārga*) is assured. However, only the path of contemplation (*bhāvanāmārga*), which follows the path of knowledge, can bring final liberation.

What is the connection between the path leading to liberation and knowledge of all the dharmas? In order to answer this question, we must examine the beginning of the path, in particular the four applications of mindfulness (*smṛtyupasthāna*).[220] In Dharmaśreṣṭhin's representation,

220 Often the thirty-seven dharmas helpful to enlightenment (*bodhipakṣya/*

the disciple first contemplates the body (*kāya*) as impure, impermanent, painful, and not the self, according to its characteristic marks. Then he contemplates in the same fashion sensations (*vedanā*), mind (*citta*), and the dharmas, which are here subdivided into mental dharmas (*caitta/caitasika dharma*), conditioned factors separated from the mind (*cittaviprayukta saṃskāra*), and dharmas in general. We recognize the four categories of conditioned dharmas enumerated in the Pañcavastuka. These dharmas are contemplated in the applications of mindfulness first in their subdivision into categories and then all together. These applications of mindfulness, however, are a prerequisite for the next steps on the path to liberation, as it is from them that certain wholesome roots (*kuśalamūla*) are produced that make the liberating process possible. In other words, liberation is not possible without knowledge of which dharmas are to be contemplated, and therefore without knowledge of all the dharmas.[221]

The structure of Dharmaśreṣṭhin's *Abhidharmahṛdaya* appears to be determined by the four noble truths.[222] This would mean that correct knowledge of the four noble truths—liberating knowledge—implies knowledge of the dharmas.

Note at this point that in Dharmaśreṣṭhin's representation of the path leading to liberation there is no mention of meditation at all. In particular, the four stages of meditation (*dhyāna*) are missing. The same is also true for the stages of attainment (*samāpatti*), which had gained an important position in Buddhist teaching although they did not originally belong to it. As for other Buddhists, these stages of meditation play a major role in Dharmaśreṣṭhin's cosmology. It is thus doubly

---

bodhipākṣika dharma) are placed at the beginning of the path leading to liberation; see Cox 1992: 73–74.

221 Thus, when Frauwallner (1995: 180 (= 1971: 99)) asserts that the Sarvāstivādins' use of *smṛtyupasthāna* is only as a convenient canonical starting point for their own doctrine, he overlooks the self-justifying aspect of this usage; cf. Cox 1992: 74–75.

222 Willemen 1975: xix–xx; Dessein 1999: I: xxxv–xxxvi. This structure is valid only for chapters 1 to 7, because the remaining chapters are additions. Cf. also La Vallée Poussin 1937a: 165.

interesting to see that, for the Sarvāstivādins, these stages survived in their cosmology but played no role in their path to liberation.[223]

We have so far dealt with only three of the Indian Buddhist schools: primarily the so-called Sarvāstivāda, and in passing the Theravāda and the Pudgalavāda. Schools, as the word is used here, are distinguished from each other by divergent doctrinal opinions. Beyond schools, Buddhism also has sects or groups called *nikāyas*. Heinz Bechert describes the meaning of this word for modern Theravāda: "Those monks belong to one and the same nikāya who recognize reciprocally and without reservation the validity of each other's ordination and who perform together formal legal acts in the spirit of the order's rule or 'communal negotiations.'"[224] The situation was probably not very different during the early centuries of Buddhism. The initial points of dispute between nikāyas, if there were any, mainly concerned the interpretation and application of Vinaya prescriptions.[225] This is why we speak of "Vinaya schools." Certain doctrinal opinions developed within, and remained associated with certain nikāyas. Theravāda and Sarvāstivāda are examples: they were and remained Vinaya schools, each with its own works on Vinaya, within which Buddhist doctrine developed in its own specific way. But doctrinal positions do not always need their own nikāyas, and inversely, nikāyas do not always need distinctive doctrinal positions. The Pudgalavādins appear to have used the monastic rules of the Sarvāstivādins. If this is true, Pudgalavāda was from the start a philosophical school, not a Vinaya school.[226]

In this volume we are more interested in philosophical schools than in Vinaya schools. The names of many philosophical schools are

223 The practice of the thirty-seven dharmas helpful to enlightenment (*bodhipakṣya dharma*), on the other hand, as well as the ascetic life in the forest, are valued by certain Abhidharma texts; see Cox 1992a: 159.

224 Bechert 1985: 26.

225 This opinion is disputed by Sasaki in a series of articles (1989, 1992, 1993, 1994, 1995, 1996) and may have to be revised for the early period.

226 Bechert 1985: 42.

known to us,[227] but for the details of their teachings we depend on sources that are much more recent than the schools themselves. If we can trust those sources, then the differences between these teachings almost always concerned details of dogma. It is possible and even likely that many of these schools started as nikāyas, i.e., Vinaya schools, and did not develop their own teachings until later. We will concentrate here on only one of them, namely the one whose adepts called themselves Sautrāntikas.

The history of the Sautrāntikas is not known in detail,[228] but it seems to be primarily a reaction against Sarvāstivāda. The famous work of Vasubandhu, the *Abhidharmakośabhāṣya*, often mentions positions of Sautrāntikas next to those of the Sarvāstivādins. The author then mostly takes sides with the former. This is not tantamount to saying that Vasubandhu always presents the scholastic positions of the Sautrāntikas correctly; he sometimes seems to use this name to refer to his own opinions.[229]

The most important doctrines of the Sautrāntikas are the following:[230] They take exception to the Sarvāstivāda doctrine concerning the reality of past and future; for Sautrāntikas only the present really exists. The unconditioned (*asaṃskṛta*) dharmas do not really exist either. The same is true of the conditioned factors separated from the mind (*cittaviprayukta saṃskāra*).[231]

Denying the reality of past and future has certain consequences. The existence of the three times allowed the Sarvāstivādins to explain how past mental dharmas can have an effect much later. We have seen this in connection with "obtaining" (*prāpti*), and also in our discussion of

227 See mainly Bareau 1955.

228 See Kato 1989; cf. Cox 1995: 37–38; Mimaki 1988.

229 Kato 1989: French part, p. 10; Japanese part, pp. 74–75. Kritzer (1999: esp. 19–20, 175ff.) thinks that in reality Vasubandhu presents here the Abhidharma of the Yogācāra.

230 Abhidh-k(VP) vol. 1, p. LIII f.; Kato 1989: French part, pp. 11–12; Japanese part, pp. 145–46.

231 For an analysis of the disputes between Vasubandhu and the Sarvāstivādin Saṃghabhadra, see Cox 1995: 65–66 (introductory commentaries).

the reawakening from the state of cessation (*nirodha*). Although temporally distinct from each other, former dharmas were said to exist at the time of their effect. Such an explanation was not possible for the Sautrāntikas, who did not recognize the existence of past and future, nor that of obtaining. They were obliged to explain the relation between earlier and later dharmas differently. They tried to do this by assuming the existence of "seeds" (*bīja*).[232] Unlike obtaining, seeds do not exist independently; rather, they are part of the aggregates (*skandha*)—the dharmas that make up a person. But they have the capacity to produce certain dharmas and are thereby able to establish a relation with earlier dharmas. With the help of these seeds, it was no longer necessary to postulate a direct effect of past dharmas.

The Sautrāntikas had other doctrines, but these suffice to show how much this school opposed the Sarvāstivāda, and at the same time, how much its way of thinking was conditioned by that of the Sarvāstivāda. That said, of the Sarvāstivāda *system* little survived in Sautrāntika. It is perhaps no coincidence that, according to tradition, Vasubandhu soon abandoned the Sautrāntikas and joined the Yogācāra school of the Mahāyāna.

Concluding Observations

In our examination of the Sarvāstivādins' systematization of the dharma theory, we noted that nothing similar is found in the preserved Abhidharma texts of the Pāli school. Erich Frauwallner, the Austrian scholar who opened up the field of Abhidharma in his *Studies in Abhidharma Literature*, contrasts a Sarvāstivāda text—Dharmaśreṣṭhin's *Abhidharmahṛdaya*—with some texts of the Pāli school—Upatissa's *Vimuttimagga* and Buddhaghosa's *Visuddhimagga*—in the following words: "In the former, we find a doctrinal system, theoretical considerations and clear, systematic thought. In the latter we have a path to

232 Cox 1995: 93–94; Jaini 1959b; Sanderson 1994: 42. Sanderson remarks that the Sautrāntika notion of the seed is already mentioned in Nāgārjuna's *Mūlamadhyamakakārikā* (MadhK(deJ) 17.6–10).

liberation, practical considerations and a good deal of imagination."[233] Although the Sarvāstivādins' earlier texts cannot compare in their degree of systemization with the *Abhidharmahṛdaya*, it is certain that, from the time of the Pañcavastuka on, the Sarvāstivāda tradition fundamentally distinguished itself from the Pāli school in its attempt to order the doctrine systematically. Indeed, the *Kathāvatthu*, a text of the Pāli school, clearly reveals in its criticism of the Sarvāstivādins that its author did not correctly understand the Sarvāstivādin arguments supporting their doctrine that past and future exist.[234]

What is meant here by "systematizing" is probably clear by now. Many elements of Sarvāstivāda doctrine purport to safeguard the doctrine—to make it autonomous and internally consistent. It is, or at least tries to be, a "system" in the sense that its elements are coherent and corroborate each other; the Sarvāstivādins took pains to shape their doctrine in such a way that critical questions could be answered. The doctrine was *rationalized*, in other words, an attempt was made to make it resistant to rational attacks.

What this suggests is that the Sarvāstivādins did indeed have to defend their doctrine against rational attacks. Rational attacks are radically different from other types of attacks. A religious doctrine can for instance be forbidden or its adepts persecuted. Or the doctrine can lose influence through social or political developments. Rationalization is of no help against such attacks. Rationalizing a doctrine only helps where its adherents feel threatened by disputes with those who think differently. This presupposes a situation where those who think differently are ready to listen to the proponents' doctrine and where they are themselves listened to.

The later history of Indian philosophy repeatedly illustrates how a rational tradition, once it has gained a foothold, can influence or even completely change a school's doctrinal positions. It is yet not at all certain that such a rational tradition already existed in India when the Sarvāstivādins began their systematization. The development of the

233 Frauwallner 1995: 130 (= 1971a: 125 [13]).
234 Bronkhorst 1993b.

Pāli school shows that the incentive for rationalization was not equally strong in every part of India. As Frauwallner says:[235] "The Pāli school demonstrates that the process of development in the Sarvāstivāda school was by no means the rule and that things could take quite a different course."

The debates found in Vedic literature, particularly in the Upaniṣads, also have little to do with rational exchanges. Walter Ruben contrasts them to later rational debates:

> The type of debates found in the *Bṛhadāraṇyaka-* and *Chāndogya-Upaniṣad*s, which is the same as that in the Brāhmaṇas, is completely different from the later type of debates. In later debates, one protagonist proposes a thesis, the opponent proposes another thesis, and then both refute each others' theses with counter-arguments and defend their own view, until one of the theses proves to be right. But in the old Upaniṣads or in the Brāhmaṇas, one person asks questions and the other answers, until the first has nothing more to ask, or the second no longer knows how to answer: the winner is the one who has the last say. We could sum this up by means of the following formula: in the old Upaniṣads one had to know more, in later times one had to know better. In the old Upaniṣads, the point is not to fight for the victory of one theory and against another, wrong, theory, as it later happens in India; what is at stake—as long as it is not a verbal quarrel for its own sake—is to establish who is the greatest brahman, who knows the most.[236]

---

235 Frauwallner 1995: 131 (= 1971a: 125 [13]). Concerning the other Buddhist schools' attempts to systematize, he remarks that "it would have been natural, once one important system or other became common knowledge, for other schools to attempt their own version. Similarly it would have been natural in such a case to attempt to give their own doctrines a systematic form." (1995: 133 (= 1971a: 127 [15]))

236 Ruben 1928: 238–39. Cf. p. 241: "In the old Upaniṣads each participant accepts without resistance and without hesitation the opponent's apodictically affirmed

These remarks show that the Vedic debates had little to do with rationality in our sense of the term. How then can we explain the emergence of rationality within the Sarvāstivāda school?

We noted above that the rationalization of Sarvāstivāda teaching had begun by at least the middle of the second century BCE. At that time the Pañcavastuka, and most of the dharmas it contains, were already part of this school's teaching. The geographical location of the school in those days is well known: it was a missionary school, owing its existence to Aśoka's missions. Already in the oldest times this school belonged to the northwest of the Indian subcontinent. The Pāli school was also a missionary school, but one that, in all probability, developed in and around the town of Vidiśā, nowadays Gwalior, about two hundred miles south of Delhi.[237] What difference between Gandhāra and Vidiśā could possibly explain the Sarvāstivādins' attempts at rationalizing and its relative absence in the Pāli school?

One important fact is that there were Greek kingdoms in the northwest of India during the centuries preceding the Common Era. The rational tradition in Greek and Hellenistic culture is well known. Hellenistic kings liked to take a personal interest in philosophy and other forms of knowledge. Wise men frequented the court, and it appears that the kings debated with them.[238] We know that the inhabitants of the Greek kingdoms in the northwest of India held to their Hellenistic culture, which included Greek thought. Indeed, a Greek philosopher named Clearchus, a direct pupil of Aristotle, visited that region at

---

answer." Ruben describes (p. 243) Vedic investigations as "a pre-logical associating, an intuition without logical argumentation." In connection with the Vedic Brāhmaṇas, Gonda (1960: 176–77) speaks about "the—to modern eyes—uncritical and insufficiently formed modes of reasoning and argumentation, by means of which the endless search for connections and causalities is cultivated." See further Witzel 1987. For debates in the old Buddhist discourses, see Manné 1992.

237 Frauwallner 1956b: 18ff.; 1995: 40–42 (= 1971: 104–6); cf. Lamotte 1958: 327–28: 364–65; Lamotte 1944–80: III: XI–XII.

238 Préaux 1978/1989: 212–38; Avi-Yonah 1978: 50ff.

the beginning of the third century BCE.[239] Archaeological excavations have also brought to light a Greek philosophical papyrus.[240]

Despite their lack of interest in Indian culture,[241] the Greeks in northwest India exerted a deep influence on Buddhist visual arts.[242] We cannot rule out that the Buddhists were also indebted to the Greeks in other respects.[243] It would be especially interesting to know whether the Buddhists had regular discussions with the Greeks, and whether it was through these that they learned to present their positions in such a manner that an outsider could not reject them as incoherent.

It may be impossible to *prove* Greek influence of this nature. It is highly unlikely that the Buddhists, who themselves had inherited a rich store of ideas, would simply have taken over ideas from the Greeks; indeed we find no trace of this. The question is rather whether they learned the art of rational discussion from the Greeks.[244] This hypothesis would make the shape of their teaching substantially more understandable. Furthermore, Buddhist literature contains no trace of acquaintance with the Greeks, whom the Buddhists in the northwest must yet have known. There is one exception, and this exception concerns a discussion between a Greek king and a Buddhist monk about religious questions. This is the famous *Milindapañha*, the "Questions of Milinda," cited above. Although little in this text is Greek besides

---

239 Robert 1973; Rapin 1992: 128, 389.

240 Rapin 1992: 115–21.

241 This purported absence of interest should not be exaggerated. Lafont (1994: 46 with note 139) emits certain doubts against this supposition, and in this connection draws attention to a column found in India (Basnagar) that was dedicated to the Indian god Vasudeva and erected by a certain Heliodoros.

242 Lamotte 1958: 469–87, where also other possible Greek influences on Buddhism are discussed. Cf. also Nehru 1989, with references to further literature.

243 The Hellenistic influence on Indian astronomy is an example; Pingree 1978, esp. vol. I: 3–4. Equally important may be the fact that the Indo-Greeks seem to have been the first to found an era in India; Daffinà 1987: 55–56; also Thundy 1993: 256–57.

244 A tradition of rational debate does not develop automatically, even in complex societies. An important example is China, where such a tradition never obtained a footing; see, for example, Jullien 1995.

the name of the king,[245] its very existence is a testimony that Buddhists and Greeks discussed religious and related questions, or at least that the Buddhists remembered the Greeks as partners in discussions. It is therefore reasonable to postulate Greek influence on the Sarvāstivādins.

From this early time onward, a rational element found its way into Buddhist thinking. This does not mean that Indian Buddhism has developed in only a "rational" way ever since: this is certainly not the case, as we will see. It means that from time to time thinkers tried to present the Buddhist doctrine of their respective schools in a coherent way that would resist rational attacks. Moreover, more and more discussions took place with people who held different opinions, Buddhists and non-Buddhists. In other words, a tradition of rationality established itself.

And where there is a rational tradition, it becomes more difficult for divergent opinions to coexist without influencing each other. For the main characteristic of a rational tradition is that the different parties listen to each other. This certainly does not mean that one is convinced by the other. On the contrary, an exchange of ideas can emphasize or even bring to light differences that played no role previously. Nevertheless, the likelihood of mutual influence is increased.

This influence can take various forms. Particularly interesting are reactions against a specific system, giving rise to currents of thought that do not agree with a part, or even with the totality of another one. If these reactions are produced in rational exchanges, they can give rise to new systems of thought. As we have seen, this may have happened in the case of the Sarvāstivāda system, which may have come about in an attempt to arm itself against Greek criticism, real or imagined. As we will see in the next chapter, criticism of Sarvāstivāda, in turn, gave rise to new systems within Buddhism and Brahmanism.

245 Halbfass 1988: 19. The Indian original of the two preserved Chinese translations of this text probably defended Sarvāstivāda doctrinal opinions; Lamotte 1958: 465; Demiéville 1924: 74. On Menander, see Fussman 1993; Bopearachchi 1990.

3. Mahāyāna

Early Mahāyāna

THE OLDEST BUDDHIST TEXTS make no distinction between the Buddha's liberation and that of his disciples. In both cases the word *arhat* is used, translated here as "accomplished one." Everyone who has attained liberation, including the Buddha, is called an arhat. This changed later. Dissention arose as to what exactly characterizes an arhat and whether an arhat can lose his arhat status.[246]

These controversies did not concern buddhahood. Already in the old sūtras, the Buddha was said to possess distinctive signs and powers that arhats lack;[247] these distinctive features were further emphasized in the school of the so-called Mahāsāṃghikas.[248] In this school, the Buddha's actions were considered illusory, since otherwise actions were tantamount to creating karma and thereby propelling rebirth. In other schools, too, features such as omniscience were ascribed to the Buddha but denied to the arhat.[249] It is understandable that certain Buddhists were no longer satisfied with arhatship as a goal and sought instead the higher goal of buddhahood. And just as the old texts call the historical

246 Bareau 1957.

247 On the development of buddhology in the so-called Hīnayāna, see Weber 1994.

248 Concerning the influence of Mahāsāṃghika on early Mahāyāna, see Hirakawa 1963: 57–58; Harrison 1982; also Williams 1989: 18–19. This was not the only school that exerted such an influence; Durt 1994: 771.

249 Cf. Jaini 1992.

Buddha before his enlightenment a "being destined for enlightenment" (*bodhisattva*),[250] likewise, these Buddhists did not merely want to follow the "path of the listeners" (*śrāvakayāna*) but rather the "path of beings destined for enlightenment" (*bodhisattvayāna*).[251]

Inscriptions show that this new movement remained a minority view for several centuries.[252] Inscriptions also suggest that this movement came to find its principal support in the community of monks and not among the laymen, though this does not necessarily rule out the hypothesis that the movement began among the laity.[253] The role of women seems to have been negligible in the origin of the bodhisattva path.[254] Even before the beginning of the Common Era, the movement began to develop its own writings,[255] and in these, along with the designation *bodhisattvayāna*, the name Mahāyāna ("Great Path") is also frequently used.[256] It is to be distinguished from the path of the

250 For interpretations of the term *bodhisattva*, see Dayal 1932: 4–5; Basham 1981: 21–22; Kajiyama 1982.

251 This ideal is not totally unknown to the texts of the Śrāvakayāna; see Durt 1994: 801, with a reference to the Abhidh-k-bh(P) p. 182.

252 See various articles by Gregory Schopen, e.g., "Mahāyāna in Indian Inscriptions" (1979), and "The Inscription on the Kuṣān Image of Amitābha and the Character of the Early Mahāyāna in India" (1987: esp. 124–25).

253 Against the idea that the laity played an important role, see mainly Schopen 1975; 1979: 9; 1984: 25–26; also 1991; Williams 1989: 20–21; Warder 1983: 14–15; Harrison 1995; Durt 1991; 1994: 775–76; and Fussman 1996: 783–84. The main protagonists of this position are Hirakawa (1963), Lamotte (1954; 1958: 89–90, 686–87), Kajiyama (1993: 142–43), and Vetter (1994b); cf. also Kottkamp 1992: 166–68n4.

254 Harrison 1987: 78; Vetter 1994b: 1254n26.

255 Gombrich (1988a: 29–46) is of the opinion that the rise and spread of Mahāyāna can be explained by the use of writing. This view does not enjoy universal support; see Hinüber 1989: 28n55; Vetter 1994b: 1243–44n4. Cf. also Lopez 1995.

256 *Yāna* can mean "path" as well as "vehicle"; cf. PW s.v. *yāna*. The texts often play on the double meaning of this word; see, e.g., Braarvig 1993: I: xcvii, which cites the *Gaganagañjaparivarta* of the Mahāsaṃnipāta; further Durt 1994: 781. The name Mahāyāna was slow to gain prominence; an early Chinese translation of this appellation is *ta tao* 大道 "the great/noble path," whereas later *ta ch'êng* 大乘 "the great vehicle" was commonly used; see Durt 1994: 778–79; Leon Hurvitz in Fujita 1975: 120 note n. The question as to the

listeners (*śrāvakayāna*), also called the Hīnayāna ("Low Path") by its opponents.[257]

Mahāyāna, then, is first and foremost characterized by the aspiration to attain perfect buddhahood rather than to gain enlightenment as an arhat. In what way does the career of beings destined for enlightenment differ from that of listeners? Details of the career of the Buddha Śākyamuni—the historical Buddha—are known from the so-called Jātakas, stories about his previous lives. These describe how he helped other living beings in many ways, sometimes at the cost of his own life. Accordingly, one of the main characteristics of a bodhisattva is that he seeks not just his own liberation but the liberation of all other beings as well.[258] At least this is how the Mahāyāna texts describe the difference between Mahāyāna and other Buddhists, and it seems clear that they look down upon the other Buddhists' goal of mere personal liberation.

Mahāyāna was not a new sect (*nikāya*). Monks who chose the path to buddhahood remained members of the same monastic community and continued to submit to the same monastic rules.[259] On the doctrinal level there were initially no points of dispute either. And why should there be? Doctrine and order were not at stake. Strictly speaking, nothing was at stake, for only a personal motivation was involved. Undoubtedly, the adepts of Mahāyāna studied the same texts as the other Buddhists, and from the point of view of Buddhist doctrine, one would hardly expect the birth of Mahāyāna to produce significant changes.[260]

---

exact difference between Śrāvakayāna and Mahāyāna is not easy to answer; see Cohen 1995.

257 The Buddhists also designated a third path, between these two, namely, the path of a solitary buddha (*pratyekabuddha*). On this type of buddha in Pāli literature, see Kloppenborg 1974; Wiltshire 1990.

258 See e.g. Conze 1974: 127, with reference to the ASP(Vaidya) chap. 11, p. 116. Mahāyāna inscriptions too seem to care about the well-being of all creatures; Schopen 1984: 42.

259 Cf. Bechert 1985: 51–52; 1963.

260 An Shigao, perhaps one of the earliest translators of Hīnayāna texts into Chinese, was probably himself an adept of Mahāyāna; Forte 1995: 70–71.

In reality, events took a different course. Mahāyāna distinguished itself ever more through its own doctrinal developments. In most cases, their starting points can be traced to non- or pre-Mahāyāna Buddhism, but their full development belongs to Mahāyāna. In these cases one can say that certain tendencies that also existed outside and before the birth of Mahāyāna asserted themselves more strongly here. Moreover, these new doctrines do not exclusively concern the main claims of emergent Mahāyāna, such as the nature of a buddha being different from that of an arhat. Many important developments within Mahāyāna have little or nothing to do with these claims. Mahāyāna developed doctrine in new and unexpected directions, and this happened at a time when the development of Buddhist doctrine outside Mahāyāna had for the most part lost its dynamism. This is all the more astonishing in view of the fact that for a long time the adepts of Mahāyāna remained less numerous than the non-Mahāyānists.

Why should such enthusiastic innovations in Buddhist doctrine take place within this minority movement—innovations that had nothing to do with its main aspirations?

It may be impossible to give a full answer to this question. One factor probably played a major role. It seems that the adepts of emergent Mahāyāna were engaged in contemplative practices—perhaps more so than other Buddhists. It is even possible that at least some of the Mahāyāna sūtras were inspired by meditational experiences, or by ideas about such experiences.[261] Experiences gained in certain meditative states—or, more likely, ideas about the experiences to be gained in these states—likely contributed to their worldview.

Before discussing the specific doctrinal developments that may have been influenced or even determined by contemplative practice (or reflections about them), we will first summarize the Mahāyāna path to liberation. This path is not always clearly depicted in the oldest Mahāyāna texts, but when it is, it often takes the following shape. When somebody has taken the resolve called "mind of enlightenment" (*bodhicitta*) and has thus become a bodhisattva, it is his duty

---

261 Harrison 1978: 54; 1990: xx.

to cultivate, one after the other, a long series of qualities and practices. Prominent among these are the thirty-seven dharmas helpful to enlightenment detailed in chapter 2.[262] Sometimes, the four immeasurables (*apramāṇa*)—benevolence (*maitrī*), compassion (*karuṇā*), sympathetic joy (*muditā*), and equanimity (*upekṣā*)—are emphasized.[263] We know that this enumeration of qualities and practices was looked upon as a list of the most essential points of Buddhist doctrine and practice long before the birth of Mahāyāna. It is a concise representation of the path to arhatship. Thus the bodhisattva follows the same path as the arhat up to a certain point. And if we can believe an old text, he even runs the risk of unwittingly becoming one.[264] In order to avoid this, he fulfills (*paripūrayati*) the dharmas helpful to enlightenment but stops short of realizing (*sākṣātkaroti*) them.[265]

The Mahāyānist bodhisattva aspires for more than mere arhatship. His path to complete enlightenment, to buddhahood, therefore consists of more than the thirty-seven dharmas helpful to enlightenment. A bodhisattva also cultivates the so-called perfections (*pāramitā*).[266] Initially there were six of these, namely the perfection of generosity (*dāna*), of morality (*śīla*), of patience (*kṣānti*), of energy (*vīrya*), of meditation (*dhyāna*), and of wisdom (*prajñā*).[267] Four additional perfections were added subsequently.

Most of these perfections are primarily connected with the mode of life of the adepts of Mahāyāna, but the last one, the perfection

---

262 Dayal 1932: 80–81; Gethin 1992: 275 with notes 36 and 37. Pagel (1995: 307–8) discusses the position of the *bodhipākṣika dharmas* on the Buddhist path to liberation. Hedinger (1984) describes the career of a bodhisattva according to Śāntideva's *Śikṣāsamuccaya* (ca. 700).

263 See, e.g., Pagel 1995: 133–45. For the early history of these stages, which are also called "abodes of Brahma," see Bronkhorst 1993: 93–94.

264 Harrison 1987: 82. See also Braarvig 1993: I: 82; II: 331; I: 132; II: 503.

265 Lamotte 1944–1980: III: 1133–34, 1138–39.

266 Dayal 1932: 165–66. Apart from the perfections, the literature concerning this subject also mentions a number of "degrees" (*bhūmi*)—usually ten—as well as five paths (*mārga*).

267 For a discussion of these six perfections, especially with reference to the so-called *bodhisattva-piṭaka*, see Pagel 1995: 145–316.

of wisdom, has a direct connection with the doctrine. This perfection of wisdom was held in high esteem, especially in the so-called *prajñāpāramitā* sūtras, "discourses concerning the perfection of wisdom." Rāhulabhadra's *Prajñāpāramitāstotra*, for instance, calls it the only way to liberation. The *Aṣṭasāhasrikā Prajñāpāramitā* ("Perfection of Wisdom in Eight Thousand Verses"), which is perhaps the oldest Mahāyāna sūtra,[268] describes it as the leader of the five (remaining) perfections; these five perfections are subsumed in the perfection of wisdom. Other texts express similar views.[269]

What is this perfection of wisdom? The question is discussed in many Mahāyāna texts, particularly in the prajñāpāramitā sūtras. These texts emphasize that the phenomenal world does not really exist. This belief is not new in Buddhism, as we have already noted. It strongly marked Abhidharma Buddhism, which, however, did not so much stress the *unreality* of the phenomenal world as the *reality* of the dharmas. Nevertheless, the Sarvāstivādins already called themselves *śūnyavādins*—"adepts of the doctrine of emptiness"—in the old *Vijñānakāya*; here it means that they did not recognize the existence of the person.[270] We saw also that they went further and concluded from the nonexistence of the person that no composite objects really exist. It is therefore understandable that the *Vibhāṣā*—another Sarvāstivāda text—declares that only the principle according to which all things are empty and without self can be recognized as the highest truth.[271] The prajñāpāramitā sūtras do not hesitate to place this unreality of the phenomenal world in the foreground and emphasize its absurdity. For if the phenomenal world does not really exist, they say, the Buddha does not really exist either, nor do the bodhisattvas. The following passage from the *Aṣṭasāhasrikā Prajñāpāramitā* illustrates this:

268 Lancaster 1969; 1975.

269 Mahāyāna inscriptions confirm the importance of attaining the highest knowledge (*anuttarajñāna*); see Schopen 1984: 39.

270 La Vallée Poussin 1925: 358–59.

271 La Vallée Poussin 1937a: 164.

> The lord said to the venerable Subhūti, the elder: Make it clear now, Subhūti, to the bodhisattvas, the great beings, starting from perfect wisdom, how the bodhisattvas, the great beings, go forth into perfect wisdom! [...]
>
> Whereupon the venerable Subhūti, by the Buddha's might, said to the Lord: The Lord has said, "make it clear now, Subhūti, to the bodhisattvas, the great beings, starting from perfect wisdom, how the bodhisattvas, the great beings, go forth into perfect wisdom!" When one speaks of a "bodhisattva," what dharma does that word *bodhisattva* denote? I do not, O Lord, see that dharma "bodhisattva," nor a dharma called "perfect wisdom." Since I neither find, nor apprehend, nor see a dharma "bodhisattva," nor a "perfect wisdom," what bodhisattva shall I instruct and admonish in what perfect wisdom? And yet, O Lord, if, when this is pointed out, a bodhisattva's heart does not become cowed, nor stolid, does not despair nor despond, if he does not turn away or become dejected, does not tremble, is not frightened or terrified, it is just this bodhisattva, this great being, who should be instructed in perfect wisdom. It is precisely this that should be recognized as the perfect wisdom of that bodhisattva, as his instruction in perfect wisdom. When he thus stands firm, that is his instruction and admonition.[272]

Later in the same chapter, the following words are attributed to the Buddha:

> *The Lord*: Here the bodhisattva, the great being, thinks thus: countless beings I should lead to nirvāṇa and yet there are none who lead to nirvāṇa, or who should be led to it. However many beings he may lead to nirvāṇa, yet there is not any being that has been led to nirvāṇa, nor that has led others to it. For such is the true nature of dharmas, seeing that their

272 ASP(Vaidya) pp. 2–3; tr. Conze 1958: 1–2.

> nature is illusory. Just as if, Subhūti, a clever magician, or magician's apprentice, were to conjure up at the crossroads a great crowd of people and then make them vanish again. What do you think, Subhūti, has there anyone been killed by anyone, or murdered, or destroyed, or made to vanish?
>
> *Subhūti*: No, indeed, Lord.
>
> *The Lord*: Even so a bodhisattva, a great being, leads countless beings to nirvāṇa, and yet there is not any being that has been led to nirvāṇa, nor that has led others to it.[273]

There are many similar passages. Here we should notice the comparison with magic, which occurs in many texts. The phenomenal world is not essentially different from a magic show. Only the highest knowledge is free from it. It is hardly surprising that the Mahāyāna texts often attribute great magic powers to the advanced bodhisattvas. Being themselves free from everyday illusions, they can modify at will the unreal delusion to which other beings are continually subject. This is, of course, connected with the supernatural powers that those advanced on the path of liberation already cultivated before the rise of Mahāyāna, for example, in the four constituent parts of supernatural power (*ṛddhipāda*) that are part of the dharmas helpful to enlightenment. In Mahāyāna these supernatural powers blend more smoothly with the overall picture of reality than had been the case before.[274] They play an especially important role in later times, in tantric forms of Buddhism.[275]

Mahāyāna did not stop at denying the reality of the phenomenal world. Radically, it went on to deny the reality of the dharmas themselves.[276] It would be difficult to overestimate the importance of this step. The dharma theory had practically become identical with

---

273 ASP(Vaidya) p. 10; tr. Conze 1958: 8.

274 Cf. Gómez 1977: 221–61.

275 Williams 1989: 185–86.

276 Strictly speaking, the perfection of wisdom negated in the above passage is a dharma; see Schmithausen 1977: 45.

Buddhist doctrine,[277] and the negation of its absolute truth, therefore, was a rupture of the highest order. The negation of the reality of the dharmas fundamentally modified the Buddhist worldview. Since the dharma theory enumerates what really exists, and explains how the dharmas constitute our phenomenal world, if the dharmas themselves no longer exist, nothing is left. Before examining the consequences of this revolutionary change, we must first ask how this could take place at all.

The sheer delight with which the authors of the prajñāpāramitā sūtras emphasize the unreal nature of many things, including even buddhas and bodhisattvas, must have made the further step toward the unreal nature of the dharmas very tempting. However, these authors were Buddhists and would, therefore, have hesitated to reject the central doctrine of Buddhism without support from the old canonical texts.[278] In order to understand how they interpreted these texts, we must briefly deal with a linguistic problem in Middle Indic.

We have already dealt with the doctrine of not-self. We saw that the Buddha rejected the idea that one can reach liberation through knowledge of the self. The concept of the self he referred to was hardly different from the one current among certain non-Buddhists. This self was eternal, blissful, not subject to change. This concept was soon succeeded by another one, which saw the person as the totality of all its component parts. The negation of *this* self was closely connected with the view that composite objects do not exist.

The development of the Buddhist doctrine of not-self did not end here, however. In order to understand its subsequent development, we have to remember that the oldest Buddhist tradition did not use

277 Stcherbatsky was right to call his book on the dharma theory *The Central Conception of Buddhism* (reprint Delhi: Motilal Banarsidass 1983). Williams (1989: 30) wonders whether the prajñāpāramitā sūtras react against Abhidharma Buddhism. We should not however forget that Mahāyāna, especially the school of Yogācāra (to be discussed below), had its own Abhidharma.

278 Lamotte (1973) discusses a few further purported examples of canonical support.

Sanskrit but a Middle Indic language that has not survived.[279] It was different from the other Indian languages in which the old canon is now extant—mainly (Buddhist) Sanskrit and Pāli.[280] Pāli, too, is a Middle Indic language, which differs from Sanskrit on a point that is important for this discussion.

Consider some canonical statements related to the doctrine of not-self. It is often stated that all the dharmas, or other things, are not the self.[281] In all of these statements, the Pāli uses the singular substantive *anattā* "not self," which belongs to the *n*-stem *attan* "self." But in Pāli, as in other old Middle Indic languages, the *n*-stems often change under the influence of *a*-stems.[282] This means that *anattā* can also be the plural of *anatta*, rather than the singular of *anattan*. In this case, *anattā* is a plural adjective meaning "without self" or "selfless." In Sanskrit this confusion is impossible: the singular substantive is *anātmā*, the plural adjective *anātmānaḥ*.

Fortunately, the Pāli canon contains many passages that allow us to ascertain that *anattā* is a singular substantive, meaning "not self."[283] Buddhist texts in Sanskrit likewise confirm this interpretation.[284] Nevertheless, certain variant readings suggest that the alternative interpretation was found attractive already at an early date. Sometimes, the Pāli commentaries interpret *anattā* to mean "without self."[285] In other places, we find a modified reading for *anattā* that only allows for the interpreta-

279 Bechert 1980.

280 Hinüber 1986: 36. For the name Pāli, see Hinüber 1994b.

281 In Pāli e.g.: *sabbe dhammā anattā*. For references, see PTC pp. 114–15. s.v. *anatta*. PDhp 375 (p. 131) has *sabba-dhammā anattā*. Cf. GDhp 108.

282 Hinüber 1986: 153 § 348.

283 E.g., *rūpaṃ anattā, [...], viññāṇaṃ anattā* (PTC s.v. *anatta*). Here *anattā* can only be the singular substantive "not self"; the adjective "without self" would be—beside the neuter *rūpaṃ* and *viññāṇaṃ*—*anattaṃ*. See also Tokunaga 1995: 97–98, with references to further literature.

284 E.g., *rūpam anātmā, [...] vijñānam anātmā* (CPS pp. 15.3, 4, 5, and 27e.8 (2x); Mvu III.446). Vetter (1996: 48n7) refers to the reading *rūpaṃ [...] nātmā* in the *Saṅghabhedavastu*; *nātmā* (= *na ātmā*) means "[is] not the self."

285 CPD I.146 s.v. *an-atta(n)*.

tion "without self."[286] Certain Sanskritizations also show that *anattā/anātman* was often taken to be an adjective.[287] At times, the adjective *anatta* is not used but its meaning is expressed differently; as in the sentence "forms are empty of self, or empty of what belongs to a self."[288] This means the same as "forms are without a self...."

This technical discussion allows us to understand how an important change in the Buddhist worldview that took it away from the Buddha's words could take place without anyone noticing. For the difference between "the dharmas are not the self" and "the dharmas are without self" is highly significant. The first sentence only states that there is no self among the dharmas. Combined with the belief that only the dharmas really exist, this justifies the conclusion that no self exists. Indeed, the sentence "the dharmas are not the self" does not say anything about the dharmas; it concerns something (the self) that is found—or would be found if it existed—outside the dharmas. The sentence "the dharmas are without self," on the other hand, says something about the dharmas. It can be interpreted to mean that the dharmas have no nature of their own, so they do not really exist.[289]

286 E.g., the variant *anattaṃ* in the expression *rūpaṃ anattā [...] viññāṇaṃ anattā*; MN III.19 (NDPS p. 81); SN III.78, 179. *anatta* as an adjective is also found in SN III.114: *anattaṃ rūpam anattaṃ rūpan ti yathābhūtaṃ na pajānāti, anattaṃ vedanaṃ, anattaṃ saññaṃ, anatte saṅkhāre, anattaṃ viññāṇaṃ anattaṃ viññāṇan ti yathābhūtaṃ na pajānāti.* SN III.56 is identical, the only difference being that every second time *anatta* reads *anattā*. Cf. also Ud 8.2 (p. 80), where the truth (*saccaṃ*), which seems to be nirvāṇa, is described as *anattaṃ* "without self."

287 E.g., *rūpam anātmā [...] vijñānaṃ anātma* (Mvu III.335; for *anātma* there are the variant readings *anātmā* and *anātmaṃ*); *anātma* can only be an adjective here. In Uv 12.8 *sarvadharmā anātmānaḥ*, *anātman* is likewise an adjective, and means therefore "without self." Abhidh-k-bh(Pā) p. 466.24 cites the same sentence in exactly the same words. Mvu I.173 reads *ye dharmā anātmīyā*; here *anātmīya* has the same meaning as the adjective *anātman*.

288 SN IV.54: *rūpā suññā attena vā attaniyena vā.*

289 Williams 1989: 46. Among Mahāyāna authors, Bhāvaviveka (or Bhāviviveka, Bhāviveka, Bhavya; see Lindtner 1995: 37–39) holds a special place, in the sense that—insofar as Hīnayāna is concerned—he clings to the old (and originally correct) interpretation. In his *Prajñāpradīpa* he explains the expression *anātman* in the old discourses as "not self" rather than "without self"; Lopez 1987: 98, 105.

This idea soon became popular. The texts mention the "emptiness of the dharmas" (*dharmaśūnyatā*) or the "selflessness of the dharmas" (*dharmanairātmya*), to be contrasted with the older "selflessness of the person" (*pudgalanairātmya*). More precisely, the selflessness of the dharmas came to be seen as an extension of the selflessness of the person. As we have observed in our analysis of the word *anattā*, this development appears to have already started in canonical times.[290] A few non-Mahāyāna Buddhist schools subsequently adopted this idea,[291] which became important in Mahāyāna.[292]

The doctrine of the emptiness, or selflessness, of the dharmas cannot be fully explained by a linguistic misunderstanding of the Middle Indic word *anattā*. It fits too well into the developments outlined above. The change of interpretation of the word *anattā* was therefore very convenient. The linguistic ambiguity helped the development, and gave it a certain direction. But we should not conclude from this that without this ambiguity there would have been no further development in approximately the same direction.

What hides behind this tendency to deny the reality of the phenomenal world and the dharmas? Its first beginnings can be found in the old discourses, which claim, for instance: "Sensual pleasures are impermanent, hollow, false, deceptive; they are illusory, the prattle of fools."[293] It has been suggested that the doctrine of the illusory nature of appearances was the reflection of a spiritual state, and simultaneously an indicator of how to reach it.[294] The corresponding spiritual

---

290 Lamotte 1944–80: IV: 2005–6, 2140–44; Deleanu 1993.

291 Like the Pūrvaśailas, and likewise Harivarman's *Satyasiddhi Śāstra*; see Williams 1989: 16, 43.

292 Snellgrove (1987: 90) believes that the link between this idea and Mahāyāna was due to mere chance. And indeed, an extant Mahāyāna sūtra, the *Ajitasenavyākaraṇanirdeśa Sūtra*, incarnates Mahāyāna ideals but does not defend the doctrine of *dharmaśūnyatā*; see Dutt 1939: 73–74; Cohen 1995: 4–5.

293 MN II.261; tr. Ñāṇamoli & Bodhi 1995: 869. Cf. Schmithausen 1973a: 182. Schmithausen also refers to a Chinese parallel and to other passages with a similar content in the ancient texts.

294 Schmithausen 1973a: 180–81; Frauwallner 1956a: 144.

state would be the *attainment of cessation of ideation and feeling* (*saṃjñāvedayitanirodhasamāpatti*), also referred to as *attainment of cessation* (*nirodhasamāpatti*). We noted earlier that no spiritual processes can take place in this state and that, in the ancient understanding, the highest enlightenment could therefore not take place in it. But we cannot rule out that the lack of ideations and sensations in this state came to be interpreted to mean that ideations and sensations do not correspond to the highest reality. In other words, the world is empty. The Mahāyāna doctrine of the illusory nature of the world could be the ontological equivalent of this state, now understood to be the experience of the unreal nature of the phenomenal world.

There are indeed passages that describe how a bodhisattva can reach the concentration on emptiness (*śūnyatāsamādhi*). In this concentration, the aggregates (*skandha*) must be visualized (*pratyavekṣ-*) as empty.[295] Mental activity, which is responsible for the phenomenal world, must be abandoned. The aim of such exercises is to "empty" the phenomenal world. A passage of the *Kāśyapaparivarta* is more explicit:[296] "Enter into the state of attainment of the cessation of ideation and feeling! [For] when a monk has entered into the state of attainment of the cessation of ideation and feeling, he has nothing further left to do." If the monk has nothing left to do, he has reached liberation.

If it is true that the doctrine of the unreal nature of appearances is a reflection of the state of attainment of cessation[297]—or, more likely, the reflection of ideas about this state[298]—then we are allowed to draw certain conclusions. For we have seen that the attainment of cessation originally belonged to another, non-Buddhist circle of ideas and practices. This state entered into Buddhist practice at an early date but without fundamentally changing the ideas about liberating knowledge. In Mahāyāna a further step was taken: even the content of the

295 ASP(Vaidya) p. 183; Braarvig 1993: II: cviii–cix.

296 KP § 144; tr. Schmithausen 1973a: 181, with modifications.

297 Schmithausen 1978: 114 leaves this question open.

298 Sharf, in an interesting and important article (1995: 237–38), rightly remarks that nothing obliges us to suppose that the Yogācāra masters had themselves experienced such states.

highest liberating knowledge is now determined by the state of attainment of cessation. Since the latter is empty of ideations and feelings, liberating knowledge itself, i.e., the perfection of wisdom, has the emptiness of the phenomenal world as its object. Seen this way, the non-Buddhist ideology that the Buddha had tried to keep out had now definitely found its way in to Buddhist doctrine and practice.

Buddhist texts also link the doctrine of the emptiness of the world with other meditative states. In early Mahāyāna, the spiritual technique of visualizing had gained prominence.[299] This technique is often linked with the "meditation on the buddhas" (*buddhānusmṛti*), which is already mentioned in the old discourses. Initially, this practice had nothing to do with visualizing. This new element appears at a time when visualizing the divinities had also started to play a role outside of Buddhism.[300] The *Pratyutpanna-buddha-saṃmukhāvasthita-samādhi Sūtra* ("Discourse on the concentration in which [the yogi is] situated face to face with the buddhas existing at that time"), one of the oldest Mahāyāna texts preserved, emphasizes the fundamentally unreal nature of the objects experienced during this concentration and compares them to things experienced in a dream. The sūtra then goes on to explain the emptiness of all the dharmas.[301]

Unlike the attainment of cessation (*nirodhasamāpatti*), the practice of visualization is less directly connected with the emptiness of all dharmas. On the basis of visualization practices, it would likewise be possible to reach the conclusion that the phenomenal world is shaped by the mind, and is therefore unreal, and that only the mind really exists. This is indeed stated in a passage of the *Pratyutpanna-buddha-saṃmukhāvasthita-samādhi Sūtra*, which declares: "This [entire world]

---

299 Forman (1990: 7) sees an essential difference between "visionary experiences" and experiences that cannot be described as sensual experiences or mental representations. Only the latter, he proposes, should be called mysticism.

300 Beyer 1977; Harrison 1978; 1992; Lamotte 1944–80: IV: 1927–28n2; also Gómez & Silk 1989: 20–21 and 69–70 (introduction and partial translation of the *Samādhirāja Sūtra*); Rawlinson 1986; 1983; Kloppenborg & Poelmeyer 1987.

301 Harrison 1990: xix; 1978.

consisting of the three spheres is mind only (*cittamātra*)."[302] We will see below that this point of view came to occupy a central place in the so-called Yogācāra.[303] The present passage, on the other hand, appears to interpret meditation experiences (or ideas about them) as corroborating the new doctrine of emptiness. Seen this way, there is no one-way road between spiritual praxis and doctrine. Certain doctrinal positions were probably inspired by meditation experiences (or, in the case of the attainment of cessation, by the lack of any such experiences)—or by ideas about such experiences or non-experiences. Inversely, certain meditation experiences were interpreted in the light of these doctrinal positions. There is in this way a constant feedback loop between doctrine and contemplative praxis, in which it is impossible to decide in every instance how exactly they influenced each other.

We have to be attentive, however. In the context of Indian religions, it is customary to claim that the doctrinal positions of this or that school are based on the direct perception of reality by certain spiritually advanced beings. In the context of Brahmanism, such beings are mostly the seers (*ṛṣi*) of yore, or yogis; in the context of Jainism, it is the Jina. Yogis, for example, are supposed to perceive directly the categories and subcategories of the Brahmanical school of the Vaiśeṣika: among these, one's own and other people's souls; substances such as space, direction, and time; atoms, wind, the mind, inherence, and so on.[304] No modern scholar is likely to take these Vaiśeṣika claims seriously.[305] Its ideas are *not* taken from meditative practices. Nevertheless, it looks as if the Vaiśeṣika felt somehow obliged to postulate a connection between its own doctrines and meditative practices, even though the school had no particular link with traditions of meditation.

In Buddhism the situation is completely different. Here meditative practices are constantly discussed and analyzed. It is indeed hard to imagine that any new doctrine could have been accepted in Buddhism

302 Harrison 1990: xx, 42; Schmithausen 1973a: 175–76.

303 For other textual occurrences of this sentence, see Griffiths 1986: 173n4.

304 WI p. 45 §§ 241–42.

305 But see Bronkhorst 1993c.

without it being looked upon, implicitly or explicitly, as the object of experience of spiritually advanced adepts. Hence it is justified to ask whether the Buddhist assertion that this or that truth is perceived during meditation still means anything at all. We have therefore to examine whether and to what extent the doctrine of the unreal nature of appearances can be understood as continuous developments out of older forms of Buddhism.

In the old discourses, liberation takes place in the fourth stage of meditation (*dhyāna*); the knowledge that leads to liberation concerns the four noble truths. The same role was also attributed to other types of knowledge in ancient Buddhism, especially the knowledge of not-self or selflessness. Mahāyāna Buddhism developed the doctrine of selflessness and widened its interpretation so as to include the selflessness of the dharmas. This reinterpreted selflessness is the emptiness of the world, knowledge of which leads to the perfection of wisdom. Thus it turns out that this perfection of wisdom is not a break with the past, but rather the partial reinterpretation and extension of an element already present before Mahāyāna Buddhism.[306]

For Mahāyāna then, both the phenomenal world and its constituent dharmas are without reality. But is there anything beyond the phenomenal world and the dharmas that does exist? Many passages in the prajñāpāramitā literature seem to evoke this possibility. Erich Frauwallner summarizes their content as follows:

> The idea of a highest existence is central [...]. In conformity with the general development of Buddhism, the texts sharply emphasize the ungraspable and indeterminable nature of this highest existence. Only rarely is it described as a spotless and luminous mind (*prabhāsvaraṃ cittam*), following an old idea found here and there in the canon and later taken over by the Mahāsāṃghikas. Generally, it is stated again and again that no determinations apply to it. It

306 Schmithausen 1978: 112–13.

is without origin and end, uncreated and unchanging, and has not entered existence at all. It is unthinkable, imponderable, immeasurable, uncountable, and without equal. It is limitless, i.e., without beginning, middle, or end, and thus spatially unlimited. It is also temporally without beginning, without present, and without end, and thus it lies outside the three time zones. In short, it is naturally pure and free from all determinations. It is as a result also unimaginable (*avikalpa*), and no cognitive processes can take place in it. Due to its unlimited and ungraspable nature, it is frequently likened to empty space.

As a consequence of this, it is not touched by what happens in the phenomenal world. It is neither bound nor released, neither stained nor purified, and it exercises no influence itself. Whether recognized or not, it remains unmoved. It does not thrive when it is taught, nor does it decline when it is not taught.

As a designation of the highest existence, we often find the expressions "essence of the dharmas" (*dharmāṇāṃ dharmatā*) and "element of the dharmas" (*dharmadhātu*), and also "culminating point of the real" (*bhūtakoṭi*). More characteristic and equally favored is its designation as thusness (*tathatā*), which can already be found in the canonical writings. This name seems to express the ungraspable nature of highest existence, which is only similar to itself. In later times, it was thought to express its unchangable nature. Even more typical, though less coṃmon, are its designations as emptiness (*śūnyatā*), as without characteristics (*ānimitta*), and as undesired (*apraṇihita*), expressions already in use in the Hīnayāna but with a different meaning. For these expressions strongly emphasize the undefinable nature of the highest existence, and their importance is further heightened by the fact that they—and their contemplation—are called the gates to liberation (*vimokṣamukha*).

As the essence of all things, this highest existence is also

> the essence of the Buddha (*tathāgatatva*); it is omniscience (*sarvajñatā*) and the perfection of wisdom (*prajñāpāramitā*).[307]

The texts clearly create the impression of recognizing a highest existence. At least for some of them, however, this impression is wrong. The highest truth is that there is no highest existence:

> *Subhūti*: Even nirvāṇa, I say, is like a magical illusion, is like a dream. How much more so anything else? ... Even if perchance there could be anything more distinguished, of that too I would say that it is like an illusion, like a dream.[308]

The old Mahāyāna texts confront us in this way with a contradiction. In reality, the contradiction is only apparent, since the highest reality is not ontologically different than other dharmas. The example of eternity makes this clear.[309] For instance, we know that according to early Mahāyāna, the phenomenal world and the dharmas are empty—without highest reality—because they do not really exist; they cannot be produced and cannot disappear. In this sense, they are without beginning and without end. The same holds for the so-called highest existence. It is also ultimately unreal and has no beginning and no end. This is stated in the following passage with reference to the perfections: "The perfection of wisdom (*prajñāpāramitā*) has not perished, does not perish, will not perish; and thus the perfections of meditation (*dhyānapāramitā*), energy (*vīryapāramitā*), patience (*kṣāntipāramitā*), morality (*śīlapāramitā*), and generosity (*dānapāramitā*) have not perished, do not perish, will not perish; that is because there is no birth of those dharmas, and what has no birth, how can that be known to undergo perishing?"[310] And the *Aṣṭasāhasrikā Prajñāpāramitā* declares: "The perfection of wisdom

307 Frauwallner 1956a: 147–48 (translated).
308 ASP(Vaidya) p. 20.21–24; tr. Conze 1958: 18.
309 Studied by Braarvig 1993: II: esp. lviii–xciv.
310 AdSP(Conze) (60) p. 83.14–18; tr. Braarvig 1993: II: lxvii note 2.

is immeasurable, eternal, without end. Why? Because the perfection of wisdom does not exist."[311] The passage then goes on to make a comparison with space (*ākāśa*): just as the latter has no measure, no duration, no end, similarly the perfection of wisdom has no measure, no duration, and no end.

In this representation there can ultimately be no difference between so-called highest existence on the one hand and the phenomenal world and the dharmas on the other. Both are unreal and therefore without beginning or end. The following passage from the thirteenth chapter of the *Aṣṭasāhasrikā Prajñāpāramitā* places highest existence and the phenomenal world on the same level:

> *Subhūti*: Deep, O Lord, is perfect wisdom. Certainly as a great enterprise has this perfection of wisdom been set up, as an unthinkable, incomparable, immeasurable, incalculable enterprise, as an enterprise that equals the unequaled.
>
> *The Lord*: So it is, Subhūti. And why is it an unthinkable enterprise? Because unthinkable are tathāgatahood, buddhahood, self-existence (*svayaṃbhūtva*), and omniscience (*sarvajñatva*). And on these one cannot reflect with one's thought, since they cannot be an object of thought, or of volition, or of any of the dharmas that constitute thought. And why is it an incomparable enterprise? Because one cannot reflect on tathāgatahood, etc., nor compare it. And why is it immeasurable? Because tathāgatahood, etc., is immeasurable. And why is it incalculable? Because tathāgatahood, etc., is incalculable. And why is it an enterprise that equals the unequaled? Because nothing can be equal to the Tathāgata, to the fully enlightened one, to the self-existent, to the omniscient, how much less can anything be superior to him?
>
> *Subhuti*: Do these five attributes apply only to tathāgatahood, etc., or also to the aggregates (*skandha*) and to all dharmas?

311 ASP(Vaidya) pp. 230–31; cf. Braarvig 1993: II: lxviii.

> *The Lord*: They apply to them also. Also the aggregates and also all dharmas are unthinkable. For with regard to the true essential nature of form, etc., there is no thought, nor volition, nor any of the dharmas that constitute thought, nor any comparing. For that reason the aggregates and all dharmas are also unthinkable and incomparable. They are also immeasurable, because one cannot conceive of a measure of form, etc., since such a measure does not exist, in consequence of the infinitude of all dharmas. They are also incalculable, because they have risen above all possibility of counting. They are also equal to the unequaled, because all dharmas are the same as space.[312]

This passage mentions the five aggregates (form, sensation, ideation, conditioned factors, consciousness), as well as all the dharmas in general, in the same breath as the essence of the perfected one, buddhahood, existence of the self, and omniscience. In other words, the text does not differentiate between the phenomenal world (embodied in the dharmas) and the so-called highest existence. This highest existence is described in the same terms as the phenomenal world and the dharmas because neither of them really exists. Both are without origin and without end because they ultimately do not exist; and that which does not exist cannot disappear, nor be compared, measured, or counted.

We may yet wonder whether these authors—who repeatedly discuss the essence of the dharmas (*dharmāṇāṃ dharmatā*), the element of the dharmas (*dharmadhātu*), the culminating point of the real (*bhūtakoṭi*), thusness (*tathatā*), emptiness (*śūnyatā*), the essence of a buddha (*tathāgatatva*), omniscience (*sarvajñatā*), and the perfection of wisdom (*prajñāpāramitā*)—really rejected the idea of a highest existence. This plethora of designations only made sense if their users had some idea of what they represented. One cannot but think of the comparison with space (*ākāśa*), which is often used in the texts. Space is presented as being nothing at all and therefore without measure, duration, or end.

312 ASP(Vaidya) pp. 138–39 (shortened); tr. Conze 1958: 101.

But in India, space is not solely looked upon as being nothing. Since ancient times, a more positive concept of space has also been known. In the older Upaniṣads, space is an element that is sometimes identified with the highest Brahman.[313] Within Buddhism, as we have seen, the Sarvāstivādins considered space an unconditioned (*asaṃskṛta*) dharma, and therefore an existent. Even though the Sautrāntikas rejected this, seeing space instead as pure absence and therefore as nothing at all, the authors of the prajñāpāramitā sūtras were no doubt aware that space was sometimes conceived as a positive phenomenon.[314]

It looks as if these authors were playing with ideas that in the end they rejected. They discussed something very similar to a highest existence, but in the end they returned to the position that this highest existence is also empty and therefore unreal. Whatever the case, further developments within Mahāyāna show a great need for a highest reality. Increasingly, the expressions enumerated above tended to be interpreted positively, but the ambiguity between highest existence and nothingness was not abandoned.

Before examining some of these developments below, we first deal with Madhyamaka, a development that links the tradition of the prajñāpāramitā sūtras with Sarvāstivāda rationality.

Madhyamaka

The early Mahāyāna sūtras appear to react against the Abhidharma Buddhists' overall attempts at systematization. However, they did not as a rule attack isolated doctrinal positions adopted by the Sarvāstivādins. This would not have been possible without examining these ideas in depth and dealing with them rationally. Such rational discussions were not sought by the adepts of early Mahāyāna. They preferred to dedicate themselves to contemplative practice rather than hair-splitting disputation.

313 Qvarnström 1988: 24–25; Ruegg 1978: 176.

314 These two opposite concepts of space also play a role in the polemic between Buddhists and Vedāntins; see Qvarnström 1988.

There was one Mahāyāna adept, however, who answered the Sarvāstivādins' challenge on their own terms.[315] This was Nāgārjuna, who probably lived during the second century CE.[316] Using the utmost skill and virtuosity, Nāgārjuna turned the Sarvāstivādins' own rationality against them. His major work is the *Mūlamadhyamakakārikā* ("Foundational Verses of the Middle Way"), probably not called thus by Nāgārjuna himself. We know that the Buddha's path to liberation was called "middle path" already in the old discourses. Nāgārjuna borrows the idea but reinterprets it in his own way.[317] As the name of a school, Madhyamaka or Mādhyamika is only attested later.[318]

The *Foundational Verses of the Middle Way* do not merely attack Sarvāstivāda doctrine. The method they develop goes much further, and no doubt at times it made even non-Sarvāstivādins shake their heads in wonder. Nāgārjuna did not merely assert that the phenomenal world does not exist; he actually managed to prove it. Nāgārjuna thus belongs to those thinkers, of whom there are also examples in ancient Greece and China, who put the new instrument of logic to this use.[319] We must remember that most Buddhists of Nāgārjuna's time were *a priori* convinced of the outcome of his arguments that the phenomenal world is unreal. Unfortunately for the Abhidharma Buddhists, however, a side effect of Nāgārjuna's method was to prove that their conception of the world—the dharma theory—could not be correct either.

A proof that shows that the phenomenal world does not exist should

---

315 Warder's assertion (1973) that Nāgārjuna was not a Mahāyānist is implausible; cf. May 1979: 473–74; Ruegg 1981: 6n13; Lindtner 1982: 21n67.

316 Vikn pp. 71–77; Lamotte 1944–80: III: XL, LII–LIII; Robinson 1967: 25–26. There is no consensus as to Nāgārjuna's date and place; see e.g. Ruegg 1981: 4–5n11; 1982 (p. 507: 150–200 CE); Ichimura 1992; 1995; and now Walser, 2002.

317 Ruegg 1981: 1. A survey of the use of the expression "middle path" is provided by Mimaki & May 1979: 456–57. For presumed parallels in the Pāli canon, cf. Gómez 1976.

318 May 1979: 472; Ruegg 1981: 1; Vetter 1982a: 100–101 with note 28a.

319 For China, see Graham 1989: 75–76. A comparison between Nāgārjuna and the Eleatics is found, e.g., in Siderits & O'Brien 1976; likewise Jacobi 1911: 1 (559) note 2; McEvilley 1981; also Hayes 1988: 51–52.

interest everyone who is interested in philosophy, even non-Buddhists, and indeed these latter were not slow to react. We will concentrate, however, on some of the arguments that mainly concern Abhidharma Buddhism. In so doing, we will see that even when Nāgārjuna attacks doctrines specific to these Buddhists, his argumentation has implications that go well beyond these doctrines.

To grasp many of Nāgārjuna's arguments, we must understand the following. Nāgārjuna's starting point, shared by most Buddhists of his time, was that the objects of the phenomenal world are somehow conditioned by words. We discussed this understanding of the relation between things and their labels while dealing with the arrangement of the doctrine in the early centuries following the Buddha's demise. Nāgārjuna did not feel compelled to go against this prevalent belief. On the contrary, his new method consisted in using this belief—or better, this conviction—in a new fashion.

In so doing, however, he did not, like most Buddhists before him, limit its scope to individual words: he also analyzed propositions. His premise was that the words that occur in a proposition each correspond to an object or event in the situation described by it. For instance, the proposition "Nāgārjuna reads a book" describes a situation in which there is a book, Nāgārjuna, and the activity of reading. In other propositions, such a direct connection with the phenomenal world is difficult to maintain. An example is the proposition "Nāgārjuna writes a book." This proposition describes a situation in which Nāgārjuna and the activity of writing have their place. But the book is not yet there; it is there only when the writing is over. Faced with this difficulty, one might conclude that the hypothesis according to which the words in a proposition correspond to objects or events in the situation described is not correct. For Nāgārjuna, this conclusion was unimaginable. For him, difficulties like this were merely proof that the phenomenal world does not really exist. Like other Buddhists, he knew this beforehand. Contradictions of this nature only showed that the unreality of the phenomenal world could now also be proved.[320]

320 On Nāgarjuna's argumentation, see Bronkhorst 1997.

Let us now turn to some passages from the *Mūlamadhyamakakārikā* that deal with Sarvāstivāda doctrinal positions. As we said before, the arguments are not aimed exclusively at the Sarvāstivādins; they have a wider scope. However, here and there Nāgārjuna takes Sarvāstivāda doctrinal positions as his starting point.

We start with the seventh chapter, which deals with the "characteristics of the conditioned" (*saṃskṛtalakṣaṇa*). These are the conditioned factors separated from the mind (*cittaviprayukta saṃskāra*)—birth (*jāti*), old age (*jarā*), existence (*sthiti*), and impermanence (*anityatā*)—which we discussed in a previous chapter. Their number varies: sometimes there are four of them, sometimes three. Nāgārjuna leaves out old age. Instead of the expressions birth (*jāti*), existence (*sthiti*), and impermanence (*anityatā*), he uses origination (*utpāda*), existence (*sthiti*), and destruction (*bhaṅga*), respectively. The role of these dharmas remains the same: they are responsible for the arising, existence, and cessation of each conditioned dharma. Nāgārjuna says:

> If there is a characteristic of the conditioned other than origination (*utpāda*), existence (*sthiti*), and destruction (*bhaṅga*), there would be infinite regress (*anavasthā*). If there is no such [characteristic], these are not conditioned (*na saṃskṛta*).[321] (7.3)

This concerns a problem that we encountered before. Conditioned (*saṃskṛta*) dharmas need a dharma called birth (*jāti*), or origination (*utpāda*), in order to come into being. But the dharma *birth* is itself conditioned (*saṃskṛta*) and therefore needs such a dharma itself, which could then be called *origination of origination* (*utpādotpāda*). This origination of origination, however, too is a conditioned dharma, and would therefore need a further dharma called *origination*. This series has no end, and this is what Nāgārjuna calls infinite regress (*anavasthā*).

We saw already how the Sarvāstivādins sought to solve this problem:

321 MadhK(deJ) 7.3–4. Here and in what follows I use Kalupahana's (1986) translation, with liberal modifications. See also May 1959: 107–8.

the primary origination brings about the origination of origination, and the origination of origination brings about the primary origination. These are the exact words Nāgārjuna puts in the mouth of his opponent:

> The origination of origination is exclusively the origination of primary origination. Again, the primary origination produces the origination of origination. (7.4)

Here Nāgārjuna points out how problematic mutual causes are:

> If the origination of origination is for you the origination of the primary origination, not being produced by the primary [origination], how can the [former] produce the [latter]? (7.5)

> If, produced by the primary [origination], it produces the primary [origination], how can that primary [origination], not being produced by it, produce it? (7.6)

In other words, something has first to be produced itself in order to produce something else. The next verse elaborates:

> This, while being produced, may, if you so desire, produce that, if this, [though as yet] unborn (*ajāta*), can produce that. (7.7)

Here Nāgārjuna attributes to his opponent the following explanation:

> As a light will illuminate itself as well as other things, so does origination produce both itself and other things. (7.8)

Nāgārjuna submits this example of a light to the following destructive analysis:

> There exists no darkness either in the light or in whatever place it is situated. What does light illuminate? For illumination is the destruction of darkness. (7.9)
>
> How can darkness be destroyed by light that is arising, when the light that is arising does not reach the darkness? (7.10)
>
> On the other hand, if darkness is destroyed by light that has not reached it, then that [light], while remaining here, will destroy the darkness present in all the worlds. (7.11)
>
> If light illuminates both itself and other things, then certainly darkness too will conceal itself and other things. (7.12)

Nāgārjuna then returns to the dharma *origination* (*utpāda*):

> How can this non-arisen origination (*utpāda*) produce itself? If it produces having arisen, then, it having been born, what is it that is produced again? (7.13)
>
> Neither that which is presently arising, nor what has arisen, nor what has not arisen, arises in any way. This has already been explained by means of [the road] being traveled, [the road] traveled, and [the road] not traveled. (7.14)

In this last verse, Nāgārjuna refers to an argument he used in the second chapter, where he concluded that traveling, the traveler, and the road being traveled do not exist:[322]

> If there were a traveling of [a road] that is being traveled,

322 MadhK(deJ) chap. 2. See also May 1959: 51–52. According to Bareau (1964: 156) this chapter concerns "the course of time," but he gives no arguments to support this interpretation; cf. Bhattacharya 1985: 8.

> there would be two [acts of] traveling: the [traveling] by which that [road] is being traveled, and again that traveling on it. (2.5)

> If there were two [acts of] traveling, there would be two travelers. For there can be no traveling without a traveler. (2.6)

Nāgārjuna is here analyzing the verbal expression: "The road presently being traveled is being traveled." In this proposition, the verb "to travel" is used twice, and this is sufficient for Nāgārjuna to conclude that there must be two acts of traveling. Nāgārjuna used this example of the road being traveled as a touchstone for other proofs. He not only refers to it here in the discussion of the characteristics of the conditioned, he does the same in the third chapter, for example, when showing the Buddhist doctrine of perception to be untenable.

Another central tactic in Nāgārjuna's reasoning is tersely expressed in verse 17:

> If something that has not arisen exists somewhere, it could arise. Since no such thing exists, what arises?

This is clearer if we apply the question to a concrete example. In the proposition "the pot comes into existence," the question arises: how *can* the pot come into existence if it isn't there? The pot must exist in order to accomplish any kind of activity. In the present case, the activity is that of coming into existence. Therefore, the pot must exist in order to come into existence. But if it already exists, it no longer needs to come into existence, because it is already there.

As in the proposition above about the verb "to travel," Nāgārjuna is capitalizing on a linguistic feature to undermine the reality of the phenomenal world. In so doing, he is following his Buddhist predecessors in eliding any distinction between words and the objects they point to. The phenomenal world is, after all, conditioned by language, and the proposition "the pot comes into existence" should therefore correspond to a situation in the phenomenal wherein the pot and its coming into existence coexist. That this turns out to be impossible demonstrates that the phenomenal world has no absolute reality. Nāgārjuna pushes this method of argumentation further, however, showing that the existence of dharmas—such as origination—is no more defensible than the existence of things like pots.

Nāgārjuna then submits the two remaining characteristics of the conditioned to a similar and equally destructive analysis. He concludes the chapter with the following two verses:

> Since origination, existence, and destruction are not established, the conditioned (*saṃskṛta*) does not exist. Given that the conditioned is not established, how will the unconditioned (*asaṃskṛta*) be established? (7.33)

> Origination, existence, and destruction have been declared to be like an illusion, like a dream, like a city of the *gandharvas*. (7.34)

This conclusion clearly shows what remains of Sarvāstivāda ontology in the hands of Nāgārjuna. Not only do the three (or four) dharmas known as the characteristics of the conditioned turn out to be unprovable or even nonexistent, all conditioned (*saṃskṛta*) and unconditioned (*asaṃskṛta*) dharmas undergo the same fate. Since for the Sarvāstivādins, the conditioned and unconditioned dharmas are the only things that really exist, without an answer to Nāgārjuna's attack, their whole ontology breaks down.

Here we turn to the first chapter of the *Mūlamadhyamakakārikā*, which deals with the Abhidharma Buddhists' doctrine of causality. We have noted above that this doctrine is an important part of the dharma theory. For it is causality that connects the momentary dharmas produced one after the other and that conditions their production. The Sarvāstivādins had made a distinction between different sorts of conditions (*pratyaya*), as we saw in the previous chapter: the producing condition (*hetu-pratyaya*), the support (*ārambaṇa-* or *ālambana-pratyaya*) or object of knowledge, the immediately contiguous condition (*samanantara-pratyaya*), and the determining condition (*adhipati-pratyaya*). They are mentioned in the second verse:

> There are four conditions (*pratyaya*), namely, the producing condition (*hetu*), the support (*ārambaṇa*), the immediately contiguous condition (*anantara*), and the determining condition (*ādhipateya*). A fifth condition does not exist.[323] (1.2)

Nāgārjuna then proceeds to demolish the idea of cause and effect:

> Activity is not constituted of conditions (*pratyaya*) nor is it not constituted of conditions. Conditions are neither constituted nor not constituted of activity. (1.4)

> These are conditions, because depending upon them these [others] arise. So long as these [others] do not arise, why are they not non-conditions? (1.5)

> A condition of something that is nonexistent or of something that is existent is not proper. What nonexistent [thing] has a condition? Of what use is the condition of an existent [thing]? (1.6)

> Since a thing that is existent or nonexistent or both existent and nonexistent does not produce, how could there be, such being the case, a producing condition? (1.7)

It is easy to show that Nāgārjuna's logic, here as well as in the examples discussed above, leaves much to be desired.[324] However, this observation, though correct, does not do sufficient justice to Nāgārjuna's presuppositions. For him—as we have already noted above—the role

---

323 MadhK(deJ) 1.2ff.

324 This is what Frauwallner (1956a: 176) does.

of language in interpreting the phenomenal world is decisive. Language demands that a cause have an effect and vice versa. However, cause and effect do not exist at the same time. When a cause exists, its effect does not exist. And once the effect is there, its cause often exists no longer. How then can they be dependent on each other? To convince Nāgārjuna that his conclusions are false, one should not teach him a better logic but a different worldview.[325] Given his presuppositions, his arguments are largely faultless in their logic.

After this overarching criticism, it is easy for Nāgārjuna to prove in the verses that follow that the four types of conditions mentioned above are untenable. Here again, he reaches the conclusion that coming into being is not really possible. In the first verses of the nineteenth chapter, Nāgārjuna uses the same type of argument to prove that time does not exist:

> If the present and the future depend upon the past, then the present and the future will be in the past time. (19.1)
>
> Again, if the present and the future do not exist therein [i.e., in the past], how could the present and the future depend upon it? (19.2)
>
> Moreover, not depending upon the past, the [present and future] cannot be established. Therefore, neither the present nor the future time exist. (19.3)[326]

In the fifteenth chapter, Nāgārjuna deals with another notion we have met before, namely, the Sarvāstivādins' concept of the dharmas' "own-nature" (*svabhāva*). This is supposed to be eternal and beyond the scope of time. According to Nāgārjuna, such an own-nature stands in contradiction with causal dependence. He states:

---

325 Cf. Oetke 1991: 320–21; 1989: 10–11.

326 MadhK(deJ) 19.1–3. On this topic, see Oetke 1990; also Bronkhorst 1997.

> The occurrence of the own-nature through causes and conditions is not proper. An own-nature that has occurred as a result of causes and conditions would be something that is made. (15.1)
>
> Again, how could there be an own-nature that is made? Indeed, an unmade own-nature is independent of something else. (15.2)
>
> In the absence of an own-nature (*svabhāva*), whence can there be an other-nature (*parabhāva*)? For the own-nature of an other-nature is called an other-nature. (15.3)
>
> How can there be something that is without own-nature and other-nature? For something is established only when there is own-nature and other-nature. (15.4)
>
> When something is not established, [its] absence is also not established. It is, indeed, the change of something that people generally call its absence. (15.5)[327]

While reading this passage, it is important to keep in mind that only that which "exists" in the highest sense of the term can be or have an own-nature. We have already seen that whatever has originated from causes and conditions does not really exist. It is therefore not surprising to see that Nāgārjuna starts from the premise that if things were to possess an own-nature, they would have to be without origin.[328]

We have touched upon Nāgārjuna's position on causality but without mentioning the doctrine of conditioned origination. This doctrine is of the highest interest to him. For Nāgārjuna, it is proof that the dharmas cannot really exist. For this doctrine connects the dharmas

327 MadhK(deJ) chap. 15. Hayes (1994: 308–9) discusses the false conclusions of chapter 15.

328 Oetke 1989: 14.

with each other and shows their mutual dependence. We have seen that for Nāgārjuna dependence implies simultaneity. However, the dharmas arise one after the other, leading to a contradiction. From this Nāgārjuna concludes that all the dharmas are empty—without real existence:

> We state that conditioned origination is emptiness. It is mere designation depending on something, and it is the middle path. (24.18)
>
> Since nothing has arisen without depending on something, there is nothing that is not empty. (24.19)[329]

For Nāgārjuna, conditioned origination is emptiness, just as for the Sarvāstivādins conditioned origination was the conditioned dharmas. Since for Nāgārjuna there are no dharmas (because the dharmas are empty), conditioned origination is also empty, or, as he says here, "emptiness." For Nāgārjuna, therefore, neither the objects and events of the phenomenal world nor the dharmas exist in highest reality. Ultimately, for him, nothing exists at all. This knowledge constitutes the middle way, as verse 18 appears to state.

To conclude this section on the *Mūlamadhyamakakārikā*, we will examine Nāgārjuna's treatment of the problem of the self. We know how important a role this problem had played in the history of Buddhism before him. The relevant canonical passages had been interpreted in various ways. Originally, they rejected the concept of the self one finds in, for instance, the old Upaniṣads and the liberating knowledge that was associated with it. But soon, knowledge of not-self became liberating knowledge in its own right, and these passages started to be seen as confirming the idea that composite things do not really exist. Finally, certain Buddhists came to see in these very passages proof that the dharmas do not really exist.

We encounter most of these ideas in the *Mūlamadhyamakakārikā*.

329 MadhK(deJ) 24.18–19.

For Nāgārjuna, the dharmas are empty and do not really exist. For him, too—as we will soon see—knowledge of the not-self plays a decisive role in reaching liberation. Finally, he shares the opinion that composite things do not really exist.

This last idea is closely connected with the conception of the person as a collection of dharmas. The Pudgalavādins accepted this concept, but it was known as well to those Buddhists who explicitly rejected it. The Pudgalavāda, we saw earlier, asserted the reality of the phenomenal world in a limited way. The Pudgalavādins maintained that the person really exists and is no mere illusion. In a certain sense, the Pudgalavādins and Nāgārjuna, who brought the negation of the phenomenal world to new heights, are complete opposites; contrary to the Pudgalavādins, Nāgārjuna's highest reality is empty. His phenomenal world, however, contains many things, including persons and other composite objects, and while discussing the person, Nāgārjuna starts from premises that resemble those of the Pudgalavādins. His discussion begins by analyzing the relationship between the person and the aggregates (*skandha*):

> If the self were identical with the aggregates, it would arise and cease. If it were different from the aggregates, it would not have the characteristics of the aggregates. (18.1)
>
> In the absence of a self, how can there be something that belongs to the self? From the appeasement of the self and of what belongs to the self, one is free from "mine" and "I." (18.2)
>
> No one is free from "mine" and "I." Whoever sees someone who is free from "mine" and "I" sees wrong. (18.3)[330]

The point of the last verse is that someone who is free from the belief in "mine" and "I" must nevertheless be a person, a self; but a self does not exist.

330 MadhK(deJ) chap. 18. Cf. Vetter 1982: 176–77.

The verses that follow are especially interesting. Up to this point, Nāgārjuna has merely brought to light the internal contradictions of the phenomenal world. Beside this, he has refuted certain worldviews, among them that of the Sarvāstivādins. The idea that the phenomenal world is unreal, however, was the common property of almost all Buddhists in his day. Nāgārjuna's own contribution is to provide a method to prove it. His proof concerns a relatively minor part of the Buddhist religion. The latter's main aim is liberation. In what way is Nāgārjuna's method of use for attaining this aim? The next verses of the eighteenth chapter deal with this question:

> When views pertaining to "mine" and "I," whether associated with the internal or the external, have ceased, then clinging (*upādāna*) ends. With the ceasing of that, birth ceases. (18.4)

Here again, Nāgārjuna does not state anything new. The old discourses and even the Buddha's so-called first discourse call the knowledge of not-self liberating knowledge. The same, or a similar, knowledge still seems to play a comparable role for Nāgārjuna. The text continues:

> Liberation (*mokṣa*) results from the cessation of actions (*karman*) and defilements (*kleśa*). Actions and defilements result from representations (*vikalpa*). These from false imagining (*prapañca*). False imagining stops in emptiness (*śūnyatā*). (18.5)

> The Buddhas have communicated that there is a self. They have taught that there is no self. And they have taught that there is neither self nor not-self. (18.6)

> The nameable (*abhidhātavya*) has ceased; the domain of mind (*cittagocara*) has ceased. For the essence of dharmas (*dharmatā*) is without arising and disappearing, like nirvāṇa. (18.7)

It is easy to recognize here certain themes we have seen earlier. The diversity of the phenomenal world is conditioned by representations and by naming—by words—but it disappears when representations and cognizing stop.[331] This happens when the practitioner gains insight into emptiness. Emptiness is precisely what Nāgārjuna's method teaches. In this emptiness, the diversity of the phenomenal world is removed, representations disappear, followed by actions and defilements, and liberation takes place. At the same time, Nāgārjuna offers a solution to the problem that preoccupied the Pudgalavādins and their opponents. Both can, with some justification, cite passages in support of their point of view. In reality, the Buddha—more precisely, the Buddhas—enunciated these contradictions in order to proclaim the highest truth.

It is hardly necessary to emphasize that Nāgārjuna's thought raises—and indeed has raised through the ages—many more questions than have been dealt with above. It has given rise to many different points of view in modern research too, often based on faulty interpretations.[332] What is important here is that Nāgārjuna's thought is determined, to a significant extent, by the difference between limited truth (*saṃvṛtisatya*) and highest truth (*paramārthasatya*). The phenomenal world does not exist in highest truth, but it has limited reality. Likewise the Buddha, his teaching, liberation, and even Nāgārjuna's arguments only have limited reality. But this limited reality has its use and is even necessary in order to reach liberation, nirvāṇa. This is what Nāgārjuna explains in the twenty-fourth chapter of the *Mūlamadhyamakakārikā*:

> (Objection:) If all this is empty and there is no arising and ceasing, then there are no four noble truths for you. (24.1)
>
> In the absence of the four noble truths, understanding,

---

331 Lindtner (1994: 273) surely goes too far when he cites this passage in order to show that the *Mūlamadhyamakakārikā* was a manual of practical yoga.

332 See Oetke 1988a and 1989, for a presentation and refutation of many of these points of view.

relinquishing, cultivation, and realization will not be possible. (24.2)

In the absence of this [fourfold activity], there are no four noble fruits. In the absence of the fruits, neither those who have attained the fruits nor those who have reached the way [to such attainment] exist. (24.3)

If the eight types of individuals do not exist, there will be no congregation (Saṅgha). In the absence of the noble truths, there is no true doctrine (Dharma). (24.4)

When the doctrine and the congregation are nonexistent, how can there be an enlightened one (Buddha)? Speaking in this manner, you contradict the three jewels. (24.5)

You [also] contradict emptiness, the reality of the fruits, both evil and virtue, and all worldly conventions. (24.6)

(Answer:) We say that you do not comprehend the purpose of emptiness, emptiness, and the meaning of emptiness. That is why you are repelled. (24.7)

The teaching of the doctrine by the Buddhas is based upon two truths: truth in a limited sense (*saṃvṛtisatya*) of ordinary life and truth in the highest sense. (24.8)

Those who do not understand the distinction between these two truths do not understand the profound truth embodied in the Buddha's message. (24.9)

Without relying upon convention, the ultimate fruit is not taught. Without understanding the ultimate, nirvāṇa is not attained. (24.10)[333]

333 MadhK(deJ) 24.1–10; cf. Oetke 1989: 28–29.

Nāgārjuna does not merely state his conclusions; he often tries to prove them. Reflections on the correct way to draw conclusions began early in India, and it is possible that Nāgārjuna himself contributed a treatise in this field, the *Upāyahṛdaya*.[334] Although some of his arguments are not convincing from a logical point of view, many others are logically irreproachable. Logic and epistemology underwent a noteworthy development in India after Nāgārjuna (perhaps in part inspired by him), primarily linked with the names of Vasubandhu and Dignāga (both perhaps belonging to the fifth century). Some of Nāgārjuna's followers, starting with Bhāvaviveka (sixth century), took pains to present their master's arguments in a manner that agrees with the requirements of the logic of their time. However, whether the arguments are formulated in Nāgārjuna's own terms or in those imposed by later developments of logic, their main weakness is not, as some scholars seem to think,[335] their logic, but the premises on which they are based. These premises primarily concern ideas about the relationship between words and things.

The question of Nāgārjuna's influence on later Indian thinkers must be reserved for a separate study.[336] The question will come up briefly below, in connection with Dignāga. Here we must briefly examine if and how the Sarvāstivādins—who were among the main targets of Nāgārjuna's attacks—reacted to his criticism. No explicit response of the Sarvāstivādins to Nāgārjuna has survived; perhaps it never existed. To my knowledge, modern research has never dealt with this problem.[337] We can therefore only make a brief, but important, observation: the Sarvāstivāda system was to a fair extent immune to Nāgārjuna's main attacks. Nāgārjuna maintains that an object can only originate if it already exists. But this is Sarvāstivāda doctrine, according to which past and future exist. A future object already exists before it is produced,

334 Kajiyama 1991.

335 So Hayes 1994.

336 Bronkhorst 1999, an English translation of which is in preparation.

337 Hayes (1994: 299) even claims that the Ābhidharmikas did not at all defend themselves against Nāgārjuna's attacks.

i.e., before it enters into the present. The difference is that only a present object is endowed with efficiency. Many of Nāgārjuna's arguments, which are often concerned with causality, are in this way answered in a more or less satisfactory fashion.

Further Developments in Mahāyāna

With the prajñāpāramitā sūtras and Madhyamaka, Buddhism had, in a certain sense, developed in this particular direction as far as it could possibly go. The idea that the phenomenal world does not really exist had become prominent some centuries after the death of the historical Buddha. This trend had started with the negation of the person and had soon been extended to all composite objects. The dharmas were all that was left. In the prajñāpāramitā sūtras and Madhyamaka, no place remains even for the dharmas, or for any kind of higher existence. As we have said, it is impossible to go further in this direction.

We should not however think that the development of Mahāyāna ends with the prajñāpāramitā sūtras. Quite on the contrary, Mahāyāna Buddhism is characterized by a variety of different views and doctrines. We have seen that the prajñāpāramitā sūtras allude to some kind of highest existence. And indeed, Mahāyāna literature—or at least that part of it that has come down to us—contains much that cannot easily be fitted into the scheme of completely "emptying" the world. One Mahāyāna sūtra, the *Saṃdhinirmocana Sūtra*, goes so far as to state that the teaching was proclaimed in three "turns of the wheel of Dharma."[338] The first "turn" concerns the teaching of the Śrāvakayāna. The descriptions of the second and third turns are so unclear that they have given rise to various interpretations.[339]

338 Saṃdhis(ÉLa) VIII 30, pp. 206–7.

339 Harris 1991: 70–71; cf. Powers 1993: 78–79. Harris believes that the interpretations referring to different schools of Buddhism are relatively late. The *Aṣṭasāhasrikā Prajñāpāramitā* (ASP(Vaidya) p. 101.19–20) already mentions a second turn of the wheel of dharma, which corresponds to the doctrine of the prajñāpāramitā sūtras. The *Mahāprajñāpāramitāśāstra* attributed to Nāgārjuna (Lamotte 1944–80: II: 1074, 1095) distinguishes between a threefold teaching,

Whatever their correct interpretation, they testify to an awareness of the differences between the various developments that took place in Mahāyāna. Views arose that are quite independent of notions of the emptiness of the world. Moreover, these views at first betrayed little or no mutual relationship. The historical study of many of these views still stands in its infancy, so that it is impossible to give a satisfactory and complete picture of it. We must restrict ourselves to a brief presentation of a few of them in their historical development. This will convey a first impression of the complicated early history of Mahāyāna teachings. It is important to distinguish this early history from the attempts by later thinkers to harmonize these manifold ideas into a single coherent picture. It would be a mistake to imagine that all Buddhists have always tried to reach internal consistency in their ideas. Such efforts seem to have been the exception rather than the rule.

We will first discuss the concept of *dharmakāya* ("body of teaching"), whose origin is to be looked for in the old discourses. Shortly before his death, the Buddha told his disciple Ānanda: "It may be that you will think: 'The Teacher's instruction has ceased, now we have no teacher!' It should not be seen like this, Ānanda, for what I have taught and explained to you as Dhamma (Skt. *dharma*) and discipline (*vinaya*) will, at my passing, be your teacher."[340] Elsewhere, too, the Buddha identifies himself with his teaching: "Who sees the teaching sees me; who sees me sees the teaching."[341] And once, the expression *dhammakāya* (Skt. *dharmakāya*) is used as an adjective qualifying the Buddha, in the sense of "whose body is the doctrine."[342] Paul Harrison has shown that the expression *dharmakāya* was retained for some time, even in the later Mahāyāna sūtras, in the sense of "whose body is the teaching," or "who is embodied in the teaching."[343] This expression

specified as [Sūtra-]Piṭaka, Abhidharma, and emptiness. See Snellgrove 1987: 79–80.

340 DN II.154; tr. Walshe 1995: 269–70; see also Franke 1913: 242. Cf. MPS 386–87.

341 SN III.120.

342 DN III.84; cf. Franke 1913: 276; Harrison 1992a: 50.

343 Harrison 1992a.

here always designates the Buddha, or the buddhas, who is/are embodied in the teaching.

The expression *dharmakāya*, however, was also beginning to be used as a substantive with several meanings, because its two constituent words *dharma* and *kāya* have two meanings each. *Dharma* means "the teaching" and "mental property" (and of course "element of existence," a meaning that became all-important in Buddhism). *Kāya* means "body" as well as "collection." *Dharmakāya* can therefore mean "collection of the teaching,"[344] but very soon it is also found in the sense "collection of mental properties," where it designates the special mental properties that belong to a buddha. The meaning of *dharmakāya* as "collection of dharmas" or even "totality of dharmas" appeared somewhat later.

So far, the use of the expression *dharmakāya* is in no way different from what can be found in non-Mahāyāna Buddhist teachings. In certain sūtras, however, the expression receives a broader meaning in accordance, it seems, with the need for a highest existence. Thus, the *Anūnatvāpūrṇatvanirdeśa* declares on the one hand that the dharmakāya consists of all the good properties of a perfected being, and on the other, that it is a thing that has no parts.[345] This implies that the dharmakāya is thought of as something that really exists.[346] *Dharmakāya* is here equated with *dharmadhātu* "element of the dharmas," i.e., with the totality of what exists.[347]

An even more interesting equivalence is found in the texts of the so-called Tathāgatagarbha tradition.[348] *Tathāgatagarbha* means "embryo of the Buddha."[349] This expression springs from the idea that all liv-

344 According to Harrison (1992a: 56), only the plural analysis as "collection of the doctrines" is possible; but this is not convincing.

345 Griffiths et al. 1989: 21. Cf. Takasaki 1966: 39–40.

346 Harrison (1992a: 75) is justified in asking whether a less reifying interpretation of the word *dharmakāya* is possible in all these passages. Further studies will perhaps answer this question.

347 Griffiths et al. 1989: 22. On *dharmadhātu*, see also Sutton 1991: 117–18.

348 Takasaki 1966: 32–33; Ruegg 1969: 275–76; Brown 1991.

349 *Garbha* can also mean "womb," and sometimes it is not clear in the texts which meaning they refer to. See, e.g., King 1995: 2.

ing beings carry, and have always carried, in themselves their own buddhahood in a latent form, veiled by external impurities caused by passions and other earthly factors. When the living being is freed from these accidental impurities and its "support is transformed" (*āśrayaparivṛtti*),[350] then the tathāgatagarbha, the "buddha embryo," becomes the *dharmakāya*, the "body of the teaching (*dharma*, singular) and of the perfected properties (*dharma*, plural)," i.e., the absolute aspect of fully realized buddhahood.[351] In their essence, tathāgatagarbha and dharmakāya are therefore identical. Moreover, the tathāgatagarbha is conceived of as something that really exists. It is indeed the "highest reality," which has no fundamental connection with the doctrine of universal emptiness.[352]

Various texts use epithets for the tathāgatagarbha and the dharmakāya like "eternal" (*nitya*), "unchanging" (*dhruva*), "joyful" (*sukha*), "self" (*ātman*), and "pure" (*śubha, śuci*).[353] We see in these the concept of the self that had been rejected by the Buddha. It appears that this idea held such a powerful sway that certain Buddhists could not resist it. We have already seen one reason for this attraction: it was unclear to many Buddhists why and how the Buddhist path could lead to liberation from rebirths. This explanation does not rule out the possibility that the notion of the tathāgatagarbha as an eternal and joyful self may have originated within Buddhism, without non-Buddhist influence; or even that later non-Buddhists may have borrowed this notion from the Buddhists, as some scholars hold.[354] There is no need to examine these possibilities in detail. Certainly the similarity between this notion of the tathāgatagarbha and the self of the non-Buddhists is so striking that the Buddhist texts themselves comment on it. The *Laṅkāvatāra Sūtra*

350 See note 388 below.

351 Schmithausen 1973: 129.

352 Schmithausen 1973: 133.

353 *Śrīmālādevīsiṃhanāda Sūtra*, cited in Nakamura 1961: 59; Ruegg 1969: 392; 1989: 19–20; Wayman & Wayman 1974: 45–46, 98, 102. On the equivalence tathāgatagarbha = ātman, see Vikn p. 56 (reference to the *Mahāparinirvāṇa Sūtra*); Laṅkāv(V) 10.746, 754–55, pp. 156–57.

354 Ruegg 1989: 19–20, 38–39, 50–51; cf. Williams 1989: 100.

contains a passage where the bodhisattva Mahāmati asks the Buddha the following question:

> Now the Blessed One makes mention of the tathāgatagarbha in the sūtras, and verily it is described by you as by nature bright and pure, as primarily unspotted, endowed with the thirty-two marks of excellence, hidden in the body of every being like a gem of great value that is enwrapped in a dirty garment, enveloped in the garment of aggregates (*skandha*), elements (*dhātu*), and realms of the senses (*āyatana*), and soiled with the dirt of greed, anger, folly, and false imagination, while it is described by the Blessed One to be eternal, permanent, wholesome, and unchangeable. Is not this tathāgatagarbha taught by the Blessed One the same as the self (*ātman*) taught by the non-Buddhist philosophers (*tīrthakara*)? The self as taught in the systems of the non-Buddhist philosophers is an eternal creator, unqualified, omnipresent, and imperishable.[355]

It is hardly surprising that this representation of the tathāgatagarbha—outrageous from a Buddhist point of view—was soon weakened.[356] In one of the solutions proposed this doctrine was looked upon as not ultimate, as requiring an interpretation (*neyārtha*);[357] it was not to be taken literally (*nītārtha*). Another solution was to interpret it in the light of other Mahāyāna doctrines, mainly the doctrines of selflessness (*nairātmya*) and of emptiness (*śūnyatā*). This new interpretation may have been responsible for the fact that the tathāgatagarbha doctrine in India became more or less absorbed by the Yogācāra school,

355 Laṅkāv(V) 2.137, p. 33.10–11; tr. Suzuki 1932: 68–69. Ruegg (1989: 38) remarks that the representation of the tathāgatagarbha in the *Laṅkāvatāra Sūtra* differs in some points of detail from that found in other texts. According to Sutton (1991: 55–56) the tathāgatagarbha has a didactic but not an ontological value here.

356 Ruegg 1989: 26–27.

357 On this expression, see Ruegg 1995: 574; and the final chaptet below.

as seems to have happened.[358] Certain works of this school attributed to Maitreyanātha contain ideas that are still very close to the tathāgatagarbha doctrine.[359]

Yogācāra means "activity of yoga" and also "one whose activity is yoga," i.e., a "yogin."[360] The word *yoga* here appears in a Buddhist context, in the sense of "spiritual practice."[361] This sense of the term *yogācāra* is not found in the old discourses, but outside Buddhism it was used early in this sense, especially in the *Mahābhārata*, the great Sanskrit epic,[362] where it designates the path leading to liberation that is characterized by effort; the first meaning of *yoga* is "yoking," hence "effort." In the *Mahābhārata*, the path of effort is opposed to the path of knowledge (*sāṃkhya*).[363] For our purposes, we can note simply that epic yoga consists of ascetic practices in which physical and mental immobility play a major role.[364] Although Buddhism adopted such practices at an early date, it does not use the term *yoga* to refer to them until much later. Accordingly, it is likely that Buddhist and non-Buddhist ascetics were in contact not only at the beginning (as has been argued in chapter 2) but also later. The adoption of the word *yoga* in Buddhism undoubtedly indicates some interchange of non-Buddhist and Buddhist currents.

Returning to Yogācāra:

> This school is usually considered to belong to Mahāyāna. Indeed, all later Yogācāra texts propagate primarily the

358 Takasaki 1966: 57–58.

359 Frauwallner 1951. Maitreyanātha's historical reality is controversial; May 1971: 292–93.

360 It is not clear whether the term *yogācāra* should be taken in the sense of a determinative compound (*tatpuruṣa*) or of a possessive compound (*bahuvrīhi*); Madhav Deshpande, Indology (email discussion group) 15 February 1996.

361 An early occurrence of the term *yogācāra* (in the sense "the one whose activity is yoga") is found in the *Brahmaparipṛcchā*, cited by Candrakīrti and Bhāvaviveka; Lindtner 1994: 273. See also Schlingloff 1964: 28–29 and 237–38 s.v. *yoga* etc.

362 For the use of this and other related words, see Crangle 1994: 99–100.

363 Edgerton 1924; 1965: 35–36.

364 Bronkhorst 1993: 45–46.

> Mahāyāna path to liberation. But the oldest materials found in the voluminous *Yogācārabhūmi*,[365] which was compiled at the latest at the beginning of the fourth century CE, contain not only passages of a clearly Mahāyāna orientation, but also passages which still entirely rest on traditional, so-called Hīnayāna Buddhism.[366]

Yogācāra is rooted, so to speak, in pre- or non-Mahāyāna Buddhism.[367] This is especially true of various ideas that this school used and adopted while developing its doctrine.

One of the most important works of classical Yogācāra is Asaṅga's *Mahāyānasaṃgraha* ("Summary of Mahāyāna"), which was written around the fourth century.[368] This work exposes the main tenets of the school and discusses them in detail. By looking briefly at some of the concepts discussed in this work with an eye on their historical development,[369] we will see that they had to be profoundly modified before they could take their place in the classical system.

As we have seen, contemplative practice (or reflections on it) may have influenced or even determined certain developments within Mahāyāna; the doctrine of the unreal nature of appearances was discussed as an example. This doctrine, we saw, may be the ontological equivalent of the state called attainment of cessation (*nirodhasamāpatti*). It was also connected with visualization practices.

The same is possibly true of the notion of *ālayavijñāna*, a term sometimes translated as "fundamental consciousness." This notion, destined to play an important role in Mahāyāna, is very different from the doctrine of the unreal nature of appearances. Nevertheless, there are reasons to suppose that the ālayavijñāna was, at its inception, closely

---

365 Schmithausen (1969a) has shown that the *Yogācārabhūmi* is a compilation.

366 Schmithausen 1978: 113.

367 Kritzer (1999: 280) wonders whether the Dārṣṭāntikas and the Sautrāntikas should not be considered Hīnayāna Yogācāras.

368 Lamotte 1973a. This text has become more easily accessible thanks to Nagao 1994. Cf. also Keenan 1992.

369 For an overview of Yogācāra, see May 1971.

connected with reflections about the attainment of cessation. This is Lambert Schmithausen's thesis, which seems to find confirmation in the texts. The link is found in the problem that the ālayavijñāna may have been invented to solve.

Attainment of cessation is a meditative state wherein there is neither ideation (*saṃjñā*) nor feeling (*vedayita*). This was understood to mean that mind (*citta*) and mental dharmas (*caitasika*) are absent. While discussing the Pañcavastuka, we saw that consciousness (*vijñāna*) was subsumed under mind (*citta*). There is therefore no consciousness in attainment of cessation: it represents an interruption of the sequence of mental dharmas. How then can a person who has sojourned in this state return to consciousness? Mental dharmas normally succeed each other in a continuous sequence, the current mental dharma acting as the primary cause for the next one. After an interruption like the attainment of cessation, there are no mental dharmas that could produce succeeding ones. Nevertheless, the ancient discourses proclaim that it is possible to return from the attainment of cessation.

This problem was not exclusive to the Yogācāras. The Sarvāstivādins, too, had to confront it, but they had their own solution. For them the past exists. Past mental dharmas can therefore directly bring forth new dharmas, despite the distance in time.[370] In Yogācāra this solution was not possible because it did not accept the existence of the past.

At least one canonical text claims that there is consciousness (*vijñāna*) in attainment of cessation. How is this possible? A passage of the *Yogācārabhūmi*, called "Initial Passage" by Schmithausen, answers the question this way:

> When [a person] has entered [Attainment of] Cessation (*nirodha*(*samāpatti*)), his mind and mental [factors] have ceased; how, then, is it that [his] mind (*vijñāna*) has not withdrawn from [his] body?—[Answer: No problem;] for [in] his [case] Ālayavijñāna has not ceased [to be present] in the material sense-faculties, which are

370 See Cox 1995: 117–18.

> unimpaired: [Ālayavijñāna] which comprises (/possesses / has received) the Seeds of the forthcoming [forms of] mind (*pravṛttivijñāna*), so that they are bound to re-arise in future (i.e., after emerging from this attainment).[371]

It is likely that in this passage the word *ālayavijñāna* is used in its oldest meaning. The presence of the ālayavijñāna explains how one can survive a sojourn in attainment of cessation and how one can come out of it and obtain consciousness again. It becomes clear that in this case the ālayavijñāna, though called consciousness (*vijñāna*), is not conscious. For were it conscious, experience would be possible in attainment of cessation, and this would contradict the definition of this state.

The problem that is solved by postulating the ālayavijñāna has in itself nothing to do with specifically Mahāyāna concerns. It is possible that this concept had existed for a long time in non-Mahāyāna circles before it was adopted into Mahāyāna. It is neither possible nor necessary to examine here the complicated history of the meaning of this word, as this has been done by Schmithausen, but some of the new functions that came to be attached to the ālayavijñāna in later times can be considered.[372] The ālayavijñāna came to be considered the individual substratum of the cycle of rebirths (*saṃsāra*) and even of liberation. It also came to serve as a link between actions and their effects by acting as a repository for karmic activity. It bore the impressions (*vāsanā*) and seeds (*bīja*) of mental and physical actions until such time as the conditions came together for these to ripen in later experiences. Sometimes ālayavijñāna itself was considered a seed having a future effect. It was the basis for the sense of "I," and it was the factor responsible for a new life after death.

This enumeration of functions shows how close the later ālaya-

---

371 Tr. Schmithausen 1987: I: 18; cf. II: 276–77nn146–47.

372 Schmithausen 1987: I: 4–5, with II: 244–45nn12–13. Waldron (1995) considers the ālayavijñāna as the center of a theory of the mind that amounts to a paradigm shift from the preceding dharma theory.

vijñāna came to the notion of a self.[373] By rejecting the self, Buddhism had created a problem that kept cropping up in various ways in the course of its history. The doctrine of not-self had given rise to the developed dharma theory, and to the doctrine of emptiness in the prajñāpāramitā sūtras and Madhyamaka. In Mahāyāna, we find different examples of the way in which Buddhist thinkers tried to find a substitute for the self. One of these is the ālayavijñāna.

The notion of the ālayavijñāna found a place in classical Yogācāra beside another doctrine that became famous under the names *mind only* (*cittamātra*) and *making-known only* (*vijñaptimātra*). According to this doctrine, any cognition or perception has as object an image that exists in cognition itself, not a real object that exists outside cognition. Knowledge is "mind only" or "making-known only"; no corresponding external object is cognized. The doctrine is sometimes called "idealism" in modern scholarly literature for this reason, though it is not always obvious that the existence of external objects is denied.[374] The existence of the external world could yet easily be reconciled with the manifold series of individual consciousnesses that are accepted in the texts.[375]

As far as the origin of this doctrine is concerned, it is once again Schmithausen who has emphasized, and tried to prove, its connection with the practice of meditation, especially with the spiritual technique of visualizing.[376] We know that spiritual experiences were used to demonstrate the emptiness of all dharmas. We also know that, at least on one occasion, the conclusion was drawn from meditative experiences or conceptions of them that the mind creates the phenomenal world

373 See the etymological explanation of the word ālayavijñāna: "It is [called] *ālayavijñāna* because living beings stick to it (*ālīyante*) as to [their] self" (*Mahāyānasaṅgraha* and *Abhidharmasamuccayabhāṣya*, cited in Schmithausen 1987: II: 274–75n137). The world mostly sees the self in consciousness (*vijñāna*); *Abhidharmasamuccayabhāṣya*, cited in Schmithausen 1987: II: 331n386.

374 Oetke (1992) has for instance shown that one of the major works of classical Yogācāra, Vasubandhu's *Viṃśatikā*, contains no such denial. See also Oetke 1996: 196–97.

375 Wood (1991) deals with this problem without considering this as a possible solution.

376 Schmithausen 1973a: 163–64.

and that only the mind is real. This idea subsequently became an essential part of Yogācāra doctrine.

Thus in the *Saṃdhinirmocana Sūtra*, the "Discourse of the Unraveling of the Hidden Meaning," we find the claim that the images that are made the objects of contemplation are not different from the mind, for they are nothing beyond "making-known only" (*vijñaptimātra*). To prove this, the sūtra adduces a saying of the Buddha, which is apparently interpreted as a proof of the ideal—i.e., not objectively real—nature of the objects of contemplation.[377] The *Saṃdhinirmocana Sūtra*, however, goes one step further. In the paragraph that immediately follows, it explains that ordinary objects, too—the objects of ordinary perception—are not different from the mind and are not external to the act of making known. They are mere images in the mind. Schmithausen concludes from these and other similar reflections that the Yogācāras' idealism arose from reflections about a certain spiritual practice.[378]

This main doctrine of the Yogācāras could also be explained differently.[379] We have met the doctrine of mere designation (*prajñaptimātra*) before, for the first time in the dialogue between the monk Nāgasena and King Menander. Later, this doctrine became the common property of various Buddhist schools, whether or not they were Mahāyāna. The doctrine of making-known only (*vijñaptimātra*) shares certain elements with the doctrine of mere designation (*prajñaptimātra*), and we cannot rule out that the former arose from the latter. For the doctrine of mere designation states that the objects of the phenomenal world are nothing but designations or denominations. Who gives the objects their designations? If we assume that we are the ones who do this—and for the Buddhists there is no other possibility—we must conclude that the phenomenal appearances denoted by these denominations are likewise attributed to the objects by us. They are therefore, in reality, our representations. Only a small step remains between this and the conclusion that knowledge is mind only.

377 See also Schmithausen 1984.

378 Schmithausen 1973a: 185.

379 Frauwallner 1956a: 268–69; cf. Schmithausen 1973a: 171–72.

One more point must be added. The rejection of the person was a perpetual source of problems in Buddhism. For instance, if there is no person, how can the dharmas of one person be distinguished from those of another? And how can the continuity of a person be explained if there is no person? The fruit of an action belongs to the person who has performed it. How is this possible? We have seen how the Sarvāstivādins tried to solve this problem and also that the later Yogācāra used the ālayavijñāna as a connection between actions and their results. The Sarvāstivādins' solution, however, was not universally accepted, and the solution of the later Yogācāra does not help us to understand the early history of this school.

We know that the Buddhists cultivated the notion of a "series" or "uninterrupted succession" (*saṃtāna*). The so-called *uninterrupted succession of mind* (*citta-saṃtati* or *-saṃtāna*) often played the role of a "pseudo-self."[380] This uninterrupted succession of mind made it possible to explain the relation between actions and their fruits. The circumstance that, in Buddhism, actions, whether physical or not, always had a mental component, made this explanation all the more convincing.[381] Only the fruits of actions posed a problem, for they are not always mental. For instance, when a being is punished for past crimes in hell, his or her experiences are not only mental: the guardians of hell play an important role in these punishments.[382]

The *Abhidharmakośa* makes the following general statement: the diversity of the world is produced by actions.[383] How is it possible for actions to produce non-mental effects? This problem would at least partly be resolved if one could believe that "this [whole world] consisting of three spheres is mind only (*cittamātra*)," as the *Pratyutpanna-buddha-saṃmukhāvasthita-samādhi Sūtra* in the oldest known passage dealing with this topic puts it. This is also what Vasubandhu says in the commentary to his *Viṃśatikā*:

380 Conze 1962: 132.

381 Cf. Sanderson 1994.

382 This example is taken from Vasubandhu's *Viṃśatikā* (v. 4); Vasubandhu's commentary adds that these guardians of hell do not really exist. Cf. Frauwallner 1956a: 368; see also Mus 1939: 209–10.

383 Abhidh-k-bh(P) p. 192.5. Cf. Schmithausen 1987: 203 with 491n1301.

> You imagine that elements arise and change in a particular way for the inhabitants of hell due to their actions. The impression (*vāsanā*) of those actions attaches to their continuity of consciousness, not somewhere else. Why then do you not accept that where the impression is, its results appear as well, namely in a corresponding change of consciousness? Why do you think that its fruit could appear where the impression is not?[384]

It would be vain to try to choose between the various explanations we have considered. It is likely that they supported and strengthened each other. It is probably impossible to determine whether the idealism of the Yogācāra really arose from experiences of meditation (or ideas about such experiences) and was subsequently strengthened by reflections about the doctrine of "designation only," or the other way round, and we will not try to do so. The important point is that the idealistic doctrine of Yogācāra was not born in a vacuum. Here too, as is so often the case in the development of Buddhist doctrine, there is continuity with older ideas and practices.

Although it may no longer be possible to establish which role the doctrine of designation-only (*prajñaptimātra*) played in the development of the doctrine of making-known only (*vijñaptimātra*), it is possible, and even important, to mention the mutual relationship between these two doctrines in classical Yogācāra. This can be done by considering the doctrine of the triple nature, or the threefold constitution of things, to which we now turn.

The starting point of this doctrine is the two truths—limited truth (*saṃvṛtisatya*) and highest truth (*paramārthasatya*).[385] Limited truth, known also as "real in a limited sense" (*saṃvṛtisat*), is conditioned by

---

384 Commentary on *Viṃśatikā* verse 7 translated in accordance with Frauwallner 1956a: 370.

385 Cf. Nagao 1991: 61–62. Concerning the term *saṃvṛti*, Nagao believes that the two forms *saṃvṛti* and *saṃvṛtti* are used, the second being preferred by the Vijñānavādins; see pp. 13–14.

language, as we have repeatedly observed. In Yogācāra, the situation is somewhat more complicated than elsewhere in Buddhism. To put it briefly, in Yogācāra there is an additional level situated between the truth conditioned by language and the highest truth. As for other Buddhists, the truth conditioned by language is ultimately no truth at all. Rather, it is an imagined reality, which is properly speaking unreal. In the case of the Yogācāra school, this is the world of the objects that make up the phenomenal world. We imagine that these objects exist independently of our consciousness, but according to Yogācāra, this is not the case. For nothing exists except the act of making known.

The texts speak of the *imagined* (*parikalpita*) nature (*svabhāva*) or characteristic (*lakṣaṇa*) of things. This nature or characteristic is unreal, because the doctrine of making-known only (*vijñaptimātra*) recognizes no objects outside ourselves, only the act of making known. In other words, the dharmas that figure in the doctrine of conditioned origination (*pratītyasamutpāda*) and elsewere only condition the acts of making known and play no role in the objects of the phenomenal world, because these latter do not exist. In this context one speaks of the *dependent* (*paratantra*) nature or characteristic of things. This is not the highest truth, which the Yogācāras call the *perfected* (*pariniṣpanna*) nature or characteristic of things. The perfected nature of things is identical with the dependent nature except that it is free from any representations, which give rise to the belief that the imagined nature is real.

The doctrine of the triple constitution of things is already formulated in the *Saṃdhinirmocana Sūtra*. The following passages contain its most important tenets. Here the Buddha is speaking to the bodhisattva Guṇākara:

> The dharmas, Guṇākara, have three characteristics. Which are these three? The imagined characteristic (*parikalpitalakṣaṇa*), the dependent characteristic (*paratantralakṣaṇa*) and the perfected characteristic (*pariniṣpannalakṣaṇa*).
>
> What, Guṇākara, is the imagined characteristic of the dharmas? It is each establishment of a name and of a

convention for the dharmas according to essence or particularity, in order to designate them in everyday linguistic usage.

What, Guṇākara, is the dependent characteristic of the dharmas? It is the dependent origination of the dharmas, namely, when this exists, that comes into being, following the production of this, that arises, namely, depending on ignorance the conditioned factors arise—(here follows the whole series of elements of conditioned origination, up to)—and thus this great mass of suffering arises.

What, Guṇākara, is the perfected characteristic of the dharmas? It is the thusness (*tathatā*) of the dharmas. It is seen by bodhisattvas through their energy and correct observation, and through the realization of the practice of this vision. [This is] the realization of the highest perfect enlightenment.

[...]

As the association with color in the case of a clear crystal, Guṇākara, likewise we must consider, in the case of the dependent characteristic, its impregnation—belonging to the imagined characteristic—by linguistic usage. Just as the mistaken perception of the clear crystal as sapphire, ruby, emerald, or gold, similarly we must consider the mistaken assumption of the dependent characteristic as the imagined characteristic. As the clear crystal itself, so we must consider the dependent characteristic. Just as the clear crystal is not established stably and lastingly as a sapphire, ruby, emerald, or gold, and is unreal, just so we must consider the perfected characteristic, insofar as the dependent characteristic is not established stably and lastingly as the imagined characteristic and is unreal.

We can recognize the imagined characteristic, Guṇākara, if we base ourselves on the names linked with the images of the phenomenal world. We can recognize the dependent characteristic if we base ourselves on the conception of the

> dependent characteristic as imagined characteristic. And we can recognize the perfected characteristic if we base ourselves on the nonconception of the dependent characteristic as imagined characteristic.[386]

In this passage, the connection between imagined nature and designations is explicit. It speaks, for instance, of the impregnation of this nature by linguistic usage. Later, in Asaṅga's *Mahāyānasaṃgraha*, it is said that the seeds (*bīja*) of imagination (*parikalpa*) are the impressions of words (*abhilāpavāsanā*). Dependent own-nature (*paratantra svabhāva*), on the other hand, is the act of making-known only (*vijñaptimātra*); and acts of making known have no existing objects.[387]

Fundamental consciousness (*ālayavijñāna*), the act of making-known only (*vijñaptimātra*), and the triple nature of things are essential concepts of classical Yogācāra, which are accordingly abundantly discussed in Asaṅga's *Mahāyānasaṃgraha*.[388] This work also knows the concept of dharmakāya, but interprets it differently from the Tathāgatagarbha school. This latter school should perhaps be understood as a reaction against the Yogācāra interpretation of this concept.[389] Nevertheless, the dharmakāya of the Yogācāra school, too, seems to come close to the idea of a highest truth. This may be deduced from the attributes that the *Mahāyānasaṃgraha* assigns to it.[390] The dharmakāya is, for example, eternal (*nitya*), inconceivable (*acintya*), neither existing nor nonexisting, neither conditioned (*saṃskṛta*) nor unconditioned, not produced by actions (*karman*), neither many nor

---

386 Powers 1995: 81–82; cf. Frauwallner 1956a: 285–87. See further Saṃdhis(ÉLa) VI.3–10, pp. 60–63, 188–90.

387 Lamotte 1973a: II: 87–88, 99, 107, 108. Boquist (1993) attempts to present the development of the doctrine of the triple nature in different Yogācāra texts.

388 Lamotte 1973a: II: 12–152. Sakuma (1990) has dealt with another concept of the Yogācāra, namely, the transformation of the support (*āśrayaparivṛtti* or *-parāvṛtti*), which cannot be taken into account here. See also Schmithausen 1969b: 90–91n34.

389 So suggests John P. Keenan in Griffiths et al. 1989: 20–21. Concerning the influence of the Tathāgatagarbha school on Yogācāra, see also Keenan 1982.

390 Lamotte 1973a: 268–69; Griffiths et al. 1989: 49–50.

one. It can be reached through knowledge free from representations (*nirvikalpakajñāna*). This dharmakāya is the support (*āśraya*) of the various buddhas' bodies of enjoyment (*saṃbhogakāya*) and bodies of magical transformation (*nirmāṇakāya*). Together these three bodies (*kāya*) are the main constituents of the so-called *doctrine of the three bodies* of the Yogācāra school, a topic we will not cover further in this volume but which has nonetheless played a central role in Mahāyāna Buddhist teachings.

The Logico-Epistemological School

Buddhist teaching as we have examined it so far had much to say about the nature of reality. Quite early, the reality of the phenomenal world had come to be denied. Only the dharmas really exist according to the ancient systematizers. The reality of these dharmas, too, was subsequently subjected to doubt, especially by Mahāyāna thinkers. Some of them went so far as to claim that in reality nothing exists at all. They even believed that they could logically prove this. Others claimed that our experience is mind-only, or making-known only, and came close to denying external reality. It seems that with Dignāga, who was active around the beginning of the sixth century, a change took place that allowed Buddhism to successfully combine various threads of its history. This change is expressed in Dignāga's main work, the "Collection of Valid Means of Knowledge," *Pramāṇasamuccaya*.

It is almost certain that Dignāga did not deny the existence of external reality.[391] This does not mean that he accepted the existence of the dharmas, as the adepts of the Śrāvakayāna did. According to Dignāga, external reality is the object of perception (*pratyakṣa*). It is also completely indescribable, for the very essence of perception is that it is free from representations (*kalpanā*).[392] The object of perception is the "own-characteristic" (*svalakṣaṇa*) of things. It is opposed to the reality described by words, which concerns the general characteristic (*sāmānya-*

391 Katsura 1991: 138n42.

392 Prs 1.3; Hattori 1968: 25.

lakṣaṇa).[393] Perception, then, concerns external reality, while the reality described by words concerns representations found in the mind. The latter also applies to the reality reached by inference.[394] The realm of language and logic is therefore that of the general characteristic; it has a mental nature. The two realms—the realm of the own-characteristic and the realm of the general characteristic—are completely different from each other and do not overlap, according to Dignāga.

In this binary division, we may recognize the division between a highest reality and a reality conditioned by language that we met while discussing the Śrāvakayāna. What is missing in Dignāga is a description of external reality in terms of the dharma theory. This means that Dignāga's external reality, unlike the dharma theory, is immune to Nāgārjuna's criticism. With Dignāga, Buddhism is once again in a position in which external reality can have its place without this time being endangered by Nāgārjuna's arguments and those of his school.

What about the realm of the general characteristic? This realm consists of representations in the mind. It does not therefore belong to external reality. Dignāga might have asserted, without running into difficulties, that it is nothing but a delusion without internal structure. Moreover, he might have defended the opinion that the realm of language and logic is subject to the contradictions brought to light by Nāgārjuna. But he did not do so. On the contrary, he developed a theory concerning the relationship between words and things—or, better, between language and reality—that permanently protects the reality that is conditioned by language against Nāgārjuna's attacks. This is the so-called *apoha* theory, which was perhaps not exclusively invented for this reason, but which nonetheless annihilated once and for all the threat posed by the Mādhyamikas' destructive arguments.

We know that Nāgārjuna's main arguments are based on the conviction that there is a close parallel between words and things. The words found in the proposition "Nāgārjuna writes a book" should, each of them, correspond to a thing or event in the situation described. But the

393 PrsV 1.2; Hattori 1968: 24–25.

394 See Frauwallner 1959: 103–4 (779–80).

book does not exist while it is being written, and therefore this proposition poses a problem, at least to Nāgārjuna and his disciples. This problem can, however, be solved in two different ways: either by admitting that the book somehow already exists before coming into existence; or by refusing to accept that the word "book" designates the concrete book that is being written.

The Sarvāstivādins did indeed believe that objects already exist before coming into existence. Certain Brahmanical thinkers, especially those belonging to the schools of Sāṃkhya and Yoga, followed the Sarvāstivādins in this respect. For them, Nāgārjuna's attacks were therefore no real problem. Other non-Buddhists who were confronted with Nāgārjuna's challenge proposed various solutions that have one point in common, namely, that words do not exclusively designate individual objects.[395] In this context, the Naiyāyikas' point of view was particularly important. They believed that words designate species (*jāti*); more precisely, that words can designate individual things (*vyakti*), forms (*ākṛti*), and species (*jāti*). According to this theory, the word *book* in the proposition "Nāgārjuna writes a book" already designates something before the book has come into existence, for the species exists already before the individual book comes into being. The Naiyāyikas, and all of those who shared this view, could therefore stick to the premise that the words that occur in a proposition each correspond to a thing or event that are part of the situation described. For according to the Naiyāyikas, species are things, too. This solution was not acceptable to the Buddhists, because they had no place for species in their ontology. Thus, those Buddhists who did not share the Sarvāstivādins' point of view still feared Nāgārjuna's challenge.

This is where the *apoha* theory finally brought relief. The *apoha* theory made it possible to explain the denotation of words in such a way that all the advantages of the assumption of species could be used, but without having to accept their existence. This was of course a revolutionary change in a tradition which had always taken for granted that words correspond to something, even if not necessarily to individual

395 See Bronkhorst 1996.

things. According to Dignāga, words no longer correspond to something, not even to something that is only real in a limited sense. There is simply nothing that corresponds to words. And yet, denotation takes place in such a manner that it looks as if there were species.

How does Dignāga manage to develop and support such a theory? Note here that Dignāga was a competent logician, who made an important contribution to this field. In logic the following rule applies: In a correct inference the consequence must be present where the reason is present, and where the consequence is not present, the reason is not present either. Dignāga had, as a matter of fact, been the first in India to formulate this insight clearly.[396] An example will elucidate what it is about. The statement "There is fire on the mountain because there is smoke" is the traditional example of a correct inference. It is correct, because wherever there is smoke, there is fire, too. The opposite is not always true: there can be fire without smoke. But where there is no fire, there is certainly no smoke either. This last observation shows that a correct inference necessarily involves exclusion. For instance, it says something about all objects that are without fire, and about all objects that are without smoke, namely, "where there is no fire there is no smoke." The collection of all objects without fire is a subgroup of the collection of all objects without smoke.

Dignāga now claims that denotation takes place in a way that is similar, or even identical, to inference. A word—for instance *book*—refers to a great number of objects, namely, to all books. It is not always possible to establish the precise relationship between the word and all these objects. What is certain is that whatever is *not* a book is *not* connected with the word *book*.[397] From this point of view, denotation is exclusion (*apoha*). The word *book* does not designate all books: rather, it excludes all *non*-books.

Denotation as exclusion explains without difficulty how expressions

396 See Frauwallner 1957: 29 (744); 1959: 85–86 (761–62).

397 Frauwallner 1959: 100–101 (776–77); Hayes 1988: 297–98. The Naiyāyika Uddyotakara's criticism of the doctrine of *apoha* also contains a summary of Dignāga's point of view; see Much 1994.

like "white lotus" can be used. The two words *white* and *lotus* do not designate two objects. On the contrary, together they designate one object, namely a white lotus, or as the case may be, all white lotuses. But a white lotus is not a combination of everything that is white and everything that is lotus. Rather, the word *white* excludes everything that is not white, and the word *lotus* excludes everything that is not a lotus. What remains after this double exclusion is a white lotus, or, as the case may be, all white lotuses. Note further that since the two words *white* and *lotus* in the expression "white lotus" designate together one single object, they do not in this case designate anything on their own.[398]

This way of understanding the relationship between words and things—which was new for the Buddhists—had important consequences. Previously words had been linked to individual objects, and on this basis it had been impossible to say much about the structure of reality as conditioned by language. This situation now changes drastically. In the *apoha* theory, different words no longer simply stand next to each other on the same level. A clear hierarchy is established among words, and therefore also among the things conditioned by words. To put it differently, the world conditioned by words has a structure. Consider the word *śiṃśapā*. It designates a tree of a certain species, or, according to the *apoha* theory, it excludes all objects that are not *śiṃśapā* trees. By a similar process of exclusion, the word *tree* designates a collection of objects that includes all *śiṃśapā* trees. Thus the word *tree* is hierachically superior to the word *śiṃśapā*. It is, on the other hand, inferior to the word earthen (i.e., made of earth), for all trees are earthen, but not all earthen things are trees. *Earthen* is in its turn subordinated to the word *substance*, and so on. In this way a pyramidal structure develops.

On the top of this pyramid the all-encompassing concept *knowable* (*jñeya*) is found. The knowable is either existent (*sat*) or nonexistent (*asat*). Not much can be said about the nonexistent. The existent, on the other hand, is said to be of three kinds: it is substance (*dravya*), property (*guṇa*), or activity (*karman*). We shall not go into the further

398 Prs + PrsV 5.14–20; Hayes 1988: 278–79.

subdivisions of these three categories. Suffice it to say that for Dignāga the structure of reality, which can be grasped by words, displays a great similarity with the structure of the Brahmanical system of Vaiśeṣika. In both cases, the existent is first divided into substances, properties, and activities.[399] This is not surprising in itself, for both Dignāga and the Vaiśeṣika system follow the model of language—i.e., the Sanskrit language—to systematize reality.[400] And the Sanskrit language contains primarily substantives, adjectives, and verbs, to which substances, properties, and activities correspond.[401]

If we now summarize Dignāga's understanding of reality, we must note that he preserves the two traditional "levels" of Buddhism; for him, too, there is a highest reality and an apparent reality. Highest reality cannot be described by words and is only accessible through perception. Apparent reality, on the other hand, cannot only be described by language, it is conditioned by it. But neither highest reality nor apparent reality are contradictory in themselves. Apparent reality obtains in this way internal coherence; and highest reality is free from contradictions for the simple reason that nothing can be said about it.

It can, however, be perceived. It seems as if this pure perception, unconnected with representation, was a goal to be pursued. Dignāga does not explicitly say so. He only mentions the yogins' perception, which is free from representation (*vikalpa*).[402] It is likely that for Dignāga this pure perception constituted liberating insight, just as perception without representation was liberating insight for other adepts of Mahāyāna, as we have seen. This perception—and strictly speaking it is the only perception there is—cannot have a false object, for false objects are only mistakes of the mind.[403]

---

399 Katsura 1979; 1991: 131–32.

400 See Bronkhorst 1992a.

401 PrsV 1.3 also distinguishes, apart from substantives, adjectives and verbs, proper nouns and "substance-words" (*dravyaśabda*); the latter designate things or people that are characterized by a substance, as for example "carrying a stick" (*daṇḍin*).

402 Prs + PrsV 1.6; Hattori 1968: 27, 94–95; cf. Steinkellner 1978.

403 Prs + PrsV 1.17; Hattori 1968: 36, 122.

Why does Dignāga not explain in his *Pramāṇasamuccaya* how to reach liberation? This is probably to be accounted for by his purpose, which was not to write a religious but rather a logico-epistemological work. In his introduction, he states that the aim of his book is to refute other theories in this field and to display his own theory.[404] He does not say what the knowledge it describes is good for, presumably because this would have been obvious to every Buddhist.

With Dignāga, Buddhism reached a new phase in its development. An advanced logic and theory of knowledge made it possible to renew traditional ideas and to develop a refined ontology. This development did not end with Dignāga. Other Buddhist and non-Buddhist thinkers continued to discuss, criticize, and develop his ideas. For our purposes here, it suffices to say that the fundamental ingredients of these later developments were already present in Dignāga's work.

404 PrsV 1.1; Hattori 1968: 23–24.

4. Final Observations

THE PRECEDING PRESENTATION of Buddhist teaching in India is not exhaustive. Many thinkers and ideas are not dealt with. The third vehicle after the Śrāvakayāna (or Hīnayāna) and the Mahāyāna, namely, the Mantrayāna or Vajrayāna that constitutes tantric Buddhism, has been left out altogether. All that can be said here about this third vehicle is that it differs from the earlier forms of Buddhism by its frequent use of magical formulas and rites. In spite of this, the continuity that links this new vehicle with the forms of Buddhism we have studied is undeniable. The magical power of the bodhisattvas, for example, played a role in Mahāyāna and was rooted in the idea that "the true nature of dharmas is illusory." The use and potency of magical formulas is also easy to understand if we remember that for most Buddhists the phenomenal world is a reflection of language. As a result, power can be obtained over the phenomenal world through language. Similar ideas were prevalent in India outside Buddhism.[405]

Some points remain to be discussed in this final chapter. These are: (1) Buddhist hermeneutics, (2) the influence of Buddhism on other, non-Buddhist developments in India, and (3) some important landmarks in the developments described here.

405 Sanderson (1994a) shows how certain developments in Vajrayāna were directly borrowed from a non-Buddhist (Śaiva) tradition; cf. also Strickmann 1996: 22–23 and *passim* (index s.v. Śiva, śivaïsme).

Hermeneutics

The development of Buddhist teaching in India was not one-dimensional. Indeed, it would be hard to imagine greater differences than those between certain ideas and practices common in Mahāyāna and those that characterize Abhidharma Buddhism. Both, in their turn, are radically different from the teachings of the historical Buddha. Nevertheless, they are all forms of Buddhism. All the conceptions and ideas that we have discussed, and all the spiritual practices connected with them, are supposedly based on the words of the Buddha. How did the Buddhists explain this variety based on a shared claim?

There could only be one explanation. Obviously certain Buddhists had not correctly understood the words of the Buddha. Understanding them correctly was of the greatest significance. This concern gave rise to the development of hermeneutics, of a method of interpretation.

According to the older tradition, the words of the Buddha were established in various councils that were held after the Buddha's death. The word *council* is used in modern research; the Indian word—*saṅgīti* or *saṅgāyanā*—means "common recitation," emphasizing the aspect of establishing the words of the Buddha:[406] the words of the Buddha were established in the memory of the monks through common recitation. There could be no question of writing them down, at least not in the earlier days, for no script was used in India at that time.[407]

In spite of these councils, no agreement was reached as to which texts could and could not be ascribed to the Buddha. The disagreement began during the first council, supposedly held in Rājagṛha shortly after the Buddha's demise, where a monk called Purāṇa did not join the council because he preferred to remember the words of the Buddha as he had heard and marked them: "Well recited, sirs, was the doctrine and the discipline by the older monks. However, I

406 Bechert 1985–87: I: 25; Hinüber 1989: 26. On the councils, see Bareau 1958; Frauwallner 1958; Prebish 1974. The word *saṅgīti* was also applied to "councils" without common recitation; see Hallisey 1991.

407 See Hinüber 1989; Falk 1993.

will remember [these two] exactly as I heard them and received them directly from the mouth of the Exalted One."[408] Nor do the accounts of the first council agree as to what exactly was recited. Some say that the *Vinaya-piṭaka* and the *Sūtra-piṭaka* were recited. Others add to these the *Abhidharma-piṭaka*. Many modern scholars doubt that this council was ever held.

The old *Mahāparinirvāṇa Sūtra* attributes to the Buddha rules for examining the authenticity of texts and thus for their acceptance as his teaching. If a monk claims that he has heard the teaching or the discipline in this or that form from the Buddha himself, from a community of monks, from many or only one learned monk, this should neither be accepted without proof nor rejected; in such a case, one must find out whether the opinions presented agree with the sūtra in terms of doctrine, and whether they agree exactly—perhaps what is meant is "word for word"—with the Vinaya.[409]

These rules did not solve all problems. In later times, especially after the rise of Mahāyāna, a plethora of new texts appeared that were accepted by many Buddhists as the authentic words of the Buddha. The words attributed to the Buddha in this manner do not always agree with each other. If one accepts all of these texts as authentic, some will have to be interpreted in roundabout ways so as to avoid contradictions. One statement attributed to the Buddha does indeed allow one to proceed in this manner. According to this statement four rules should be observed:[410] One must rely upon the doctrine, not on the person; upon the meaning, not on the sound; upon a discourse that can be taken literally (*nītārtha*), not on one that must be interpreted (*neyārtha*); upon direct cognition (*jñāna*), not on discursive cognition (*vijñāna*). Inevitably these rules were often used to prove that one's own opinion was correct. The belief that the Buddha had pronounced certain discourses which needed interpretation (*neyārtha*) and others which were to be taken literally (*nītārtha*) was particularly helpful for those who wished

408 Hinüber 1989: 26.

409 Lamotte 1947; Bareau 1970: 222–23; Hinüber 1989: 27–28.

410 This is the so-called *Catuḥpratisaraṇa Sūtra*. Cf. Lamotte 1949.

to justify their own convictions. The question of *which* sayings need interpretation and *which* are to be taken literally predictably led to differences of opinion. The rule according to which one must rely upon direct cognition probably favored Mahāyāna Buddhism.

The Buddhists, then, had a double strategy to deal with the multiplicity of teachings that were attributed to the Buddha. First of all there were rules that were meant to distinguish between authentic and spurious discourses. Second, the authentic discourses had to be sifted, too: some were to be taken literally, others had to be "interpreted." In spite of this double strategy, differences of opinion between Buddhists did not disappear. The adepts of the Śrāvakayāna criticized the new Mahāyāna discourses, and the adepts of Mahāyāna tried to answer these criticisms.[411] Words of the Buddha that had so far been taken literally were subjected to new interpretations: the texts that corresponded to one's own doctrine were taken literally, all the others were seen as needing interpretation.[412]

One question could not be circumvented: Why did the Buddha bother to express himself in words that need interpretation and cannot be taken at their face value? To answer this question, the Buddhists made use of the concept of "skill in means" (*upāyakauśalya*).[413] Skill in means was soon recognized by Mahāyāna as one of the perfections (*pāramitā*) that a bodhisattva must seek to attain, and that a buddha possesses. Through skill in means, a buddha encourages people to seek enlightenment.

And different people need different means. A well-known parable from the *Lotus Sūtra* tells of a rich man who owns a big house with a

411 See Cabezón 1992.

412 This circumstance, even more than the difference between highest truth (*paramārthasatya*) and limited truth (*saṃvṛtisatya*), is probably responsible for the legend attested in Europe around 1800, according to which the Buddha, shortly before his death, took back all that he had said so far, explaining that he had only meant it as a parable and subsequently only taught emptiness; Droit 1997: 96–97.

413 See Pye 1978.

single door.[414] One day, while this rich man's children are playing with their toys inside, the house catches fire. When their father calls them, the children do not come out. Now the father uses skill in means if, on the basis of his knowledge of his children's tastes, he entices them to leave the house with the promise of particularly enchanting toys. In reality, he does not have these toys, but he gives them something much more valuable. The aim is to save the children. It is noteworthy that the father promises his children different types of carts, but that in the end he gives them all big carts, big vehicles (*mahāyāna*). The comparison with the three vehicles (*yāna*) of Buddhism is clear. In this comparison, Mahāyāna is represented as the best, or even as the only vehicle.[415]

Influences outside Buddhism

We have seen that Indian Buddhism cannot be rightly understood without taking into account non-Buddhist religious and intellectual currents. This is true for the early development of Buddhism, which was strongly influenced by Jainism and related movements, as well as by the idea that knowledge of the self was essential to attain liberation. Later on, the Sarvāstivāda school may have been influenced in a decisive manner by the Greek culture prevalent in northwest India, especially by its tradition of debate. In this section, we look at further interactions with other movements and the ways these may have spurred new developments in Indian Buddhism.

Buddhism was not always merely at the receiving end in this exchange of ideas and practices. With the constant growth of its importance in India, Buddhism itself started to exert an influence on other movements. In the course of the centuries, this happened in various fields. Sometimes it directly concerned Buddhist doctrine and praxis. Influences in other fields, such as the arts and literature, cannot be dealt with here. Suffice to say that Buddhism left its mark on the most important Brahmanical philosophies as well as on the practice of yoga. Attempts

414 Saddharmap(V) pp. 51–52; German translation in Glasenapp 1983: 135–36.

415 Fujita 1975.

to prove that Buddhism was already known to late Vedic literature are not always convincing.[416]

The Sarvāstivāda tendency to systematize found resonance within as well as outside Buddhism. Indeed, several thinkers tackled the question as to how to use the Sarvāstivādins' method without adopting the details of their doctrine.[417] This means that they tried to develop alternative doctrines that were systematically thought through. Others thought that the Sarvāstivādins' rationality only led to absurdities, and that one should turn away from it, or point out its absurdity. In these cases we are dealing with reactions to the doctrine, or rather the method, of the Sarvāstivādins. Thirdly, there were thinkers who simply borrowed their ideas. Influence of these kinds can be felt inside as well as outside Buddhism.

We find some early traces of Buddhist influence in the *Mahābhārata*.[418] One of its verses declares—with respect to the manifested (*vyakta*) of Sāṃkhya—that, being connected with the four characteristics (*lakṣaṇa*), it is born, grows, becomes old, and dies. The unmanifested (*avyakta*) is without them.[419] Both from the point of view of terminology and content, this may be compared with the Sarvāstivādins' four characteristics of the conditioned (*saṃskṛtalakṣaṇa*). The necessity to know all the names of the unmanifested in order to reach liberation may be an epic reformulation of the Buddhist conviction that one cannot put an end to suffering as long as there remains even a single dharma

416 It is possible that Buddhism influenced the *Maitrāyaṇīya Upaniṣad*; Bronkhorst 1993: 49, with references. Gombrich (1992: 173; 1992a: 213–14) has tried to show that the *Baudhāyana Dharmasūtra* refers to Buddhists; Tsuchida (1996) proposes a different interpretation of the same passage. According to Vetter (1996: 54n20) one cannot completely rule out that *Bṛhadāraṇyaka Upaniṣad* 4.4.6–7, which represents desire as the cause for rebirth, was composed under the influence of the oldest form of Buddhism.

417 One must consider that many of the borrowings to be discussed here come with certainty from Sarvāstivāda, and that all earlier examples *could* come from this school.

418 Lindtner (1995a) seeks to prove that Mahāyāna influenced the *Bhagavadgītā*.

419 Mhbh 12.228.29.

that is not known and correctly understood.[420] The *Mahābhārata* also knows the expression *avipraṇāśa* ("non-destruction") in connection with the theory of karma. *Avipraṇāśa* was sometimes used in Buddhism as a synonym of *avijñapti* ("non-information").[421] A clearer but still implicit reference to Buddhism is found in the *Śāntiparvan* of the *Mahābhārata* where it speaks of a fourfold *dhyānayoga*. This recalls the four stages of meditation (*dhyāna*) of Buddhism. And indeed, the goal that must be reached is called nirvāṇa, also in this passage of the *Mahābhārata*. The first stage of meditation (the only one described) contains reflection (*vicāra*) and deliberation (*vitarka*), as well as joy (*sukha*), exactly as in Buddhism.[422]

The earliest trace of borrowing of a Buddhist idea by a non-Buddhist may perhaps be found in the *Mahābhāṣya*, Patañjali's "Great Commentary." This is a commentary on Pāṇini's famous grammar and belongs to the Brahmanical tradition. As such, it has nothing to do with Buddhism, and accordingly it does not even mention that religion. The *Mahābhāṣya* was probably composed in northwest India.[423] As we know, this is also the region where the Sarvāstivādins had settled.[424]

There are several reasons to believe that Patañjali underwent the influence of Buddhism, which we considered in chapter 2. The Sarvāstivādins, as we have seen, introduced some linguistic dharmas in the context of their systematization called Pañcavastuka. These are: the word body (*nāmakāya*), the sentence body (*padakāya*), and the sound body (*vyañjanakāya*). The Sarvāstivādins' ontological preoccupations induced them to accept these dharmas in their system. These dharmas, like all the other conditioned (*saṃskṛta*) dharmas, were momentary.

Patañjali's *Mahābhāṣya* does not share the Sarvāstivādins' interest in

420 Mhbh 14.39.24; cf. also Mhbh 12.210.35.

421 Mhbh 15.42.4; Bronkhorst 1987: 67.

422 Mhbh 12.188.1–2; cf. Bronkhorst 1987: 68–69.

423 Cardona (1976: 269–70) repeats Bhandarkar's argument to the extent that Patañjali lived to the northwest of Sāketa (= Ayodhyā)—perhaps in the vicinity of Mathurā?

424 Cf. Lamotte 1958: 578. It is not ruled out that the Greek king Menander also ruled in Mathurā; cf. Fussman 1993: 91 (with note 61), 111ff.

ontological matters. Rather, the aim of his work is to discuss problems relating to Pāṇini's grammar and, whenever possible, to solve them. Thus Patañjali continues, and enlarges upon, Pāṇini's work. Nevertheless, we find considerable differences between these two thinkers. One such difference concerns the question of which parts of language are the real conveyers of meaning. According to Pāṇini, this role is fulfilled by nominal stems, verbal roots, and suffixes, in other words, by the grammatical components of words. Only a small step is needed to conclude from this that the meanings attached to words and sentences are secondary, and are deduced from the primary meanings, which belong to their parts. These ideas fit in with what we know about the linguistic ideas of those days. It is therefore all the more surprising to see that Patañjali defends the opposite view that *words* are the real conveyers of meaning. According to him, the meanings of nominal stems, verbal roots, and suffixes are secondary and can only be deduced from the meanings of words.

This difference between Pāṇini and Patañjali is fundamental and requires an explanation. Furthermore, as we have remarked above, ontological questions played no role with the grammarians. This is also true of Patañjali's disquisitions. However, some passages in his *Mahābhāṣya* reveal that for him sounds and words are truly existing things that, moreover, are eternal. Here, too, a question arises: how do we explain Patañjali's ontological interest?

Both these problems can easily be solved if we suppose that Patañjali was directly or indirectly influenced by the Sarvāstivādins. For the latters' linguistic dharmas concern sounds and words,[425] whereas nominal stems, verbal roots, and suffixes hold no interest for them. Furthermore, ontological problems are central to Sarvāstivāda. The fact that the Sarvāstivādins' linguistic dharmas are momentary, whereas Patañjali's sounds and words are eternal, is not very significant: according to the Buddhists, virtually everything is momentary, and Patañjali was not in the least bound to share the Buddhists' doctrine

425 It seems that initially the Sarvāstivādins accepted only two linguistic dharmas; see Bronkhorst 1987: 61–62.

of momentariness, even if he borrowed some of their ideas.[426] Patañjali's ontological reflections are the starting point of a development in Indian philosophy that became known as the *sphoṭa* theory. Its central concepts are quite similar to the Buddhist word body, sentence body, and sound body. In other words, the *sphoṭa* theory drew its ultimate inspiration from Sarvāstivāda.

There are further indications that strengthen the supposition that Patañjali was directly or indirectly acquainted with the doctrines and texts of the Sarvāstivādins. They cannot be dealt with at present.[427] If Patañjali were indeed influenced by the Sarvāstivādins (and there is no reason to doubt this), it is possible to establish the date of their systematizing activities. For their linguistic dharmas are part of the Pañcavastuka, without which they would have no place in the dharma theory. It is therefore likely that the Pañcavastuka had already been invented at the time of Patañjali. Patañjali's date is known. He wrote in the middle of the second century BCE.[428] Accordingly, the Pañcavastuka must have existed as early as the second century BCE.

In the case of the Brahmanical system called Vaiśeṣika, too, Buddhist influence must be postulated. The oldest texts of Vaiśeṣika do not mention Buddhism. Any conclusions as to Buddhist influence can therefore only be reached on the basis of deep similarities. Such similarities exist.[429] In order to understand this, recall the following. First, the Sarvāstivādins, and many other Buddhists with them, claimed to present an exhaustive enumeration of everything that exists in the world. This inventory existed in the form of a list of dharmas. The dharmas being all that exists, their exhaustive enumeration is an enumeration of everything that exists. Closely connected with this first claim, their second claim is that composite things do not really exist. This could

426 Kātyāyana, the author of the so-called vārttikas contained in the *Mahābhāṣya*, seems to share Patañjali's interest for the real conveyers of meaning but not his ontological positions. Kātyāyana lived during or after the reign of Emperor Aśoka, perhaps around 200 BCE; see Scharfe 1971.

427 Bronkhorst 1994; 1994b: 317–18.

428 Cardona 1976: 263–66.

429 Bronkhorst 1992a.

hardly be otherwise, for composite things are not dharmas. A third point concerns the relationship between language and what is believed to be reality: the chariot does not exist, but the word *chariot* is used when the constituent parts of a chariot are assembled. In this way, language explains how we believe that composite objects exist at all.

These three points characterized the thought of many Buddhists in those days. Momentariness and the doctrine of atoms should be added to these, positions that the Sarvāstivādins took great pains to systematize and elaborate, as we have seen.

All of the points here mentioned recur in Vaiśeṣika. Its main characteristic is certainly its advanced rationality, which at times does not hesitate to adopt risky doctrinal positions if internal consistency demands it. As explained above, this rational attitude appeared perhaps for the first time in India in Sarvāstivāda thought. It is possible that the Vaiśeṣika borrowed it directly or indirectly from that school.

Let us now examine more closely the above-mentioned points. The Buddhists had an exhaustive enumeration of everything that exists. The Vaiśeṣikas established one, too.[430] Their list had to be different from the Buddhist list of dharmas because the Vaiśeṣikas did not agree with the Buddhists' second point—that there are no composite things. The Vaiśeṣikas claimed the opposite: composite things exist and are not identical with their component parts. A pot, for example, really exists and is different from its two halves. This opinion made it impossible to agree with the Buddhists' third point. According to the Buddhists, our false belief in the existence of composite things is caused by the words of language. The Vaiśeṣikas turned this round, and assumed that *reality itself* is conditioned by language, i.e., that it corresponds to language. This also means that it is possible to draw conclusions about reality from linguistic data.

The doctrine of atoms is an essential part of Vaiśeṣika. Their atoms

430 Halbfass (1995: 85) describes the system as follows: "Classical Vaiśeṣika is a comprehensive attempt to enumerate and to classify everything that exists in the world, and to arrange it according to certain fundamental categories...i.e., substance...quality...etc."

had no spatial extension. This was the position accepted by the Sarvāstivādins, too. The Vaiśeṣikas also have a doctrine of momentariness, which is visible in their treatment of mental events. The Vaiśeṣikas likewise considered it impossible for two mental events to take place simultaneously in one and the same person, a belief held also by the Sarvāstivādins and later adopted by other Buddhists. Thus, despite many differences, the Vaiśeṣika system resembles the Buddhist system.[431] This similarity allows us to understand Vaiśeṣika as a reaction against Buddhism, and more precisely, against the Sarvāstivāda system of thought. The subsequent development of Vaiśeṣika, now combined with the school of Nyāya, is characterized by further interaction with Buddhism.[432]

Regarding Nāgārjuna's influence outside the sphere of Buddhism, the situation is less clear and has not been sufficiently studied to date. Nevertheless, we can make the following observations. Sarvāstivāda, as we noted earlier, was immune to Nāgārjuna's main attacks, because, according to the doctrine that gave it its name, objects already exist before they come into being. A similar doctrine is found in the Brahmanical system called Sāṃkhya. It became known under the name "doctrine of the effect (*kārya*) already existing (*sat*) in the cause" (*satkāryavāda*). This doctrine appeared relatively late: we meet it for the first time in Āryadeva, who was perhaps Nāgārjuna's younger contemporary. Moreover, it does not seem to fit the oldest form of Sāṃkhya that we know of.[433] It is therefore justified to wonder "whether *satkārya* itself was not perhaps only an aspect of a discussion with Mādhyamika Buddhists."[434] It may not be possible to prove this. It is possible that both Nāgārjuna and the Sāṃkhya system reacted to a problem that already existed before Nāgārjuna. It is, however, more likely that this problem—resting as it does on the hypothesis that words and things are closely correlated—ultimately had a Buddhist origin.

431 For a more detailed presentation of the classical Vaiśeṣika system, see Frauwallner 1956: 197–247; also Bronkhorst 1992a.

432 For this topic, see, e.g., Shastri 1964. For discussions between the Buddhists and other Brahmanical schools, see Kher 1992.

433 For details, see Bronkhorst 1994b: 315–16.

434 Liebenthal 1934: 9n11.

The preoccupation with this set of problems during an important part of the first millennium can be traced in the writings of all Brahmanical systems of thought, and even in Jainism. These discussions had a profound, sometimes decisive, influence on the classical shapes of the Brahmanical schools.[435]

From the time of Nāgārjuna onward, texts belonging to various systems of thought began to discuss the opinions of others. Their main aims were to defend their own positions and to show that their opponents' views were incorrect. But the unavoidable side effect of such discussions was that the schools increasingly influenced each other. A good example is the development of logic, which came into existence as a result of the constant exchange of ideas, mainly between Buddhist and Brahmanical thinkers.

The influence of Mahāyāna Buddhism on the Vedānta philosophy—especially on Advaita Vedānta—is interesting. Vedānta philosophy is primarily based on the Vedic Upaniṣads. Indeed, the term *Vedānta* means "end of the Veda" and designates the Upaniṣads. However, the relevant Upaniṣads were composed before the Common Era, whereas Vedānta philosophy became important only late—later than most of the other principal Indian philosophies.

The thinker Bhartṛhari may have considered himself to be a Vedāntin. In his major work, the *Vākyapadīya*, he quotes at one point the opinion of the *trayyantavedin* "the knowers of the end of the triple [knowledge]," i.e., "the knowers of the Upaniṣads," and there are indications that he may perhaps be quoting his own opinion.[436] Bhartṛhari's thought betrays in many ways the influence of Buddhism. Like the Buddhists, he starts with the premise that there is a close correspondence between words and things. He goes so far as to claim that the mere existence of the words *heaven* and *god* allows us to conclude that heaven and god exist.[437] Like the Buddhists, Bhartṛhari believed that

435 For details on the different positions, see Bronkhorst 1996; 1999.

436 Vkp 3.3.72. Cf. Houben 1995: 292–93; Bronkhorst 1996a: 126.

437 Bronkhorst 1996a: 128. The following observations are likewise based on this article and on Bronkhorst 1992. See also Nakamura 1972; 1973; 1981: 145.

the phenomenal world ultimately does not exist. More precisely, he believed that everything has a real and an unreal side. The real side of things is identical with the highest reality, the totality of all that exists. This highest reality is divided, by the words of language, into the things that make up the phenomenal world. Here Bhartṛhari diverges from Buddhist thinking, which does not accept that any composite things really exist. But the role of language is comparable. In both cases, *words* give to the objects of the phenomenal world a semblance of reality.

The *Āgamaśāstra*, attributed to a certain Gauḍapāda, belongs to the oldest texts of Advaita Vedānta. The influence of Mahāyāna is very clear in this case. The fourth chapter of this work, for example, was written either by a Buddhist or by a Vedāntin who was strongly influenced by Buddhism.[438]

It is not yet clear to what extent the great Śaṅkara was influenced by Buddhism.[439] Other Vedāntins leveled this accusation against him. Rāmānuja called him a crypto-Buddhist (*pracchanna-bauddha*).[440] Śaṅkara's connection with Gauḍapāda is emphasized by tradition and confirmed by a commentary on the *Āgamaśāstra* that was perhaps composed by him. Since Śaṅkara is very critical of Buddhism, it is unlikely that he borrowed much from it directly. But an indirect influence—through Gauḍapāda or other authors—cannot be ruled out.

We have already discussed some verses of the *Mahābhārata* that betray Buddhist influence on yoga. Buddhist influence on the more recent form of yoga that we call *classical yoga* was recognized long ago by modern scholarship.[441] Recall that the oldest form of yoga consisted of ascetic practices that put great emphasis on physical and mental immobility. These practices constituted a path leading to liberation different from the path of knowledge (*sāṃkhya*). This preclassical yoga influenced

---

438 Bhattacharya 1943; Vetter 1978; King 1989; 1995a; 1995b.

439 For a short description of this controversy, see Potter 1981: 20–21 and 604 notes 29–31.

440 Isayeva 1993: 14, with a reference to *Śrībhāṣya* 2.2.27. Also the *Padma Purāṇa* and Vijñānabhikṣu on *Sāṃkhya Sūtra* 1.22 use the expression in this context; Garbe 1917: 101n2.

441 La Vallée Poussin 1936–37: 223–42; Bronkhorst 1993: 68–77; Yamashita 1994.

Buddhism at an early date. Conversely, by accepting and adapting certain ideas and practices from Buddhism, preclassical yoga was able to develop its classical form, embodied in the *Yoga Sūtra* and the *Yoga Bhāṣya*.[442] In this process, Buddhism contributed the following. Preclassical, non-Buddhist yoga aimed at physical and mental immobility. The Buddhists had borrowed this interest in immobility—especially mental immobility—quite early in their history, but they did not believe that it was sufficient for reaching the highest goal. There was the additional requirement to destroy certain mental impurities; the Buddhist texts speak of taints (*āsrava*), but also of attachments (*anuśaya*), impressions (*vāsanā*), seeds (*bīja*), or intentions (*āśaya*), and sometimes of conditioned factors (*saṃskāra*). This requirement found a place in the *Yoga Sūtra*, and all the above-mentioned terms, with the exception of *āsrava*, are used in that text.[443] Concretely, this means that under the influence of Buddhism, yoga no longer exclusively sought to suppress the mind, but also—and this was new—sought to attain a lasting transformation of the mind by destroying these volitional processes.

Apart from this essential contribution of Buddhism to classical yoga, the *Yoga Sūtra* contains other parallels to Buddhist practice and theory. Among them, the four concentrations in YS 1.17—which, from the points of view of content and terminology, can be shown to be parallels of the Buddhist four stages of meditation (*dhyāna*)—the four immeasurables (*apramāṇa*) (YS 1.33), and the five faculties (*indriya*) or five strengths (*bala*) (YS 1.20). All of these were borrowed from Buddhism.

Landmarks

To conclude, let us briefly recount a few particularly important landmarks in the development of Indian Buddhism.

---

442 The *Yoga Sūtra* is mostly attributed to a certain Patañjali, and the *Yoga Bhāṣya* to a certain Vyāsa. But this is a late tradition; other testimonies attribute to Patañjali both the sūtra and the *bhāṣya*. See Bronkhorst 1984.

443 See Meisig 1988.

Buddhism originated within the so-called *śramaṇa* movement.[444] It shared various characteristics with other currents belonging to this movement, especially the belief in the cycle of rebirths conditioned by actions and the search for liberation. But Buddhism occupied a *special position* within this movement. Its understanding of what constitute actions, as well as the method it preached, are different from the actions and methods accepted by those other currents. The connection between method and liberation from the cycle of rebirths, in particular, was less obvious in Buddhism than it was in the other currents. As a result, the Buddhists were, practically from the beginning, searching for the correct method, and could sometimes not resist the attraction of the methods propounded by their competitors.

Then there is the role played by the doctrine of not-self in Buddhism. Initially it implied no more than the denial of insight into the true nature of the self as an essential element of the road leading to liberation. The idea of not-self subsequently developed into one of the fundamental dogmas of Buddhism. It gave rise to the doctrine of the nonexistence of composite things. The ultimate constituent elements, the dharmas, became in this way the only things that really exist, and the dharma theory developed into an ontology. Subsequently a further step was taken, and the existence of the dharmas themselves came to be denied; this time, too, a justification could readily be found in the doctrine of not-self.

The belief in the nonexistence of composite things gave rise to reflections on the *relationship between words and things*. Our everyday conviction that composite things, including ourselves, really exist, can be explained by linguistic usage. A chariot does not really exist; it is nothing but a word. Nāgārjuna went a step further, including also propositions in these reflections. This allowed him not only to assert, but also to prove, that phenomenal reality does not really exist.

This last development could take place because something new had become part of Buddhism—a tradition of *rationality*. This term is here used to refer to the readiness (and obligation) to discuss with people

444 I now prefer to speak of the culture of Greater Magadha; see Bronkhorst 2007.

who think otherwise. It is possible that this tradition arose as a result of contacts with the Greeks who lived in the northwestern part of the subcontinent. It soon spread throughout South Asia and came to characterize the subsequent development not only of Buddhist thought but also of Indian philosophy in general.

The last element to be mentioned is the constant interest of Buddhist thinkers for *meditative practice*. This does not necessarily mean that many of them really practiced meditation, but that ideas about such experiences often conditioned their conception of reality. Already in canonical times, Buddhist cosmology posited three levels of reality that were distinguished from each other on the basis of mental states. Later developments—such as Yogācāra idealism—were probably inspired, at least in part, by similar reflections.

The interplay of these and other factors gave Indian Buddhism its richness in doctrines and ideas. These doctrines and ideas exerted a deep influence on non-Buddhists in India. Classical Indian philosophy might never have come into existence without Buddhism, and certainly not in the way it did, and classical yoga, not itself Buddhist, was strongly influenced by Buddhism. Scholars have long asserted Buddhism's great debt to the other religious traditions of the subcontinent. However, the classical flourishing of Vedānta, Yoga, and brahmanical philosophy and practice in general owes at least as much to Buddhism as the other way around.

During its first millennium, Buddhism was a dynamic tradition that developed a great diversity of contemplative methods, soteriological aims, and ontological commitments. Much of the evidence for the roots and precise trajectories of these developments is lost to time. But by patient analysis of the extant texts of both the early Buddhists and their contemporaries, we can begin to piece together the story of how the teachings of the Buddha were passed down to succeeding generations, and how each new development bequeathed insights and complications that those who came after sought to work out. The early ascetic liberation ideal was shaped subsequently by the knowledge tradition, rationality and logic, linguistic theory, and tantra before disappearing in its birthplace by the fourteenth century. But echoes of these early debates and developments have continued to play out beyond India's borders up to the present. Some might see the presence of such persistent doctrinal fault lines as troubling, but the intellectual, creative, and contemplative output they have inspired over many hundreds of years has unquestionably enriched human civilization.

Abbreviations

The abbreviations agree, to the extent possible, with those enumerated in the *Abkürzungsverzeichnis zur buddhistischen Literatur in Indien und Südostasien, insbesondere zu den Veröffentlichungen der Kommission für buddhistische Studien der Akademie der Wissenschaften in Göttingen*, edited by Heinz Bechert (Göttingen: Vorabdruck, 1988).

AAWG	*Abhandlungen der Akademie der Wissenschaften in Göttingen*, Phil.-Hist. Kl.
AAWL	*Abhandlungen der Akademie der Wissenschaften und der Literatur*, Mainz, Geistes- und Sozialwissenschaftliche Klasse
Abhidh-avat(V)	*Abhidharmāvatāraśāstra*, see van Velthem 1977
Abhidh-hṛ(A)	*Abhidharmahṛdayaśāstra*, see Armelin 1978
Abhidh-k(VP)	*Abhidharmakośa*, tr. La Vallée Poussin 1923–31
Abhidh-k-bh(D)	*Abhidharmakośa and Bhāṣya of Ācārya Vasubandhu with Sphuṭārthā Commentary of Ācārya Yaśomitra*, pts. 1–4, ed. Swami Dwarikadas Shastri, Varanasi, 1970–73 (BBhS 5,6,7,9)
Abhidh-k-bh(Hi)	= Hirakawa 1973–78

Abhidh-k-bh(P)	Vasubandhu, *Abhidharmakośabhāṣya*, ed. P. Pradhan, rev. 2nd ed. Aruna Haldar, Patna, 1975 (TSWS 8)
Abhidh-k-bh(Pā)	= Pāsādika 1989
ABORI	*Annals of the Bhandarkar Oriental Research Institute*, Poona
ADAW	*Abhandlungen der Deutschen Akademie der Wissenschaften zu Berlin*, Klasse für Sprachen, Literatur und Kunst
AdSP(Conze)	Edward Conze (ed. and tr.), *The Gilgit Manuscript of the Aṣṭādaśasāhasrikā-prajñāpāramitā*, chapters 55 to 70, chapters 70 to 82, Roma, 1962, 1974 (SOR XXVI, XLVI)
ALB	*The Brahmavidyā*, Adyar Library Bulletin, Madras
Amṛtar(B)	= van den Broeck 1977
AN	*Aṅguttara-Nikāya*, ed. R. Morris, E. Hardy, 5 vols., London 1885–1900 (PTS); vol. 6: Indexes, by M. Hunt and C.A.F. Rhys Davids, London, 1910 (PTS)
ANISt	Alt- und Neu-Indische Studien, Hamburg
ArchOr	*Archiv Orientální*, Praha
AS	*Asiatische Studien, Études Asiatiques*, Bern
ASP(Vaidya)	*Aṣṭasāhasrikā Prajñāpāramitā*, ed. P. L. Vaidya, Darbhanga, 1960 (BST 4)
Bd.	Band
BEFEO	*Bulletin de l'École Française d'Extrême-Orient*, Paris

BEI	*Bulletin d'Études Indiennes*, Paris
BF	*The Buddhist Forum*, London: School of Oriental and African Studies, 1990ff.
BK	*Bukkyō Kenkyū*, Buddhist Studies, Hamamatsu
BM	*Bibliothèque du Muséon*, Louvain
BSOAS	*Bulletin of the School of Oriental and African Studies*, University of London, London
BSR	*Buddhist Studies Review*, London
BST	*Buddhist Sanskrit Texts*, Darbhanga
CPD	*A Critical Pāli Dictionary*, begun by V. Trenckner, ed. D. Anderson, H. Smith, H. Hendriksen, vol. I, Copenhagen, 1924–48, vol. II (fasc. 1ff.), Copenhagen, 1960ff.
CPS	*Catuṣpariṣatsūtra*, ed. Waldschmidt 1952–62
Daśo	*Daśottarasūtra*, see Mittal 1957–62
DaśoE(Trip)	= Tripāṭhī 1968
Dhsk	*Dharmaskandha*, ed. Dietz 1984
DN	*Dīghanikāya*, ed. T. W. Rhys Davids, J. E. Carpenter, 3 vols. 1890–1911 (PTS)
EĀ	*Ekottarāgama* (= TI 125)
EB	*The Eastern Buddhist*, Kyōto
EIP	*The Encyclopedia of Indian Philosophies*, ed. Karl H. Potter, Delhi, 1970ff.
FBI	*Freiburger Beiträge zur Indologie*, Wiesbaden
Festschr.	Festschrift
GDhp	*The Gāndhārī Dharmapada*, ed. Brough 1962

Hôbôgirin	Hôbôgirin, *Dictionnaire encyclopédique du bouddhisme d'après les sources chinoises et japonaises*, ed. S. Lévi, J. Takakusu, P. Demiéville, J. May. Fasc. 1ff., Tôkyô, Paris, 1929ff.
HOS	Harvard Oriental Series, Cambridge, MA
IBK	Indogaku Bukkyōgaku Kenkyū, *Journal of Indian and Buddhist Studies*, Tōkyō
IIJ	*Indo-Iranian Journal*, Den Haag, Dordrecht
IsMEO	Istituto Italiano per il Medio ed Estremo Oriente
JA	*Journal Asiatique*, Paris
JAOS	*Journal of the American Oriental Society*, New Haven
JB	*Jaiminīya Brāhmaṇa*
Jg.	Jahrgang
JGJKSV	*Journal of the Ganganatha Jha Kendriya Sanskrit Vidyapeetha*, Allahabad
JIABS	*Journal of the International Association of Buddhist Studies*
JIP	*Journal of Indian Philosophy*, Dordrecht
JORM	*Journal of Oriental Research*, Madras
JPTS	*Journal of the Pali Text Society*, London
JRAS	*Journal of the Royal Asiatic Society of Great Britain and Ireland*, London
KlSchr	*Kleine Schriften* [in der Serie der Glasenapp-Stiftung], Wiesbaden, Stuttgart
KP	*Kāśyapaparivarta*, ed. Alexander von Staël-Holstein, Shanghai, 1926

KZ	*Zeitschrift für vergleichende Sprachforschung auf dem Gebiet der Indogermanischen Sprachen*, begründet von A. Kuhn, Göttingen
Laṅkāv(V)	(*Saddharma)laṅkāvatārasūtra*, ed. P. L. Vaidya, Darbhanga, 1963 (BST 3)
LOS	*London Oriental Series*, London
MĀ	*Madhyamāgama* (= TI 26)
MadhK(deJ)	Nāgārjuna, *Mūlamadhyamakakārikāḥ*, ed. J. W. de Jong, The Adyar Library and Research Centre, Madras, 1977
MCB	*Mélanges chinois et bouddhiques*, Bruxelles
Mhbh	*Mahābhārata*, crit. ed. V. S. Sukthankar u.a., Poona, 1933–41 (BORI)
Mil	*Milindapañha*, ed. V. Trenckner, London, 1880
MN	*Majjhima-Nikāya*, ed. V. Trenckner, R. Chalmers, 3 vols., London, 1888–99 (PTS)
MPS	*Mahāparinirvāṇasūtra*, ed. Waldschmidt 1950–51
MSS	*Münchener Studien zur Sprachwissenschaft*, München
Mvu	*Mahāvastu-Avadāna*, ed. Émile Senart, 3 vols., Paris, 1882–97
MW	Monier Monier-Williams, *A Sanskrit-English Dictionary*, Oxford, 1899
NAWG	*Nachrichten der Akademie der Wissenschaften in Göttingen*, Phil.-Hist. Kl., Göttingen
NDPS	*Nālandā Devanāgarī Pāli Series*, Nālandā

ÖAW	Österreichische Akademie der Wissenschaften, Wien
OLZ	*Orientalistische Literaturzeitung*, Berlin
ORT	*Orientalia Rheno-Traiectina*, Leiden
Pa.	Pāli
PDhp	*Patna-Dharmapada*, in Roth 1980
PEFEO	*Publications de l'École Française d'Extrême-Orient*, Paris
PEW	*Philosophy East and West*, Hawaii
PIOL	*Publications de l'Institut Orientaliste de Louvain*, Louvain
Prak(Im)	= Imanishi 1977
Prs	Dignāga, *Pramāṇasamuccaya*
PrsV	Dignāga, *Pramāṇasamuccayavṛtti*
PTS	Pali Text Society, London
PW	Otto Böhtlingk, Rudolph Roth, *Sanskrit-Wörterbuch*, 7 Bde., St. Petersburg, 1855–75
RHR	*Revue de l'Histoire des Religions*, Paris
RM	*Religionen der Menschheit*, Stuttgart
RO	*Rocznik Orjentalistyczny*, Kraków, Lwów, Warszawa
RSO	*Rivista di Studi Orientali*, Roma
SĀ	*Saṃyuktāgama* (= TI 99)
Saddharmap(V)	*Saddharmapuṇḍarīkasūtra*, ed. P. L. Vaidya, Darbhanga, 1960 (BST 6)

Saṃdhis(ÉLa)	*Saṃdhinirmocanasūtra*, ed. and tr. Lamotte 1935
Saṅg	*Saṅgītisūtra and Saṅgītiparyāya*, ed. Stache-Rosen 1968
SaṅgE	= Waldschmidt 1955
SAWW	Sitzungsberichte der Akademie der Wissenschaften in Wien, Phil.-hist. Kl., Wien
Skt.	Sanskrit
SN	*Saṃyutta-Nikāya*, ed. L. Feer, 5 vols., London, 1884–98 (PTS), vol. 6 (Indexes by C. A. F. Rhys Davids), London, 1904 (PTS)
SOR	*Serie Orientale Roma*, Roma
SSAI	*Schriftenreihe des Südasien-Instituts der Universität Heidelberg*, Wiesbaden, Stuttgart
StII	*Studien zur Indologie und Iranistik*
StPhB	*Studia Philologica Buddhica*, Tokyo
STT	*Sanskrittexte aus den Turfanfunden*, Teil 1–9, Berlin, 1955–68; Teil 10ff., Göttingen, 1965ff.
SUNY	State University of New York
SWTF	*Sanskrit-Wörterbuch der buddhistischen Texte aus den Turfan-Funden*, begonnen von Ernst Waldschmidt, ed. Heinz Bechert, bearb. Georg von Simson und Michael Schmidt, Göttingen, 1973ff.
Symp	*Symposien zur Buddhismusforschung*, Göttingen [erschienen in AAWG]
TASJ	*Transactions of the Asiatic Society of Japan*, Yokohama and Tokyo

TCTL	*Ta chih tu lun* (*Mahāprajñāpāramitopadeśa*), TI 1509
TI	*Taishō Shinshū Daizōkyō oder Taishō Issaikyō*, 100 vols., Tōkyō, 1924ff.
TSWS	*Tibetan Sanskrit Works Series*, Patna
Ud	*Udāna*, ed. P. Steinthal, London, 1885 (PTS)
Uv	*Udānavarga*, ed. Bernhard 1965–68
Vikn	*Vimalakīrtinirdeśa*, tr. Lamotte 1962
Vin	*Vinayapiṭaka*, ed. H. Oldenberg, 5 vols., London, 1879–83 (PTS)
Vism(W)	Buddhaghosa, *Visuddhimagga*, ed. H. C. Warren, revised by Dharmananda Kosambi, Cambridge, MA, 1950 (HOS 41)
Vkp	Bhartṛhari, *Vākyapadīya*, ed. W. Rau, Wiesbaden, 1977
VKSKS	*Veröffentlichungen der Kommission für Sprachen und Kulturen Südasiens*, ÖAW, Wien
WI	*Word Index to the Praśastapādabhāṣya: A complete word index to the printed editions of the Praśastapādabhāṣya*, by Johannes Bronkhorst and Yves Ramseier, Delhi, 1994
WZKS	*Wiener Zeitschrift für die Kunde Südasiens*, Wien
WZKSO	*Wiener Zeitschrift für die Kunde Süd- und Ostasiens*, Wien
ZDMG	*Zeitschrift der Deutschen Morgenländischen Gesellschaft*, Leipzig, later Wiesbaden
ZMR	*Zeischrift für Missionswissenschaft und Religionswissenschaft*, Münster

Bibliography

Anacker, Stefan. 1984. *Seven Works of Vasubandhu, the Buddhist Psychological Doctor.* Delhi: Motilal Banarsidass.

Anesaki, M. 1908. "Some Problems of the Textual History of the Buddhist Scriptures." TASJ 35, 81–96.

Armelin, I., trans. 1978. *Le coeur de la loi suprême, Traité de Fa-cheng: Abhidharmahṛdayaśāstra de Dharmaśrī.* Paris: Librairie orientaliste P. Geuthner.

Avi-Yonah, Michael. 1978. *Hellenism and the East.* Published for the Institute of Languages, Literature and the Arts, The Hebrew University, Jerusalem, by University Microfilms International.

Bareau, André. 1951. *Dhammasaṅgaṇi.* Paris: Centre de Documentation Universitaire.

———. 1955. *Les sectes bouddhiques du Petit Véhicule.* Saigon. (PEFEO 38.)

———. 1957. "Les controverses relatives à la nature de l'arhant dans le bouddhisme ancien." IIJ 1, 241–50.

———. 1958. *Les premiers conciles bouddhiques.* Paris: Presses Universitaires de France.

———. 1962. *Bouddha.* Paris: Seghers.

———. 1963. *Recherches sur la biographie du Buddha dans les Sūtrapiṭaka et les Vinayapiṭaka anciens: de la quête de l'éveil à la conversion de Śāriputra et de Maudgalyāyana.* Paris: École Française d'Extrême-Orient.

———. 1964. "Der indische Buddhismus." *Die Religionen Indiens*, Bd. 3, pp. 1–213. Stuttgart. (RM 13.)

———. 1970. *Recherches sur la biographie du Buddha dans les Sūtrapiṭaka et les Vinayapiṭaka anciens: II. Les derniers mois, le Parinirvāṇa et les funérailles*, vol. I. Paris: École Française d'Extrême-Orient.

———. 1971. *Recherches sur la biographie du Buddha dans les Sūtrapiṭaka et les Vinayapiṭaka anciens: II. Les derniers mois, le Parinirvāṇa et les funérailles*, vol. II. Paris: École Française d'Extrême-Orient.

Basham, A. L. 1981. "The Evolution of the Concept of the Bodhisattva." In *The Bodhisattva Doctrine in Buddhism*, edited and introduced by Leslie S. Kawamura, 19–59. Waterloo, Ontario: Wilfrid Laurier University Press.

Bechert, Heinz. 1963. "Zur Frühgeschichte des Mahāyāna-Buddhismus." ZDMG 113, 530–35.

———, ed. 1980. *Die Sprache der ältesten buddhistischen Überlieferung / The Language of the Earliest Buddhist Tradition.* (Symp II.) Göttingen. (AAWG 117.)

———, ed. 1985–87. *Zur Schulzugehörigkeit von Werken der Hīnayāna Literatur.* 2 vols. (Symp III,1,2.) Göttingen. (AAWG 149.)

———, ed. 1991, 1992, 1997. *The Dating of the Historical Buddha / Die Datierung des historischen Buddha.* 3 vols. Göttingen: Vandenhoeck & Ruprecht. (Symp IV.)

Beck, Hermann. 1916. *Buddha und seine Lehre.* Reprint: Verlag Freies Geistesleben Stuttgart, 1958.

Bernhard, Franz. 1965–68. *Udānavarga.* 2 vols. Göttingen. (STT 10; AAWG 54.)

———. 1968. "Zur Interpretation der Pratītyasamutpāda-Formel." WZKS 12–13 (Festschr. Erich Frauwallner), 53–63.

Beyer, Stephan. 1977. "Notes on the Vision Quest in Early Mahāyāna." = Lancaster 1977: 329–40.

Bhattacharya, Kamaleswar. 1973. *L'Atman-Brahman dans le bouddhisme ancien.* Paris: Adrien-Maisonneuve.

———. 1985. "Nāgārjuna's Arguments against Motion." JIABS 8(1), 7–15.

Bhattacharya, Vidhushekhara, ed., trans., and ann. 1943. *The Āgamaśāstra of Gauḍapāda.* Reprint Delhi: Motilal Banarsidass, 1989, with a new foreword by Christian Lindtner.

Bodewitz, H. W. 1973. *Jaiminīya Brāhmaṇa I, 1–65*. Leiden: E. J. Brill.
———. 1990. *The Jyotiṣṭoma Ritual: Jaiminīya Brāhmaṇa I, 66–364*. Leiden: E. J. Brill.
Bodhi, Bhikkhu, trans. 2000. *The Connected Discourses of the Buddha: A Translation of the Saṃyutta Nikāya*. Boston: Wisdom Publications.
———, ed. 2005. *In the Buddha Words: An Anthology of Discourses from the Pāli Canon*. Boston: Wisdom Publications.
Bollée, Willem B. 1977. *Studien zum Sūyagaḍa: Die Jainas und die anderen Weltanschauungen vor der Zeitwende*. Wiesbaden: Franz Steiner. (SSAI Bd. 24.)
Bopearachchi, Osmund. 1990. "Ménandre Sôter, un roi indo-grec: observations chronologiques et géographiques." *Studia Iranica* 19(1), 39–85.
Boquist, Åke. 1993. *Trisvabhāva: A Study of the Development of the Three-Nature Theory in Yogācāra Buddhism*. Lund: Department of History of Religions. (Lund Studies in African and Asian Religions, 8.)
Braarvig, Jens. 1993. *Akṣayamatinirdeśasūtra*. Vol. I: Edition of extant manuscripts with an index. Vol. II: The tradition of imperishability in Buddhist thought. Oslo: Solum Forlag.
Bronkhorst, Johannes. 1984. "*Akālika* in the Buddhist Canon." StII 10, 187–90.
———. 1984a. "Patañjali and the Yoga Sūtras." StII 10, 191–212.
———. 1985. "Dharma and Abhidharma." BSOAS 48, 305–20.
———. 1987. *Three Problems Pertaining to the Mahābhāṣya*. Poona: Bhandarkar Oriental Research Institute. (Post-graduate and Research Department Series, 30.)
———. 1992. "Études sur Bhartṛhari, 4: L'absolu dans le Vākyapadīya et son lien avec le Madhyamaka." AS 46(1), 56–80.
———. 1992a. "Quelques axiomes du Vaiśeṣika." *Les Cahiers de Philosophie* 14 ("L'Orient de la pensée"), 95–110.
———. 1993. *The Two Traditions of Meditation in Ancient India*. Improved edition. Delhi: Motilal Banarsidass.
———. 1993a. *The Two Sources of Indian Asceticism*. Bern: Peter Lang.

———. 1993b. "Kathāvatthu and Vijñāyakāya." *Premier colloque Étienne Lamotte (Bruxelles et Liège 24–27 septembre 1989).* Louvain-la-Neuve: Institut Orientaliste, 57–61. (Publications de l'Institut Orientaliste de Louvain, 42.)

———. 1993c. "Mysticisme et rationalité en Inde: le cas du Vaiśeṣika." AS 47, 559–69.

———. 1994. "A Note on Patañjali and the Buddhists." ABORI 75, 247–54.

———. 1994a. "A Note on Zero and the Numerical Place-Value System in Ancient India." AS 48(4), 1039–42.

———. 1994b. "The Qualities of Sāṅkhya." WZKS 38 (Festschr. G. Oberhammer), 309–22.

———. 1995. "The Buddha and the Jainas Reconsidered." AS 49(2), 333–50.

———. 1995a. Review of Rospatt 1995. AS 49(2), 513–19.

———. 1996. "The Correspondence Principle and Its Impact on Indian Philosophy." *Indo-Shisōshi Kenkyū / Studies in the History of Indian Thought* (Kyoto) 8, 1–19.

———. 1996a. "Sanskrit and Reality: The Buddhist Contribution." *Ideology and Status of Sanskrit: Contributions to the History of the Sanskrit Language.* Edited by Jan E. M. Houben, 109–35. Leiden: E. J. Brill.

———. 1997. "Nāgārjuna's Logic." In *Bauddhavidyāsudhākaraḥ: Studies in Honour of Heinz Bechert on the Occasion of His 65th Birthday*, edited by Petra Kieffer-Pülz and Jens-Uwe Hartmann, 29–37. Swisttal-Odendorf: Indica et Tibetica Verlag (IndTib 30).

———. 1998. "Language, Indian Theories of." In *Routledge Encyclopedia of Philosophy*, edited by Edward Craig, vol. 5, 379–84. London and New York: Routledge.

———. 1998a. "Patañjali (c. 2nd century BC)." *Routledge Encyclopedia of Philosophy*, edited by Edward Craig, vol. 7, 248–50. London and New York: Routledge.

———. 1999. *Langage et réalité: sur un épisode de la pensée indienne.* Turnhout: Brepols. (Bibliothèque de l'École des Hautes Études, Sciences Religieuses, 105.)

———. 2007. *Greater Magadha: Studies in the Culture of Early India*. Leiden: Brill. (Handbook of Oriental Studies, Section 2 South Asia, 19.)

Brough, John. 1962. *The Gāndhārī Dharmapada*. London: Oxford University Press. (LOS 7.)

Brown, Brian Edward. 1991. *The Buddha Nature: A Study of the Tathāgatagarbha and Ālayavijñāna*. Delhi: Motilal Banarsidass.

Buswell, Robert E., and Robert M. Gimello. 1992. *Paths to Liberation: The Mārga and Its Transformation in Buddhist Thought*. Honolulu: Kuroda Institute, University of Hawaii. (Studies in East Asian Buddhism, 7.)

Buswell, Robert E., and Padmanabh S. Jaini. 1996. "The Development of Abhidharma Philosophy." EIP 7, 73–119.

Cabezón, José Ignacio. 1992. "Vasubandhu's *Vyākhyāyukti* on the Authenticity of the Mahāyāna Sūtras." In *Texts in Context: Traditional Hermeneutics in South Asia*, edited by Jeffrey R. Timm, 221–43. Albany: SUNY Press.

Cardona, George. 1976. *Pāṇini: A Survey of Research*. The Hague: Mouton. (Trends of Linguistics, State-of-the-Art Reports, 6.)

Cohen, Richard S. 1995. "Discontented Categories: Hīnayāna and Mahāyāna in Indian Buddhist History." *Journal of the American Academy of Religion* 63(1), 1–25.

Collins, Steven. 1982. "Self and Non-self in Early Buddhism." *Numen* 29(2), 250–71.

———. 1982a. *Selfless Persons: Imagery and Thought in Theravāda Buddhism*. Cambridge: Cambridge University Press.

Conze, Edward. 1958. *The Perfection of Wisdom in Eight Thousand Slokas*. Calcutta: The Asiatic Society.

———. 1962. *Buddhist Thought in India: Three Phases of Buddhist Philosophy*. London: Allen & Unwin.

———. 1974. *Buddhism: Its Essence and Development*. Second paperback edition. Oxford: Bruno Cassirer.

Cousins, L. S. 1991. "The 'Five Points' and the Origins of the Buddhist Schools." BF 2, 27–60.

———. 1994. "Person and Self." *Buddhism into the Year 2000:*

International Conference Proceedings. Bangkok, Los Angeles: Dhammakaya Foundation, 15–31.

Cox, Collett. 1988. "On the Possibility of a Nonexistent Object of Consciousness: Sarvāstivādin and Dārṣṭāntika theories." JIABS 11(1), 31–87.

———. 1992. "Mindfulness and Memory: The Scope of *Smṛti* from Early Buddhism to the Sarvāstivādin Abhidharma." = Gyatso 1992: 67–108.

———. 1992a. "The Unbroken Treatise: Scripture and Argument in Early Buddhist Scholasticism." In *Innovation in Religious Traditions: Essays in the Interpretation of Religious Change*, edited by Michael A. Williams, Collett Cox, and Martin S. Jaffee, 143–89. Berlin, New York: Mouton De Gruyter. (Religion and Society, 31.)

———. 1992b. "Attainment through Abandonment: The Sarvāstivādin Path of Removing Defilements." = Buswell and Gimello 1992: 63–105.

———. 1995. *Disputed Dharmas: Early Buddhist Theories on Existence. An annotated translation of the section on factors dissociated from thought from Saṅghabhadra's Nyāyānusāra*. Tokyo: The International Institute for Buddhist Studies. (StPhB Monograph Series, XI.)

Crangle, Edward Fitzpatrick. 1994. *The Origin and Development of Early Indian Contemplative Practices*. Wiesbaden: Harrassowitz. (Studies in Oriental Religions, 29.)

Daffinà, Paolo. 1987. "Senso del tempo e senso della storia: computi cronologici e storicizzazione del tempo." RSO 61(1–4), 1–71.

Dayal, Har. 1932. *The Bodhisattva Doctrine in Buddhist Sanskrit Literature*. Reprint: Delhi: Motilal Banarsidass, 1970.

de Jong, J. W. 1966. "The Daśottarasūtra." In *Essays in Indology and Buddhology in Honor of Dr. Yenshô Kanakura*, 3–25. Kyoto: Heirakuji Shoten.

———. 1976. *A Brief History of Buddhist Studies in Europe and America*. Varanasi: Bharat-Bharati.

———. 1991. "Buddhist Studies (1984–90)." *Chūō gakujutsu kenkyū sho kiyō* 20.

———. 1996. Review of Nolot 1995. BSOAS 59(2), 382–83.

Deleanu, Florin. 1993. "Mahāyānist Elements in Chinese Translations of Śrāvakayānist Yogācārabhūmi Texts." Unpublished lecture delivred at 34th ICANAS, August 1993.

Demiéville, Paul. 1924. "Les versions chinoises du Milindapañha (I)." BEFEO 24, 1–258.

Dessein, Bart. 1996. "Dharmas Associated with Awareness and the Dating of Sarvāstivāda Abhidharma Works." AS 50(3), 623–51.

———. 1999. *Saṃyuktābhidharmahṛdaya: Heart of Scholasticism with Miscellaneous Additions*. 3 parts. Delhi: Motilal Banarsidass. (Buddhist Tradition Series, 33, 34, 35.)

Dietz, Siglinde. 1984. *Fragmente des Dharmaskandha: Ein Abhidharma-Text in Sanskrit aus Gilgit*. Göttingen. (AAWG 142.)

Droit, Roger-Pol. 1997. *Le culte du néant: les philosophes et le Bouddha*. Paris: Seuil.

Durt, Hubert. 1991. "Bodhisattva and Layman in the Early Mahāyāna." *Japanese Religions* 16(3), 1–16.

———. 1994. "Daijô." Hôbôgirin 7, 767–801.

Dutoit, Julius. 1906. *Das Leben des Buddha*. München, Neubiberg: Oskar Schloss.

Dutt, Nalinaksha. 1939. *Gilgit Manuscripts*, vol. 1. Srinagar-Kashmir.

Edgerton, Franklin. 1924. "The Meaning of Sāṅkhya and Yoga." *American Journal of Philology* 45, 1–46.

———. 1959. "Did the Buddha Have a System of Metaphysics?" JAOS 79, 81–85.

———. 1965. *The Beginnings of Indian Philosophy: Selections from the Rig Veda, Atharva Veda, Upaniṣads, and Mahābhārata*, translated from the Sanskrit with an introduction, notes and glossarial index. London: Allen & Unwin.

Eliade, Mircea. 1951. *Le chamanisme et les techniques archaïques de l'extase*. Paris: Payot.

Falk, Harry. 1988. "Vedische Opfer im Pali-Kanon." BEI 6, 225–54.

———. 1993. *Schrift im alten Indien: Ein Forschungsbericht mit Anmerkungen*. Tübingen: Gunter Narr. (ScriptOralia 56.)

Féer, M. 1870. "Études bouddhiques: les quatre vérités et la prédication de Bénarès (Dharma-cakra-pravartanam)." JA Sixième Série, 15, 345–472.

Forman, Robert K. C. 1990. *The Problem of Pure Consciousness: Mysticism and Philosophy*. Oxford University Press.

Forte, Antonino. 1995. *The Hostage An Shigao and His Offspring: An Iranian Family in China*. Kyoto: Istituto Italiano di Cultura, Scuola di Studi sull'Asia Orientale. (Italian School of East Asian Studies, Occasional Papers 6.)

Franke, R. Otto. 1913. *Dīghanikāya: Das Buch der langen Texte des buddhistischen Kanons in Auswahl übersetzt*. Göttingen: Vandenhoeck & Ruprecht.

Frauwallner, Erich. 1951. "Amalavijñānam und Ālayavijñānam: Ein Beitrag zur Erkenntnislehre des Buddhismus." *Beiträge zur indischen Philologie und Altertumskunde: Walther Schubring zum 70. Geburtstag dargebracht*, 148–59. Hamburg: De Gruyter. (ANISt 7.) (= KlSchr pp. 637–48.)

———. 1953, 1956. *Geschichte der indischen Philosophie*. 2 vols. Salzburg: Otto Müller.

———. 1956a. *Die Philosophie des Buddhismus*. Berlin: Akademie-Verlag.

———. 1956b. *The Earliest Vinaya and the Beginnings of Buddhist Literature*. Roma. (SOR III.)

———. 1957. "Vasubandhu's Vādavidhiḥ." WZKSO 1, 104–46. (= KlSchr pp. 716–58.)

———. 1958. "Die buddhistischen Konzile." ZDMG 102, 240–61. (= KlSchr pp. 649–70.)

———. 1959. "Dignāga, sein Werk und seine Entwicklung." WZKSO 3, 83–165. (= KlSchr pp. 759–841.)

———. 1963. "Abhidharma-Studien, I." WZKSO 7, 20–36.

———. 1964. "Abhidharma-Studien, II." WZKSO 8, 59–99.

———. 1971. "Abhidharma-Studien, III." WZKS 15, 69–102.

———. 1971a. "Die Entstehung der buddhistischen Systeme." NAWG 1971, 113–27.

———. 1971–72. "Abhidharma-Studien, IV." WZKS 15, 103–21; 16, 95–152.

———. 1973. "Abhidharma-Studien, V." WZKS 17, 97–121.

———. 1973a. *History of Indian Philosophy Vol. I: The Philosophy of the Veda and of the Epic—the Buddha and the Jina—the Sāmkhya and the Classical Yoga System*. Translated by V. M. Bedekar. Delhi: Motilal Banarsidass.

———. 1995. *Studies in Abhidharma Literature and the Origins of Buddhist Philosophical Systems*. Translated from the German by Sophie Francis Kidd under the supervision of Ernst Steinkellner. Albany: SUNY Press.

Freeman, C. E. 1991. "*Saṃvṛti*, *Vyavahāra* and *Paramārtha* in the Akṣayamatinirdeśa and Its Commentary by Vasubandhu." BF 2, 97–114.

Fujita, Kōtatsu. 1975. "One Vehicle or Three?" JIP 3, 79–166.

Fussman, Gérard. 1993. "L'indo-grec Ménandre ou Paul Demiéville revisité." JA 281(1–2), 61–137.

———. 1996. "Histoire du monde indien, cours: les Saddharmapuṇḍarīka sanskrits." *Annuaire du Collège de France 1995–1996: Résumé des cours et travaux, 96e année*, 779–86. Paris.

Garbe, Richard. 1917. *Die Sâṃkhya-Philosophie. Eine Darstellung des indischen Rationalismus*. Zweite umgearbeitete Auflage. Leipzig: H. Haessel.

Gethin, R. M. L. 1992. *The Buddhist Path to Awakening: A Study of the Bodhi-Pakkhiyā Dhammā*. Leiden: E. J. Brill. (Brill's Indological Library, 7.)

Glasenapp, Helmuth von. 1938. "Zur Geschichte der buddhistischen Dharma-Theorie." ZDMG 92 (N.F. 17), 383–420. Reprint: Glasenapp 1962: 47–80.

———. 1960. "Hat Buddha ein metaphysisches System gelehrt?" *Paideuma: Mitteilungen zur Kulturkunde*, 7, 235–40. Reprinted in Glasenapp 1962: 38–46.

———. 1962. *Von Buddha zu Gandhi, Aufsätze zur Geschichte der Religionen Indiens*. Wiesbaden: Otto Harrassowitz.

———. 1983. *Pfad zur Erleuchtung: Das Kleine, das Grosse und das Diamant-Fahrzeug*. Reprint: Eugen Diederichs Verlag, Köln.

Gombrich, Richard. 1988. *Theravāda Buddhism.* London and New York: Routledge & Kegan Paul.

———. 1988a. "How the Mahāyāna Began." *Journal of Pali and Buddhist Studies* (Nagoya) 1, 29–46. (Reprint: BF 1 (1990), 21–30.)

———. 1990. "Recovering the Buddha's Message." = Ruegg and Schmithausen 1992: 5–23. (Reprint: BF 1 (1990), 5–20.)

———. 1992. "The Buddha's Book of Genesis?" IIJ 35, 159–78.

———. 1992a. "Why Is a Khattiya Called Khattiya? The Agañña Sutta revisited." JPTS 17, 213–14.

———. 1994. "The Buddha and the Jains," AS 48(4), 1069–96.

———. 1996. *How Buddhism Began: The Conditioned Genesis of the Early Teachings.* London: Athlone. (1994 Jordan Lectures.)

Gómez, Luis O. 1976. "Proto-Mādhyamika in the Pali Canon." PEW 26(2), 137–65.

———. 1977. "The Bodhisattva as Wonder-Worker." = Lancaster 1977: 221–61.

Gómez, Luis O. and Jonathan A. Silk, eds. 1989. *Studies in the Literature of the Great Vehicle: Three Mahāyāna Buddhist Texts.* Ann Arbor: Collegiate Institute for the Study of Buddhist Literature and Center for South and Southeast Asian Studies, The University of Michigan.

Gonda, Jan. 1960. *Die Religionen Indiens I: Veda und älterer Hinduismus.* Stuttgart: W. Kohlhammer. (RM 11.)

———. 1975. *Vedic Literature (Saṃhitās and Brāhmaṇas).* Wiesbaden: Otto Harrassowitz. (A History of Indian Literature, vol. I, fasc. 1.)

———. 1991. *The Functions and Significance of Gold in the Veda.* Leiden: E. J. Brill. (ORT 37.)

Graham, A. C. 1989. *Disputers of the Tao: Philosophical Argument in Ancient China.* La Salle, Illinois: Open Court.

Griffiths, Paul J. 1986. *On Being Mindless: Buddhist Meditation and the Mind-Body Problem.* La Salle, Illinois: Open Court. Third printing 1991.

Griffiths, Paul J., Noriaki Hakamaya, John P. Keenan, and Paul L. Swanson. 1989. *The Realm of Awakening: A Translation and Study of the*

Tenth Chapter of Asaṅga's Mahāyānasaṅgraha. New York: Oxford University Press.

Gyatso, Janet, ed. 1992. *The Mirror of Memory: Reflections on Mindfulness and Remembrance in Indian and Tibetan Buddhism*. Albany: SUNY Press.

Halbfass, Wilhelm. 1981. *Indien und Europa: Perspektiven ihrer geistigen Begegnung*. Basel, Stuttgart: Schwabe. (English version: Halbfass 1988.)

———. 1988. *India and Europe. An Essay in Understanding*. Albany: SUNY Press.

———. 1995. "Zum Verhältnis von Karma und Tod im indischen Denken." In *Im Tod gewinnt der Mensch sein Selbst: Das Phänomen des Todes in asiatischer und abendländischer Religionstradition*, edited by Gerhard Oberhammer, 75–95. Wien: ÖAW. (SAWW 624.)

Hallisey, Charles. 1991. "Councils as Ideas and Events in the Theravāda." BF 2, 133–48.

Hare, E. M., trans. 1935. *The Book of the Gradual Sayings (Anguttara-Nikāya) or more-numbered Suttas*, vol. IV (The Books of the Sevens, Eights and Nines). London: Pali Text Society. Reprint 1965.

Harris, Ian Charles. 1991. *The Continuity of Madhyamaka and Yogācāra in Indian Mahāyāna Buddhism*. Leiden: E. J. Brill. (Brill's Indological Library, 6.)

Harrison, Paul M. 1978. "*Buddhānusmṛti* in the Pratyutpanna-buddha-saṃmukhāvasthita-samādhi-sūtra." JIP 6, 35–57.

———. 1982. "Sanskrit Fragments of a Lokottaravādin Tradition." = Hercus et al. 1982: 211–34.

———. 1987. "Who Gets to Ride in the Great Vehicle? Self-Image and Identity among the Followers of the Early Mahāyāna." JIABS 10(1), 67–89.

———. 1990. *The Samādhi of Direct Encounter with the Buddhas of the Present*. An annotated English translation of the Tibetan version of the Pratyutpanna-buddha-saṃmukhāvasthita-samādhi-sūtra with several appendices relating to the history of the text. Tokyo: The International Institute for Buddhist Studies. (StPhB Monograph Series, V.)

———. 1992. "Commemoration and Identification in *Buddhānusmṛti*." = Gyatso 1992: 215–38.

———. 1992a. "Is the *Dharma-kāya* the Real 'Phantom Body' of the Buddha?" JIABS 15(1), 44–94.

———. 1995. "Searching for the Origins of the Mahāyāna: What Are We Looking For?" EB N.S. 28(1), 48–69.

Hattori, Masaaki. 1968. *Dignāga, On Perception: Being the Pratyakṣapariccheda of Dignāga's Pramāṇasamuccaya*. Cambridge, MA: Harvard University Press. (HOS 47.)

Hayes, Richard P. 1988. *Dignaga on the Interpretation of Signs*. Dordrecht: Kluwer. (Studies of Classical India, 9.)

———. 1994. "Nāgārjuna's Appeal." JIP 22, 299–378.

Hedinger, Jürg. 1984. *Aspekte der Schulung in der Laufbahn eines Bodhisattva*. Wiesbaden: Otto Harrassowitz. (FBI 17.)

Hercus, L. A., et al., eds. 1982. *Indological and Buddhist Studies*. Volume in honour of Professor J. W. de Jong on his sixtieth birthday. Canberra: Faculty of Asian Studies.

Hinüber, Oskar von. 1968. *Studien zur Kasussyntax des Pāli, besonders des Vinaya-Piṭaka*. München. (MSS Beiheft, 2.)

———. 1977. "Zur Geschichte des Sprachnamens Pāli." *Beiträge zur Indienforschung* (Festschr. Ernst Waldschmidt), 237–46. Berlin: Museum für Indische Kunst. (English translation: Hinüber 1994b.)

———. 1986. *Das ältere Mittelindisch im Überblick*. Wien. (VKSKS 20.)

———. 1989. *Der Beginn der Schrift und frühe Schriftlichkeit in Indien*. Stuttgart: Franz Steiner Verlag Wiesbaden. (AAWL 1989, 11.)

———. 1994. *Untersuchungen zur Mündlichkeit früher mittelindischer Texte der Buddhisten (Untersuchungen zur Sprachgeschichte und Handschriftenkunde des Pāli III)*. Stuttgart: Franz Steiner. (AAWL Jg. 1994 Nr. 5.)

———. 1994a. "Vinaya und Abhidhamma." StII 19 (Festschr. Georg Buddruss), 109–22.

———. 1994b. "On the History of the Name of the Pāli Language."

Selected Papers on Pāli Studies, 76–90. Oxford: Pali Text Society. (English translation of Hinüber 1977.)

———. 1994c. "Die neun Aṅgas: Ein früher Versuch zur Einteilung buddhistischer Texte." WZKS 38 (Festschr. G. Oberhammer), 121–35.

———. 1996. *A Handbook of Pāli Literature*. Berlin, New York: Walter de Gruyter. (Indian Philology and South Asian Studies, 2.)

Hirakawa, Akira. 1963. "The Rise of Mahāyāna Buddhism and Its Relationship to the Worship of Stupas." *Memoirs of the Research Department of the Toyo Bunko* 22, 57–106.

———. 1973–78. *Index to the Abhidharmakośabhāṣya*. 3 vols. Tokyo.

———. 1990. *A History of Indian Buddhism, from Śākyamuni to Early Mahāyāna*. Translated and edited by Paul Groner. Honolulu: University of Hawaii Press.

———. 1993. "The Meaning of 'Dharma': The Buddhist Theory of Existence." In *Premier colloque Étienne Lamotte (Bruxelles et Liège 24–27 septembre 1989)*, 17–23. Louvain-la-Neuve: Institut Orientaliste. (Publications de l'Institut Orientaliste de Louvain, 42.)

Horner, Isaline B. 1969. *Milinda's Questions*, vol. 1. London: Luzac & Co.

Houben, Jan E. M. 1995. *The Saṃbandha-samuddeśa (Chapter on Relation) and Bhartṛhari's Philosophy of Language: A Study of Bhartṛhari Saṃbandha-samuddeśa in the Context of the Vākyapadīya with a Translation of Helārāja's Commentary Prakīrṇa-prakāśa*. Groningen: Egbert Forsten. (Gonda Indological Studies, 2.)

Hu-von Hinüber, Haiyan. 1994. *Das Poṣadhavastu: Vorschriften für die buddhistische Beichtfeier im Vinaya der Mūlasarvāstivādins*. Reinbek: Inge Wezler. (StII, Monographie 13.)

Ichimura, Shōhei. 1992. "Re-examining the Period of Nāgārjuna: Western India, A.D. 50–150." IBK 40(2), (8)–(14) (=1079–1073).

———. 1995. "The Period of Nāgārjuna and the Fang-pien-hsin-lun (or Upāyahṛdayaśāstra)." IBK 43(2), (20)–(25) (=1033–1028).

Imanishi, Junkichi. 1969. *Das Pañcavastukam und die Pañcavastukavibhāṣā*. Göttingen: Vandenhoeck & Ruprecht. (NAWG Jg 1969 Nr. 1.)

———. 1977. "Über den Text des Prakaraṇa." *Annual Report of Cultural Science*, Hokkaidô University, 25,2 (March 1977), 1–37. (Pp. 4–15: Sanskrit-Fragmente des Prakaraṇa aus den Turfan-Funden; pp. 15–31: Die im Abhidharmakośa zitierten Sanskrit-Fragmente des Prakaraṇa.)

Isayeva, Natalia. 1993. *Shankara and Indian Philosophy*. Albany: SUNY Press.

Iwata, Takashi. 1991. *Sahopalambhaniyama. Struktur und Entwicklung des Schlusses von der Tatsache, dass Erkenntnis und Gegenstand ausschliesslich zusammen wahrgenomment werden, auf deren Nichtverschiedenheit*. Stuttgart: F. Steiner, 1991. (ANISt 29.)

Jacobi, Hermann. 1911. "The Dates of the Philosophical Sūtras of the Brahmans." JAOS 31, 1–29. (KlSchr II, pp. 559–87.)

Jaini, Padmanabh S. 1959. "The Development of the Theory of Viprayukta-saṃskāras." BSOAS 22, 531–47.

———. 1959a. "The Vaibhāṣika Theory of Words and Meanings." BSOAS 22, 95–107.

———. 1959b. "The Sautrāntika Theory of Bīja." BSOAS 22, 236–49.

———. 1992. "On the Ignorance of the Arhat." = Buswell and Gimello 1992: 135–45.

Jullien, François. 1995. *Le détour et l'accès: stratégies du sens en Chine, en Grèce*. Paris: Bernard Grasset.

Kajiyama, Yuichi. 1977. "Realism of the Sarvāstivāda School." In *Buddhist Thought and Asian Civilization: Essays in honor of Herbert V. Guenther on his sixtieth birthday*, edited by Leslie S. Kawamura and Keith Scott, 114–31. Emeryville, California: Dharma Publishing. Reprint: Kajiyama 1989: 129–46.

———. 1982. "On the Meaning of the Words *Bodhisattva* and *Mahāsattva* in Prajñāpāramitā Literature." = Hercus et al. 1982: 253–70. Reprint: Kajiyama 1989: 71–88.

———. 1989. *Studies in Buddhist Philosophy (Selected Papers)*. Edited by Katsumi Mimaki. Kyoto: Rinsen Book Co.

———. 1991. "On the Authorship of the Upāyahṛdaya." = Steinkellner 1991: 107–17.

———. 1993. "Prajñāpāramitā and the Rise of Mahāyāna." In *Buddhist*

Spirituality: Indian, Southeast Asian, Tibetan, and Early Chinese, 137–54. Ed. Takeuchi Yoshinori. New York: Crossroad.

Kalupahana, David J. 1974. "The Buddhist Conception of Time and Temporality." PEW 24, 181–91. Reprint: Prasad 1991: 479–89.

———. 1975. *Causality: The Central Philosophy of Buddhism*. Honolulu: The University Press of Hawaii.

———. 1986. *Nāgārjuna: The Philosophy of the Middle Way. Mūlamadhyamakakārikā*. Albany: SUNY Press.

———. 1992. *A History of Buddhist Thought*. Honolulu: University of Hawaii.

Kapani, Lakshmi. 1992. *La notion de saṃskāra, I*. Paris: de Boccard. (Publications de l'Institut de Civilisation Indienne, fasc. 59.)

Kato, Junsho. 1989. *Etude sur les Sautrāntika (Kyōryō-bu no kenkyū)*. Tōkyō: Shunjū-sha.

Katsura, Shoryu. 1979. "The Apoha Theory of Dignāga." IBK 28(1), 493–489 = (16)–(20).

———. 1991. "Dignāga and Dharmakīrti on Apoha." = Steinkellner 1991: 129–46.

Keenan, John P. 1982. "Original Purity and the Focus of Early Yogācāra." JIABS 5(1), 7–18.

———. 1992. *The Summary of the Great Vehicule by Bodhisattva Asaṅga, Translated from the Chinese of Paramārtha (Taishō, Volume 31, Number 1593)*. Berkeley, California: Numata Center for Buddhist Translation and Research. (BDK English Tripiṭaka, 46-III.)

Kher, Chitrarekha V. 1992. *Buddhism as Presented by the Brahmanical Systems*. Delhi: Sri Satguru Publications. (Bibliotheca Indo-Buddhica Series, 92.)

King, Richard. 1989. "Śūnyatā and Ajāti: Absolutism and the Philosophies of Nāgārjuna and Gauḍapāda." JIP 17, 385–405.

———. 1995. "Is 'Buddha-Nature' Buddhist? Doctrinal Tensions in the Śrīmālā Sūtra—an Early Tathāgatagarbha Text." *Numen* 42, 1–20.

———. 1995a. *Early Advaita Vedānta and Buddhism: The Mahāyāna Context of the Gauḍapādīya-kārikā*. Albany: SUNY Press.

———. 1995b. "Early Advaita Vedānta: The Date and Authorship of the Gauḍapādīyakārikā." IIJ 38, 317–55.

King, Winston L. 1992. *Theravāda Meditation: The Buddhist Transformation of Yoga*. First Indian edition. Delhi: Motilal Banarsidass.

Kirfel, W. 1920. *Die Kosmographie der Inder nach den Quellen dargestellt*. Bonn, Leipzig: Kurt Schroeder.

Klimkeit, Hans-Joachim. 1990. *Der Buddha: Leben und Lehre*. Stuttgart: W. Kohlhammer.

Kloetzli, Randy. 1983. *Buddhist Cosmology, From Single World System to Pure Land: Science and Theology in the Images of Motion and Light*. Delhi: Motilal Banarsidass.

Kloppenborg, Ria. 1974. *The Paccekabuddha: A Buddhist Ascetic. A study of the concept of the paccekabuddha in Pāli canonical and commentarial literature*. Leiden: E. J. Brill. (ORT 20.)

———. 1990. "The Buddha's Redefinition of *Tapas* (Ascetic Practice)." BSR 7 (1–2), 49–73.

Kloppenborg, Ria, and Ronald Poelmeyer. 1987. "Visualizations in Buddhist Meditation." In *Effigies Dei: Essays on the History of Religions*, edited by Dirk van der Plas, 83–95. Leiden: E. J. Brill.

Kottkamp, Heino. 1992. *Der Stupa als Repräsentation des buddhistischen Heilsweges: Untersuchungen zur Entstehung und Entwicklung architektonischer Symbolik*. Wiesbaden: Otto Harrassowitz. (Studies in Oriental Religions, 25.)

Kritzer, Robert. 1992. "Pratītyasamutpāda in the Daśabhūmikasūtra: How Many Lifetimes?" IBK 40(2), (15)–(20) (= 1072–1067).

———. 1993. "Vasubandhu on *saṃskārapratyayaṃ vijñānam*." JIABS 16(1), 24–55.

———. 1999. *Rebirth and Causation in the Yogācāra Abhidharma*. Vienna: Arbeitskreis für Tibetische und Buddhistische Studien, Universität Wien. (Wiener Studien zur Tibetologie und Buddhismuskunde, 44.)

Kubo, Tsugunari. 1992. "*Anuttarā samyak-saṃbodhi* Set against the Concept of *Parinirvāṇa* as Depicted in the Lotus Sūtra." *Indian Journal of Buddhist Studies* 4(2), 1–13.

Lafont, Jean-Marie. 1994. "Les Indo-grecs: recherches archéologiques françaises dans le royaume Sikh du Penjab, 1822–1843." *Topoi* 4, 9–68.

Lamotte, Étienne, ed. and trans. 1935. *Saṃdhinirmocanasūtra: L'explication des mystères*. Louvain: Bibliothèque de l'Université.

———. 1936. "Le traité de l'acte de Vasubandhu Karmasiddhiprakaraṇa." MCB 4 (1935–36), 151–263.

———. 1944–80. *Le traité de la grande vertu de sagesse de Nāgārjuna (Mahāprajñāpāramitāśāstra), T. 1–5*. Louvain. (BM 18, PIOL 2, 12, 24, 25, 26.) [Translates TCTL.]

———. 1947. "La critique d'authenticité dans le bouddhisme." In *India Antiqua. A volume of oriental studies presented to Jean Philippe Vogel*, 213–22. Leiden: E. J. Brill.

———. 1949. "La critique d'interprétation dans le bouddhisme." *Annuaire de l'Institut de Philologie et d'Histoire Orientales et Slaves* 9, 341–61. Bruxelles (Mélanges Henri Grégoire). English translation by Sara Boin-Webb in Lopez 1988: 11–27.

———. 1954. "Sur la formation du Mahāyāna." *Asiatica* (Festschr. Friedrich Weller), 377–96. Leipzig: Otto Harrassowitz.

———. 1958. *Histoire du bouddhisme indien, des origines à l'ère Śaka*. Louvain: Institut Orientaliste. (BM 43.) (English translation: Lamotte 1988.)

———, trans. 1962. *Vimalakīrtinirdeśa. L'Enseignement de Vimalakīrti*. Louvain. (BM 51.)

———. 1973. "Trois sūtra du Saṃyukta sur la vacuité." BSOAS 36, 313–23.

———. 1973a. *La somme du grand véhicule (Mahāyānasaṃgraha)*, vol. I: Versions tibétaine et chinoise (Hiuan-tsang); vol. II: Traduction et commentaire. Louvain-la-Neuve: Institut Orientaliste, Université de Louvain. (PIOL 8.)

———. 1977. "Die bedingte Entstehung und die höchste Erleuchtung." In *Beiträge zur Indienforschung* (Festschr. Ernst Waldschmidt), 279–98. Berlin: Museum für Indische Kunst.

———. 1988. *History of Indian Buddhism: From the Origins to the Śaka Era*. Translated from the French by Sara Webb-Boin under the supervision of Jean Dantinne. Louvain-la-Neuve: Institut Orientaliste. (Publications de l'Institut Orientaliste de Louvain, 36.)

Lancaster, Lewis R. 1969. "The Chinese Translation of the Aṣṭasāhasrikā-prajñāpāramitā-sūtra Attributed to Chih Ch'ien." *Monumenta Serica* 28, 246–57.

———. 1975. "The Oldest Mahāyāna Sūtra: Its Significance for the Study of Buddhist Development." EB N.S. 8(1), 30–41.

———, ed. 1977. *Prajñāpāramitā and Related Systems: Studies in Honor of Edward Conze*. Berkeley: University of California. (Berkeley Buddhist Studies Series, 1.)

La Vallée Poussin, Louis de. 1913. *Théorie des douze causes*. Gand: E. Van Goethem.

———. 1923–31. *Vasubandhu, Abhidharmakośa. Traduit et annoté*. 6 vols. Paris: Paul Geuthner; Louvain: J. B. Istas.

———. 1925. "La controverse du temps et du Pudgala dans le Vijñāyakāya." *Études Asiatiques* 1 (Publications de l'École Française d'Extrême-Orient, vol. XIX), 343–76.

———. 1928. *Vijñaptimātratāsiddhi: La Siddhi de Hiuan-Tsang*, vol. I. Paris: Paul Geuthner.

———. 1930. "Textes relatifs au Nirvāṇa et aux Asaṃskṛta en général." BEFEO 30, 1–28.

———. 1934. "Notes sur le 'moment' ou *kṣaṇa* des bouddhistes." RO 8 (1931–32), 1–9. Reprint: Prasad 1991: 69–77.

———. 1936–37. "Le bouddhisme et le Yoga de Patañjali." MCB 5, 223–42.

———. 1937. "La controverse du temps." MCB 5 (1936–37), 7–158.

———. 1937a. "Les deux, les quatre, les trois vérités." MCB 5 (1936–37), 159–87.

———. 1937b. "Musīla et Nārada: le chemin du nirvāṇa." MCB 5 (1936–37), 189–222.

Liebenthal, Walter. 1934. *Satkārya in der Darstellung seiner buddhistischen Gegner: Die prakṛti-parīkṣā im Tattvasaṃgraha des Śāntirakṣita zusammen mit der Pañjikā des Kamalaśīla übersetzt und ausführlich interpretiert*. Stuttgart, Berlin: W. Kohlhammer. (Beiträge zur indischen Sprachwissenschaft und Religionsgeschichte, 9.)

Lindtner, Christian. 1982. *Nagarjuniana: Studies in the Writings and*

Philosophy of Nāgārjuna. Kobenhavn: Akademisk Forlag. (Indiske Studier, 4.)

———. 1992. "The Laṅkāvatārasūtra in Early Indian Madhyamaka Literature." AS 46(1; Festschr. Jacques May), 244–79.

———. 1994. Review of Iwata 1991. IIJ 37, 272–75.

———. 1995. "Bhavya's Madhyamakahṛdaya (Pariccheda Five), Yogācāratattvaviniścayāvatāra." ALB 59, 37–65.

———. 1995a. "Lokasaṃgraha, Buddhism and Buddhi-yoga in the Gītā." In *Modern Evaluation of the Mahābhārata: Prof. R.K. Sharma Felicitation Volume*, 199–220. Delhi: Nag Publishers.

Lopez, Donald S. 1987. *A Study of Svātantrika*. Ithaca, NY: Snow Lion Publications.

———. 1988. *Buddhist Hermeneutics*. Honolulu: University of Hawaii Press.

———. 1995. "Authority and Orality in the Mahāyāna." *Numen* 42, 21–47.

Manné, Joy. 1992. "The Dīgha Nikāya Debates: Debating Practices at the Time of the Buddha." BSR 9(2), 117–36.

———. 1995. "Case Histories from the Pāli Canon I: The Sāmaññaphala Sutta hypothetical case history *or* how to be sure to win a debate." JPTS 21, 1–34.

May, Jaques. 1959. *Candrakīrti, Prasannapadā Madhyamakavṛtti. Douze chapitres traduits du sanskrit et du tibétain accompagnés d'une introduction, de notes et d'une édition critique de la version tibétaine*. Paris: Adrien-Maisonneuve.

———. 1971. "La philosophie bouddhique idéaliste." AS 25, 265–323.

———. 1979. "Chûgan." Hôbôgirin 5, 470–93.

McDermott, James Paul. 1980. "Karma and Rebirth in Early Buddhism." In *Karma and Rebirth in Classical Indian Traditions*, edited by Wendy Doniger O'Flaherty, 165–92. Berkeley: University of California Press.

———. 1984. *Development in the Early Buddhist Concept of Kamma/Karma*. New Delhi: Munshiram Manoharlal.

McEvilley, Thomas. 1981. "Early Greek Philosophy and Mādhyamika." PEW 31(2), 141–64.

McGovern, William Montgomery. 1923. *A Manual of Buddhist Philosophy, Vol. I: Cosmology*. London: Kegan Paul, Trench, Trubner.

Meisig, Konrad. 1987. *Das Śrāmaṇyaphala-Sūtra*. Wiesbaden: Otto Harrassowitz.

———. 1988. *Yogasūtra-Konkordanz*. Wiesbaden: Otto Harrassowitz. (Freiburger Beiträge zur Indologie, 22.)

———. 1992. "Zur Entritualisierung des Opfers im frühen Buddhismus." *Mitteilungen für Anthropologie und Religionsgeschichte* (Saarbrücken) 7, 213–21.

Mimaki, Katsumi. 1976. *La réfutation bouddhique de la permanence des choses (sthirasiddhidūṣaṇa) et la preuve de la momentanéité des choses (kṣaṇabhaṅgasiddhi)*. Paris: Institut de Civilisation Indienne.

———. 1988. "Kyōryōbu." *Iwanami Kôza Tôyôshisô* 8: Indo Bukkyô I, 226–60.

Mimaki, Katsumi, and Jacques May. 1979. "Chūdō: Bouddhisme ancien." Hôbôgirin 5, 456–70.

Mitchell, Donald W. 1974. "An Early View of Man in Indian Buddhism: The Sarvastivadin Concept of the Self." *International Philosophical Quarterly* 14, 189–99.

Mittal, Kusum. 1957–62. *Dogmatische Begriffsreihen im älteren Buddhismus, I: Fragmente des Daśottarasūtra aus zentralasiatischen Sanskrit-Handschriften* [I–VIII], & Dieter Schlingloff, *Dogmatische Begriffsreihen im älteren Buddhismus*, Ia: Daśottarasūtra IX–X. Berlin 1957, 1962. (STT 4, 4a.)

Mori, Sodō. 1984. *A Study of the Pāli Commentaries*. Tokyo: Sankibo Buddhist Book Store.

———. 1991. "The Time of Formation of the Twelve Link Chain of Dependent Origination." *Studies in Buddhism and Culture in Honour of Professor Dr. Egaku Mayeda on his sixty-fifth birthday*. Tokyo: Sankibo, (742)–(733) (= 39–48).

Much, Michael Torsten. 1994. "Uddyotakaras Kritik der *apoha*-Lehre (Nyāyavārttika ad NS II 2,66)." WZKS 38, 351–66.

Mus, Paul. 1939. *La Lumière sur les Six Voies: Tableau de la transmigration bouddhique*, vol. I. Paris: Institut d'Ethnologie.

Mylius, Klaus. 1985. *Gautama Buddha: Die vier edlen Wahrheiten. Texte des ursprünglichen Buddhismus.* München: Deutscher Taschenbuch Verlag.

Nagao, Gadjin M. 1991. *Mādhyamika and Yogācāra: A Study of Mahāyāna Philosophies.* Edited, collated, and translated by L. S. Kawamura. Delhi: Sri Satguru.

———. 1994. *An Index to Asaṅga's Mahāyānasaṃgraha*, part 1: Tibetan-Sanskrit-Chinese; part 2: Sanskrit-Tibetan-Chinese. Tokyo: The International Institute for Buddhist Studies. (StPhB Monograph Series, IX.)

Nakamura, Hajime. 1972. "Bhartṛhari and Buddhism." JGJKSV 28, 395–405.

———. 1973. "Buddhist Influence upon the Vākyapadīya." JGJKSV 29, 367–87.

———. 1980. *Indian Buddhism: A Survey with Bibliographical Notes.* Hirakata: Kansai University of Foreign Studies.

———. 1981. "The concept of Brahman in Bhartṛhari's philosophy." JORM 40–41, 135–49.

Nakamura, Zuiryu. 1961. *The Ratnagotravibhāga-mahāyānottaratantra-çāstra, compared with Sanskrit and Chinese, with introduction and notes.* Tokyo: Sankibo-Busshorin.

Ñāṇamoli, Bhikkhu and Bhikkhu Bodhi, trans. 1995. *The Middle Length Discourses of the Buddha: A New Translation of the Majjhima Nikāya.* Boston: Wisdom Publications.

Nehru, Lolita. 1989. *Origins of the Gandhāran Style.* Delhi: Oxford University Press.

Neumann, Karl Eugen. 1922. *Die Reden Gotamo Buddhos aus der Mittleren Sammlung Majjhimanikāyo des Pāli-Kanons zum ersten Mal übersetzt.* Erster Band. München: R. Piper.

Nolot, Édith. 1995. *Entretiens de Milinda et Nāgasena.* Traduit du pâli, présenté et annoté. Paris: Gallimard.

Norman, Kenneth R. 1981. "A Note on *Attā* in the Alagaddūpama-Sutta." In *Studies in Indian Philosophy: A Memorial Volume in Honour of Pandit Sukhlalji Sanghvi*, 19–29. Ahmedabad. (LD Series, 84.) (Reprint: Norman 1990–96: II: 200–209.)

———. 1989. "The Pāli Language and Scriptures." In *The Buddhist Heritage*, edited by Tadeusz Skorupski, 29–53. Tring: The Institute of Buddhist Studies. (Reprint: Norman 1990–96: IV: 92–123.)

———. 1990–96. *Collected Papers*. 6 vols. Oxford: PTS.

———. 1993. Review of Hinüber 1989. JRAS, Third Series, 3, 277–81.

———. 1994. "Mistaken Ideas about *Nibbāna*." BF 3 (1991–93; Papers in honour and appreciation of Professor David Seyfort Ruegg's contribution to Indological, Buddhist, and Tibetan studies; edited by Tadeusz Skorupski and Ulrich Pagel), 211–37.

Nyanatiloka. 1969. *Die Lehrreden des Buddha aus der Angereihten Sammlung Anguttara-Nikaya*. 5 vols. 3. revidierte Neuauflage. Köln: DuMont Schauberg.

Oberhammer, Gerhard, ed. 1978. *Transzendenzerfahrung, Vollzugshorizont des Heils: Das Problem in indischer und christlicher Tradition*. Wien. (Publications of the De Nobili Research Library, 5.)

Oetke, Claus. 1988. *"Ich" und das Ich: Analytische Untersuchungen zur buddhistisch-brahmanischen Atmankontroverse*. Stuttgart: Franz Steiner.

———. 1988a. "Die metaphysische Lehre Nāgārjunas." *Conceptus, Zeitschrift für Philosophie* 22, Nr. 56, 47–64.

———. 1989. "Rationalismus und Mystik in der Philosophie Nāgārjunas." StII 15, 1–39.

———. 1990. "On Some Non-Formal Aspects of the Proofs of the Madhyamakakārikā." = Ruegg and Schmithausen 1992: 91–109.

———. 1991. "Remarks on the Interpretation of Nāgārjuna's Philosophy." JIP 19, 315–23.

———. 1992. "Doctrine and Argument in Vijñānavāda Buddhism." WZKS 36, 217–25.

———. 1994. "Die 'unbeantworteten Fragen' und das Schweigen des Buddha." WZKS 38 (Festschr. G. Oberhammer), 85–120.

———. 1995. "Buddhadeva's Views on Present, Past and Future." In *Sauhṛdyamaṅgalam: Studies in Honour of Siegfried Lienhard on his 70th Birthday*, edited by Mirja Juntunen et al., 267–80. Stockholm: The Association of Oriental Studies.

———. 1996. "Gleichschaltung und Kontinuität im Mahāyāna-Buddhismus." WZKS 40, 161–222.

Oldenberg, Hermann. 1919. *Die Weltanschauung der Brāhmaṇa-Texte: Vorwissenschaftliche Wissenschaft*. Göttingen: Vandenhoeck & Ruprecht.

———. 1961. *Buddha, sein Leben, seine Lehre, seine Gemeinde*. 13th edition. Edited by Helmuth von Glasenapp. München: Wilhelm Goldman Verlag.

———. 1971. *Buddha: His Life, His Doctrine, His Order*. Translated by William Hoey. Delhi: Indological Bookhouse. Translation of Oldenberg 1961.

Olivelle, Patrick. 1993. *The Āśrama System. The History and Hermeneutics of a Religious Institution*. New York, Oxford: Oxford University Press.

Pagel, Ulrich. 1995. *The Bodhisattvapiṭaka: Its Doctrines, Practices, and Their Position in Mahāyāna Literature*. Tring: The Institute of Buddhist Studies. (Buddhica Britannica, Series continua V.)

Pāsādika, Bhikkhu. 1989. *Kanonische Zitate im Abhidharmakośabhāṣya des Vasubandhu*. Göttingen: Vandenhoeck & Ruprecht. (SWTF, Beiheft 1.)

Pauly, Bernard. 1957. "Fragments sanskrits de Haute Asie (Mission Pelliot)." JA 245, 281–307.

———. 1959. "Fragments sanskrits de Haute Asie (Mission Pelliot)." JA 247, 203–49.

Pérez-Remón, Joaquín. 1980. *Self and Non-Self in Early Buddhism*. The Hague, New York: Mouton.

Pingree, David. 1978. *The Yavanajātaka of Sphujidhvaja*. Cambridge, MA, London: Harvard University Press. (HOS 48.)

Potter, Karl H. 1981. *Encyclopedia of Indian Philosophies III: Advaita Vedānta up to Śaṃkara and His Pupils*. Delhi: Motilal Banarsidass.

Powers, John. 1993. *Hermeneutics and Tradition in the Saṃdhinirmocana-Sūtra*. Leiden: E. J. Brill. (Indian Thought, 5.)

———, trans. 1995. *Wisdom of Buddha. The Saṃdhinirmocana Sūtra*. Berkeley: Dharma Publishing.

Prasad, H. S., ed. 1991. *Essays on Time in Buddhism*. Delhi: Sri Satguru Publications. (Bibliotheca Indo-Buddhica, 78.)

Préaux, Claire. 1978. *Le monde hellénistique*, tome premier. Paris: Presses Universitaires de France. 3e édition 1989.

Prebish, Charles S. 1974. "A Review of Scholarship on the Buddhist Councils." *Journal of Asian Studies* 33(2), 239–54.

Pye, Michael. 1978. *Skilful Means: A Concept in Mahayana Buddhism*. London: Duckworth.

Qvarnström, Olle. 1988. "Space and Substance: A Theme in Madhyamaka-Vedānta Polemics." *Studies in Central and East Asian Religions* 1, 3–34.

Rapin, Claude. 1992. *La trésorerie du palais hellénistique d'Aï Khanoun: l'apogée et la chute du royaume grec de Bactriane*. Paris: de Boccard.

Rawlinson, Andrew. 1983. "The Problem of the Origin of the Mahayana." In *Traditions in Contact and Change: Selected Proceedings of the XIVth Congress of the International Association for the History of Religions*, edited by Peter Slater and Donald Wiebe, 163–70. Wilfrid Laurier University Press.

———. 1986. "Visions and Symbols in the Mahāyāna." In *Perspectives on Indian Religion: Papers in honour of Karel Werner*, edited by Peter Connolly, 191–214. Delhi: Sri Satguru.

Regamey, Constantin. 1957. "Le problème du bouddhisme primitif et les derniers travaux de Stanislaw Schayer." RO 21, 37–58.

Rewata Dhamma. 1997. *The First Discourse of the Buddha: Turning the Wheel of Dhamma*. Boston: Wisdom Publications.

Robert, Louis. 1973. "Les inscriptions." *Fouilles d'Aï Khanoum* I, 207–37.

Robinson, Richard H. 1967. *Early Mādhyamika in India and China*. Madison: University of Wisconsin Press. Reprint: Delhi: Motilal Banarsidass, 1978.

Rospatt, Alexander von. 1995. *The Buddhist Doctrine of Momentariness: A Survey of the Origins and Early Phase of This Doctrine up to Vasubandhu*. Stuttgart: Franz Steiner. (ANISt 47.)

———. 1996. Review of Zafiropulo 1993. OLZ 91(1), 79–89.

Roth, Gustav. 1980. "Particular Features of the Language of the Ārya-Mahāsāṃghika-Lokottaravādins and Their Importance for Early Buddhist Tradition Including Notes on the Patna Dharmapada." = Bechert 1980: 78–135.

Ruben, Walter. 1928. "Über die Debatten in den alten Upaniṣad's." ZDMG 83, 238–55.

Ruegg, David Seyfort. 1969. *La théorie du Tathāgatagarbha et du Gotra*. Paris: École Française d'Extrême-Orient.

———. 1978. "Mathematical and Linguistic Models in Indian Thought: The Case of Zero and *Śūnyatā*." WZKS 22, 171–81.

———. 1981. *The Literature of the Madhyamaka School of Philosophy in India*. Wiesbaden: Otto Harrassowitz. (A History of Indian Literature, vol. VII, fasc. 1.)

———. 1982. "Towards a Chronology of the Madhyamaka School." Indological and Buddhist Studies. = Hercus et al. 1982: 505–30.

———. 1989. *Buddha-Nature, Mind and the Problem of Gradualism in a Comparative Perspective*. London: School of Oriental and African Studies.

———. 1995. Review of Lopez 1988. BSOAS 58(3), 573–77.

Ruegg, David Seyfort, and Lambert Schmithausen, eds. 1990. *Earliest Buddhism and Madhyamaka*. Leiden: E. J. Brill. (Panels of the VIIth World Sanskrit Conference, 2.)

Sakuma, Hidenori S. 1990. *Die Āśrayaparivṛtti-Theorie in der Yogācārabhūmi*. 2 vols. Stuttgart: Franz Steiner. (ANISt 40.)

Sanderson, Alexis. 1994. "The Sarvāstivāda and Its Critics: Anātmavāda and the Theory of Karma." In *Buddhism into the Year 2000: International Conference Proceedings*, 33–48. Bangkok, Los Angeles: Dhammakaya Foundation.

———. 1994a. "Vajrayāna: Origin and Function." In *Buddhism into the Year 2000: International Conference Proceedings*, 87–102. Bangkok, Los Angeles: Dhammakaya Foundation.

Sasaki, Shizuka. 1989. "Buddhist Sects in the Aśoka Period, 1: The Meaning of the Schism Edict." BK 18, 181–202.

———. 1992. "Buddhist Sects in the Aśoka Period, 2: Saṃghabheda (1)." BK 21, 157–76.

———. 1993. "Buddhist Sects in the Aśoka Period, 3: Saṃghabheda (2)." BK 22, 167–99.

———. 1994. "Buddhist Sects in the Aśoka Period, 4: The Structure of the Mahāsāṃghika Vinaya." BK 23, 55–100.

———. 1995. "Buddhist Sects in the Aśoka Period, 5: Presenting a Hypothesis." BK 24, 165–225.

———. 1996. "Buddhist Sects in the Aśoka Period, 6: The Dīpavaṃsa." BK 25, 29–63.

Scharfe, Hartmut. 1971. "The Maurya Dynasty and the Seleucids." KZ 85, 211–25.

Schayer, Stanislaw. 1935. "Precanonical Buddhism." ArchOr 7, 121–32.

———. 1937. "New contributions to the problem of pre-Hīnayānistic Buddhism." *Polski biuletyn orientalistyczny (Polish Bulletin of Oriental Studies)* 1, 8–17.

Schlingloff, Dieter. 1962. *Die Religion des Buddhismus I: Der Heilsweg des Mönchtums*. Berlin: Walter de Gruyter. (Sammlung Göschen, 174.)

———. 1964. *Ein buddhistisches Yogalehrbuch*. Berlin. (STT 7.)

Schmithausen, Lambert. 1967. "Sautrāntika-Voraussetzungen in Viṃśatikā und Triṃśikā." WZKS 11, 109–36.

———. 1969. "Ich und Erlösung im Buddhismus." ZMR 53, 157–70.

———. 1969a. "Zur Literaturgeschichte der älteren Yogācāra-Schule." ZDMG, Supplementa I.3, 811–23.

———. 1969b. *Der Nirvāṇa-Abschnitt in der Viniścayasaṃgrahaṇī der Yogācārabhūmiḥ*. Wien: H. Boehlaus Nachf., Kommissionsverlag der ÖAW. (VKSKS 8.)

———. 1973. "Zu D. Seyfort Rueggs Buch 'La théorie du Tathāgatagarbha et du Gotra.'" WZKS 17, 123–60.

———. 1973a. "Spirituelle Praxis und philosophische Theorie im Buddhismus." ZMR 57, 161–86.

———. 1976. "Die vier Konzentrationen der Aufmerksamkeit." ZMR 60, 241–66.

———. 1977. "Textgeschichtliche Beobachtungen zum 1. Kapitel der Aṣṭasāhasrikā Prajñāpāramitā." = Lancaster 1977: 35–80.

———. 1978. "Zur Struktur der erlösenden Erfahrung im indischen Buddhismus." = Oberhammer 1978: 97–119.

———. 1981. "On Some Aspects of Descriptions or Theories of 'Liberating Insight' and 'Enlightenment' in Early Buddhism." In *Studien zum Jainismus und Buddhismus, Gedenkschrift für Ludwig Alsdorf*, edited by Klaus Bruhn and Albrecht Wezler, 199–250. Wiesbaden: Franz Steiner (ANISt 23).

———. 1984. "On the Vijñaptimātra Passage in Saṃdhinirmocanasūtra VIII.7." *Acta Indologica* 6 (Studies of Mysticism in Honor of the 1150th Anniversary of Kobo-Daishi's Nirvāṇam), 433–55.

———. 1986. "Critical Response." In *Karma and Rebirth: Post-Classical Developments,* edited by Ronald W. Neufeldt, 203–30. Albany: SUNY Press.

———. 1987. *Ālayavijñāna: On the Origin and Early Development of a Central Concept of Yogācāra Philosophy*. Tokyo: The International Institute for Buddhist Studies. 2 parts.

———. 1990. "Preface." = Ruegg and Schmithausen 1990: 1–3.

———. 1992. "An Attempt to Estimate the Distance in Time between Aśoka and the Buddha in Terms of Doctrinal History." = Bechert 1992: 110–47.

———. 1992a. "A Note on Vasubandhu and the Laṅkāvatārasūtra." AS 46(1; Festschr. Jacques May), 392–97.

Schneider, Ulrich. 1967. "Upaniṣad-Philosophie und früher Buddhismus." *Saeculum* 18, 245–63.

———. 1980. *Einführung in den Buddhismus*. Darmstadt: Wissenschaftliche Buchgesellschaft.

Schopen, Gregory. 1975. "The Phrase *Sa pṛthivīpradeśaś caityabhūto bhavet* in the Vajracchedikā: Notes on the Cult of the Book in Mahāyāna." IIJ 17, 147–81.

———. 1979. "Mahāyāna in Indian Inscriptions." IIJ 21, 1–19.

———. 1984. "Two Problems in the History of Indian Buddhism: The Layman/Monk Distinction and the Doctrines of the Transference of Merit." StII 10, 9–47. Reprint: Schopen 1997: 23–55.

———. 1987. "The Inscription on the Kuṣān Image of Amitābha and the Character of the Early Mahāyāna in India." JIABS 10(2), 99–137.

———. 1991. "Monks and the Relic Cult in the Mahāparinibbānasutta: An Old Misunderstanding in Regard to Monastic Buddhism." In *From Benares to Beijing: Essays on Buddhism and Chinese Religion in Honour of Prof. Jan Yün-Hua*, edited by Koichi Shinohara and Gregory Schopen, 187–201. Oakville, Canada: Mosaic Press. Reprint: Schopen 1997: 99–113.

———. 1997. *Bones, Stones, and Buddhist Monks: Collected Papers on the Archaeology, Epigraphy and Texts of Monastic Buddhism in India*. Honolulu: University of Hawaii Press. (Studies in the Buddhist Traditions, 2.)

Schubring, Walther. 1935. *Die Lehre der Jainas*. Berlin: Walter de Gruyter. (English translation: Schubring 2000.)

———. 2000. *The Doctrine of the Jainas. Described after the Old Sources*. Translated from the revised German edition by Wolfgang Beurlen. Second revised edition, with the three indices enlarged and added by Willem Bollée and Jayandra Soni. Delhi: Motilal Banarsidass.

Senart, Émile. 1900. "Bouddhisme et Yoga." RHR 43(2), 345–64.

Sharf, Robert H. 1995. "Buddhist Modernism and the Rhetoric of Meditative Experience." *Numen* 42, 228–83.

Shastri, Dharmendra Nath. 1964. *Critique of Indian Realism: A Study of the Conflict Between the Nyāya-Vaiśeṣika and the Buddhist Dignāga School*. Agra: Agra University.

Siderits, Mark, and J. Dervin O'Brien. 1976. "Zeno and Nāgārjuna on Motion." PEW 26, 281–99.

Silburn, Lilian. 1955. *Instant et cause: le discontinu dans la pensée philosophique de l'Inde*. Paris: J. Vrin.

Simson, Georg von. 1991. "Der zeitgeschichtliche Hintergrund der Entstehung des Buddhismus und seine Bedeutung für die Datierungsfrage." = Bechert 1991: 90–99.

Smith, Brian K. 1989. *Reflections on Resemblance, Ritual, and Religion*. New York: Oxford University Press.

Snellgrove, David L. 1987. *Indo-Tibetan Buddhism: Indian Buddhists and Their Tibetan Successors*. London: Serindia Publications.

Stache-Rosen, Valentina. 1968. *Das Saṅgītisūtra und sein Kommentar Saṅgītiparyāya*. Nach Vorarbeiten von Kusum Mittal bearbeitet.

Berlin. (Dogmatische Begriffsreihen im älteren Buddhismus, II; STT 9.)

Stcherbatsky, Th. 1983. *The Central Conception of Buddhism*. Reprint. Delhi: Motilal Banarsidass.

Steinkellner, Ernst. 1978. "Yogische Erkenntnis als Problem im Buddhismus." = Oberhammer 1978: 121–34.

———, ed. 1991. *Studies in the Buddhist Epistemological Tradition*. Proceedings of the Second International Dharmakīrti Conference (Vienna, June 11–16, 1989). Wien: ÖAW.

Streng, Frederick J. 1971. "The Buddhist Doctrine of Two Truths as Religious Philosophy." JIP 1, 262–71.

Strickmann, Michel. 1996. *Mantras et mandarins: le bouddhisme tantrique en Chine*. Paris: Gallimard.

Sutton, Florin Giripescu. 1991. *Existence and Enlightenment in the Laṅkāvatāra-sūtra: A Study in the Ontology and Epistemology of the Yogācāra School of Mahāyāna Buddhism*. Delhi: Sri Satguru Publications.

Suzuki, Daisetz Teitaro. 1932. *The Lankavatara Sutra: A Mahayana Text*. London: Routledge & Kegan Paul. Reprint 1968.

Takasaki, Jikido. 1966. *A Study on the Ratnagotravibhāga (Uttaratantra): Being a Treatise on the Tathāgatagarbha Theory of Mahāyāna Buddhism*. Roma: IsMEO. (SOR XXXIII.)

———. 1987. *An Introduction to Buddhism*. Translated by Rolf W. Giebel. Tokyo: The Tōhō Gakkai.

Tanaka, Kenneth K. 1985. "Simultaneous Relation (*sahabhū-hetu*): A Study in Buddhist Theory of Causation." JIABS 8(1), 91–111.

Thich Thien Chau. 1977. *Les sectes personnalistes (pudgalavadin) du bouddhisme ancien*. Paris: Université de la Sorbonne Nouvelle. Unpublished doctoral dissertation.

———. 1984. "The Literature of the Pudgalavādins." JIABS 7(1), 7–16.

———. 1987. "Les réponses des pudgalavādin aux critiques des écoles bouddhiques." JIABS 10(1), 33–53.

Thundy, Zacharias P. 1993. *Buddha and Christ: Nativity Stories and Indian Traditions*. Leiden: E. J. Brill. (Studies in the History of Religions, 60.)

Tokunaga, Muneo. 1995. "Anātman Reconsidered." *Studies in the History of Indian Thought (Indo-Shisōshi Kenkyū)* 7, 97–104.

Tripāṭhī, Chandrabhāl. 1968. "Die Einleitung des Daśottarasūtra und Nidānasaṃyukta." In *Pratidānam: Indian, Iranian and Indo-European Studies Presented to Franciscus Bernardus Jakobus Kuiper on his Sixtieth Birthday*, 275–82. The Hague, Paris: Mouton.

Tsuchida, Ryutaro. 1996. "An Interpretation of Baudhāyanadharmasūtra 2, 11, 26." *Tōyō Bunka Kenkyū Shokiyō* 130, 181–211.

van den Broeck, José. 1977. *La saveur de l'immortel (A-p'i-t'an Kan Lu Wei Lun). La version chinoise de l'Amṛtarasa de Ghoṣaka (TI 1553).* Louvain. (PIOL 15.)

van Velthem, Marcel, trans. 1977. *Le traité de la descente dans la profonde loi (Abhidharmāvatāraśāstra) de l'Arhat Skandhila.* Louvain. (PIOL 16.)

Vetter, Tilmann E. 1978. "Die Gauḍapādīya-Kārikās: zur Entstehung und zur Bedeutung von (a)dvaita." WZKS 22, 95–131.

———. 1982. "Zum Problem der Person in Nāgārjunas Mūla-Madhyamaka-Kārikās." In *Offenbarung als Heilserfahrung im Christentum, Hinduismus und Buddhismus*, edited by Walter Strolz and Shizuteru Ueda, 167–85. Freiburg: Herder.

———. 1982a. "Die Lehre Nāgārjunas in den Mūla-Madhyamaka-Kārikās." In *Epiphanie des Heils: Zur Heilsgegenwart in indischer und christlicher Religion*, edited by Gerhard Oberhammer, 87–108. Wien: Institut für Indologie der Universität Wien.

———. 1984. "A Comparison between the Mysticism of the Older Prajñā-Pāramitā-Literature and the Mysticism of the Mūla-Madhyamaka-Kārikās of Nāgārjuna." *Acta Indologica* 6 (Studies of Mysticism in Honor of the 1150th Anniversary of Kobo-Daishi's Nirvāṇam), 495–512.

———. 1988. *The Ideas and Meditative Practices of Early Buddhism.* Leiden: E. J. Brill.

———. 1991. "Zur religiösen Hermeneutik buddhistischer Texte." In *Beiträge zur Hermeneutik indischer und abendländischer Religionstraditionen*, edited by Gerhard Oberhammer, 179–92. Wien: ÖAW.

———. 1994. "Gedanken zu einer Geschichte der indischen Mystik." ZMR 78(3), 175–90.

———. 1994a. "Zwei schwierige Stellen im Mahānidānasutta: Zur Qualität der Überlieferung im Pāli-Kanon." WZKS 38, 137–60.

———. 1994b. "On the Origin of Mahāyāna Buddhism and the Subsequent Introduction of Prajñāpāramitā." AS 48(4), 1241–81.

———. 1995. "Bei Lebzeiten das Todlose erreichen: Zum Begriff *amata* im alten Buddhismus." In *Im Tod gewinnt der Mensch sein Selbst: Das Phänomen des Todes in asiatischer und abendländischer Religionstradition*, edited by Gerhard Oberhammer, 211–30. Wien: Verlag der ÖAW (SAWW 624).

———. 1996. "Das Erwachen des Buddha." WZKS 40, 45–85.

Waldron, William S. 1994. "How Innovative Is the *Ālayavijñāna*? The *Ālayavijñāna* in the Context of Canonical and Abhidharma *Vijñāna* Theory." JIP 22, 199–258.

———. 1995. "How Innovative Is the *Ālayavijñāna*? The *Ālayavijñāna* in the Context of Canonical and Abhidharma *Vijñāna* Theory, part II." JIP 23, 9–51.

Waldschmidt, Ernst. 1950–1951. *Das Mahāparinirvāṇasūtra, T. 1–3*. Berlin. (ADAW 1949, 1; 1950, 2,3.) Reprint: Kyoto: Rinsen Book Co., 1986.

———. 1951. "Vergleichende Analyse des Catuṣpariṣatsūtra." In *Beiträge zur indischen Philologie und Altertumskunde: Walther Schubring zum 70. Geburtstag dargebracht*, 84–122. Hamburg. (ANISt 7.) Reprint: Waldschmidt 1967: 164–202.

———. 1952–62. *Das Catuṣpariṣatsūtra. Eine kanonische Lehrschrift über die Begründung der buddhistischen Gemeinde*. 3 parts. Berlin. (ADAW 1952, 2; 1956, 1; 1960, 1.)

———. 1955. "Die Einleitung des Saṅgītisūtra." ZDMG 105, 298–318. Reprint: Waldschmidt 1967: 258–78.

———. 1967. *Von Ceylon bis Turfan: Schriften zur Geschichte, Literatur, Religion und Kunst des indischen Kulturraumes*. (Festgabe zum 70. Geburtstag.) Göttingen.

Walleser, Max. 1925. *Die philosophische Grundlage des älteren Buddhismus*. Zweite unveränderte Auflage. Heidelberg: Carl Winter.

Walser, Joseph. 2002. "Nāgārjuna and the Ratnāvalī: New Ways to Date an Old Philosopher." JIABS 25(1–2), 209–62.

Walshe, Maurice, trans. 1995. *The Long Discourses of the Buddha: A Translation of the Dīgha Nikāya*. Boston: Wisdom Publications.

Warder, A. K. 1971. "Dharmas and Data." JIP 1, 272–95.

———. 1973. "Is Nāgārjuna a Mahāyānist?" In *The Problem of Two Truths in Buddhism and Vedānta*, edited by Mervyn Sprung, 78–88. Dordrecht: D. Reidel.

———. 1980. *Indian Buddhism*. Second revised edition. Delhi: Motilal Banarsidass.

———. 1983. *"Original" Buddhism and Mahāyāna*. Torino. (Publicazioni di "Indologica Taurinensia," XVI.)

Wayman, Alex, and Hideko Wayman, trans. 1974. *The Lion's Roar of Queen Śrīmālā*. New York: Columbia University Press.

Weber, Claudia. 1994. *Wesen und Eigenschaften des Buddha in der Tradition des Hīnayāna-Buddhismus*. Inauguraldissertation zur Erlangung der Doktorwürde, Philosophische Fakultät, Rheinische Friedrich-Wilhelms-Universität, Bonn.

Welbon, Guy Richard. 1968. *The Buddhist Nirvāṇa and Its Western Interpreters*. Chicago: University of Chicago Press.

Wezler, Albrecht. 1984. "On the Quadruple Division of the Yogaśāstra, the Caturvyūhatva of the Cikitsāśāstra and the 'Four Noble Truths' of the Buddha." *Indologica Taurinensia* 12, 289–337.

Willemen, Charles, trans. and ann. 1975. *The Essence of Metaphysics: Abhidharmahṛdaya*. Bruxelles. (Publications de l'Institut des Hautes Études Bouddhiques, Série "Études et Textes," 4.)

———. 1996. Summary of "(Bhadanta) Dharmaśrī, Abhidharmahṛdaya or Abhidharmasāra." EIP 7, 451–70.

Williams, Paul M. 1977. "Buddhadeva and Temporality." JIP 4, 279–94.

———. 1989. *Mahāyāna Buddhism: The Doctrinal Foundations*. London, New York: Routledge.

Wiltshire, Martin G. 1990. *Ascetic Figures before and in Early Buddhism: The Emergence of Gautama as the Buddha*. Berlin, New York: Mouton de Gruyter. (Religion and Reason, 30.)

Winternitz, Moriz. 1908, 1913, 1920. *Geschichte der indischen Litteratur*. 3 vols. Leipzig: C. F. Amelangs.

Witzel, Michael. 1979. *On Magical Thought in the Veda*. Leiden: Universitaire Pers.

———. 1987. "The Case of the Shattered Head." StII 13/14, 363–415.

Wood, Thomas E. 1991. *Mind Only: A Philosophical and Doctrinal Analysis of the Vijñānavāda*. Honolulu: University of Hawaii Press. (Society for Asian and Comparative Philosophy, Monograph 9.)

Woodward, F. L., trans. 1973. *The Book of the Gradual Sayings (Anguttara-Nikāya) or more-numbered Suttas*, vol. II (The Book of the Fours). London, Boston: Routledge & Kegan Paul.

Yamashita, Koichi. 1994. *Pātañjala Yoga Philosophy with Reference to Buddhism*. Calcutta: Firma KLM.

Zafiropulo, Ghiorgo. 1993. *L'illumination du Buddha: de la quête à l'annonce de l'éveil. Essais de chronologie relative et de stratigraphie textuelle*. Innsbruck: Verlag des Instituts für Sprachwissenschaft, Universität Innsbruck. (Innsbrucker Beiträge zur Kulturwissenschaft, Sonderheft 87.)

Index

A
abhidharma. See scholasticism
Abhidharma, 63n118
Buddhism, 77, 120, 123n277, 137, 176
Buddhist, 77, 103, 135–36, 142
masters, 91, 94
Sarvāstivādins and, 90
texts, xi, 67, 103, 104n219, 107n223, 109
Abhidharmahṛdaya, 89n171, 100, 106, 109–10
Abhidharmakośa, 1–2, 90n175, 97n198, 103n216, 163
Abhidharmakośabhāṣya, 86, 91, 93–96, 101–3, 108
Abhidharma-piṭaka, 63, 82, 84, 177
Abhidharmasamuccayabhāṣya, 161n373
Abhidharmasāra, 100n209
abhilāpavāsanā. See impressions of words
accomplished one, 4, 91, 115. See also *arhat*
activity, action (*karman*), 21, 25, 80, 95–96, 127, 141–43, 148, 160, 167, 172
adattādāna. See taking what has not been given
adhipatipratyaya. See determining condition
adhvan. See times
Advaita Vedānta, 186–87
Āgamaśāstra, 187
aggregate (*skandha*), 38–39, 62, 90, 109, 127, 147, 156
classification systems and, 70, 84–85
conditioned origination and, 94
dharmas and, 82–83, 109, 127, 133–34
five aggregates, 23–31, 57, 62, 70–85, 94, 133–34
self/not-self and, 23–28, 30–31, 57, 72–76, 79, 147
aggregate of noble virtue (*śīlaskandha*), 14–15
Ajitasenavyākaraṇanirdeśa Sūtra, 126n292
ākāśānantyāyatana. See realm of infinity of space
ākiñcanyāyatana. See realm of nothingness
akuśala. See unwholesome
ālambana. See support
ālayavijñāna. See fundamental consciousness
all-pervading cause (*sarvatragahetu*), 95
Amṛtarasa, 87n167, 89n171, 98n203
Ānanda, 41, 53, 54, 61, 153,
anātman. See not the self; not-self
anavasthā. See infinite regress
Aṅguttara Nikāya, 48, 54, 62, 64
anityatā, 87, 138
antagrāhadṛṣṭi. See belief that is attached to extremes
anuśaya. See attachment
apoha. See exclusion
application of mindfulness (*smṛtyupasthāna*), 65, 69, 83n155, 105, 106n221
apramāṇa. See unmeasurables

About Wisdom

Wisdom Publications is dedicated to making available authentic Buddhist works for the benefit of all. We publish translations of the sutras and tantras, commentaries and teachings of past and contemporary Buddhist masters, and original works by the world's leading Buddhist scholars. We publish our titles with the appreciation of Buddhism as a living philosophy and with the special commitment to preserve and transmit important works from all the major Buddhist traditions.

Wisdom Publications
199 Elm Street
Somerville, Massachusetts 02144 USA
Telephone: 617-776-7416
Fax: 617-776-7841
Email: info@wisdompubs.org
www.wisdompubs.org

Wisdom is a nonprofit, charitable 501(c)(3) organization affiliated with the Foundation for the Preservation of the Mahayana Tradition (FPMT).

Studies in Indian and Tibetan Buddhism
Titles Previously Published

Among Tibetan Texts
History and Literature of the Himalayan Plateau
E. Gene Smith

Approaching the Great Perfection
Simultaneous and Gradual Methods of Dzogchen Practice in the Longchen Nyingtig
Sam van Schaik

Buddhism Between Tibet and China
Edited by Matthew T. Kapstein

A Direct Path to the Buddha Within
Gö Lotsāwa's Mahāmudrā Interpretation of the Ratnagotravibhāga
Klaus-Dieter Mathes

Foundations of Dharmakīrti's Philosophy
John D. Dunne

Freedom from Extremes
Gorampa's "Distinguishing the Views" and the Polemics of Emptiness
José Ignacio Cabezón and Geshe Lobsang Dargyay

Luminous Lives
The Story of the Early Masters of the Lam 'bras in Tibet
Cyrus Stearns

Mipham's Beacon of Certainty
Illuminating the View of Dzogchen, the Great Perfection
John Whitney Pettit

Reason's Traces
Identity and Interpretation in Indian and Tibetan Buddhist Thought
Matthew T. Kapstein

Resurrecting Candrakīrti
Disputes in the Tibetan Creation of Prāsaṅgika
Kevin A. Vose

Scripture, Logic, Language
Essays on Dharmakīrti and His Tibetan Successors
Tom J. F. Tillemans

The Svātantrika-Prāsaṅgika Distinction
What Difference Does a Difference Make?
Edited by Georges Dreyfus and Sara McClintock

Vajrayoginī
Her Visualizations, Rituals, and Forms
Elizabeth English